Pacific Prelude

MARGERY PERHAM

Pacific Prelude

A JOURNEY TO SAMOA AND AUSTRALASIA, 1929

Edited and with an Introduction by
A.H.M. KIRK-GREENE

PETER OWEN · LONDON

ISBN 0 7206 0683 7

PETER OWEN PUBLISHERS
73 Kenway Road London SW5 0RE

First published 1988

Text © The University of Oxford 1988
Introduction and Notes © A.H.M. Kirk-Greene 1988

Photoset, printed and bound in Great Britain by
WBC, Bristol and Maesteg

Contents

Illustrations

Plates 2–7 are from the collection of Margery Perham in the Rhodes House Library, Oxford, and are reproduced by kind permission of the Bodleian Library and the Executors.

For my wife

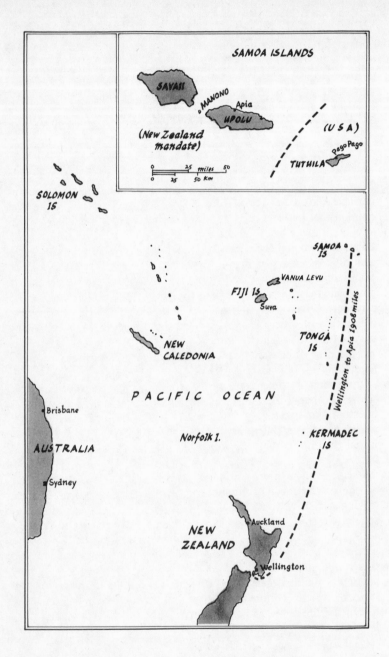

The Western Pacific, showing the Samoa Islands

Introduction

Margery Perham (1895–1982) was among the outstanding women of her age. Oxford academic from 1924 to 1963 (there are many of the opinion that had she been a man she would undoubtedly have been appointed to a Chair – or else had one created!); leading authority on comparative colonial administration; friend, confidante and adviser to countless members of Britain's colonial officials, from Secretary of State and Governor-General to first-tour cadet, from aspiring postgraduate student from overseas to nationalist leader; teacher and traveller, broadcaster and writer, lobbyist, publicist and tireless committee member, Dame Margery Perham was a conspicuously successful public figure. Perhaps all that needs to be said here about her place in public affairs is that she is an unequivocal candidate for the *Dictionary of National Biography*.*

But what of the private persona behind this prominent public figure? Probably there is no better way of beginning to answer that question than by reading the diary she kept during her first scholar's journey, as she travelled literally round the world, in 1929–31. It is the initial months of that unpublished diary which are now presented here.

Pacific Prelude offers a number of insights into our understanding of one of the most prominent women of her generation. Indeed, leaving aside her two novels, what we now have is her first serious and scholarly record – anticipating by six years her first co-authored book and by as much as eight her first individual book – in what was to be a lifetime of writing. *Pacific Prelude* enables us to meet for the first time the 'young and obscure don' (to use her own words) who, ten years later, was to earn recognition as Britain's leading authority on the study of colonial administration, a reputation she maintained for the rest of her life.

---

* A substantial sketch of Margery Perham's life prefaces *West African Passage* (Peter Owen, 1983). Rather than repeat it here, I have added a biographical calendar as an Appendix to the present volume, along with a list of principal biographical sources.

9

Pacific Prelude is the first of Margery Perham's travel diaries, though the fourth to be published. The text is essentially that which Margery had herself prepared for publication in 1972. It covers the opening months (July–October 1929) of her Rhodes Trust Travelling Fellowship, when she set out for what was originally planned as a year's research in Africa, travelling to that continent via the United States, New Zealand and Australia. The middle period of that African tour, which by the spring of 1930 had been refinanced by the Rhodes Trust to cover a second year (albeit at the sacrifice of her tutorial Fellowship at St Hugh's College, Oxford), is fully covered in the first two published volumes of her travel diaries: *African Apprenticeship* (1974), subtitled *An Autobiographical Journey in Southern Africa, 1929* but more accurately taking the narrative only from October 1929 and then, in the event, right through to March 1930; and *East African Journey* (1976), again somewhat misleadingly subtitled *Kenya and Tanganyika 1929–30* while in fact spanning the period April 1930 to January 1931. By economizing on the second allocation of what had clearly been a generous grant, Margery was able to finance a separate visit to Nigeria and the Cameroons within a matter of mere months after her return to Oxford. The diary for that journey appeared posthumously in 1983 under the title *West African Passage: A Journey through Nigeria, Chad and the Cameroons, 1931–1932.** In 1972 she had offered a two-volume diary to Faber and Faber. What she had in mind was to publish her America–Pacific–Australasia diary as the first volume of the record of her Rhodes Travelling Fellowship in 1929–31, and then, 'if all went well', to 'doing Africa . . . the most important and serious part of the diary', as the second volume (Perham MSS, Box 38, file 3, correspondence with Faber and Faber, June 1972).† As for a title, Margery tentatively suggested 'Travelling on Trust', which she had recently used for a series of four BBC radio broadcasts, or alternatively 'Travelling Fellowship', but added, in a letter to Mr du Sautoy of Faber and Faber on June 2, 1972, 'I am not good at choosing titles'.

From time to time the original manuscript diary carries the heading

---

* Page references to the diaries in this Introduction are prefaced by the abbreviations *AA (African Apprenticeship), EAJ (East African Journey)* and *WAP (West African Passage)*. Certain other page references relate to the present diary.

† The Perham papers, over seven hundred boxes in all, are still being catalogued in Rhodes House Library. They will not be open to the public before 1988. Thus no shelf mark can yet be cited. They are referred to here by box, file and folio (e.g. Perham MSS, Box 10, file 5, folio 25), which from here onwards will simply be cited as 'MSS 10/5, 25'.

'Imperial Tour' on the first sheet of its various portions (e.g. MSS 36/3). When Faber and Faber advised that the Southern and Central African sections were all that they felt able to publish at that time, Margery set aside the pre-African section. It seems she did no further work on the July–October 1929 diary in the last ten years of her life, although she had commended it to the present writer at the same time as she had handed him the Nigerian typescript in the mid-1970s. In 1985, at the invitation of Peter Owen and with the permission of the Executors, this 1929 diary was entrusted to me to prepare for publication, in advance of the date when the Perham papers will be made accessible to the general public.

It is important to make clear exactly what is now being published. It is the July–October 1929 diary as finally revised by Dame Margery for publication in June 1972. Of the two typescript 1972 versions, the one used here, with only slight textual alterations, is marked 'Edited Version 2' (MSS 38/2). This was constructed from a number of drafts and fragments, all of them retained in the Perham papers – 'very cannibalized', as she warns in a manuscript note (38/6, 1). These include: the basic 'diary', written up on her journey (some of the folios were charred in a fire in her last home in Oxford); the 'diary-letters', as she called them, sent home for typing and circulation among half a dozen close friends, often incorporating information on the same events as those written up in the diary; her working notebooks (often blue school exercise books) and ring-files, again covering many of the same events and much of the same material, but with extra data and other emphases, and very much fulfilling their role of a researcher's precious field-notes; and an accumulation of Government reports and locally published pamphlets, blue books and white papers galore. As she explains in a manuscript addition to the present diary:

> One of my problems is that of deciding how much background to give you [recipients of the letters] in order to make my own experiences and ideas comprehensible. . . . All the more serious information . . . goes into my notebooks, to be sent home with the mass of official and semi-official papers which are thrust upon me.

The diary itself, as she described it on another occasion, was really 'a sort of scrap-album into which I throw chance pictures and personal impressions that don't fit into my notes but which I may need afterwards to recreate their setting' MSS 36/3, 1).

But that is not the end of the story. For Margery, mindful perhaps of Bacon's precept 'Let diaries be brought in use', in May 1939, when her recurrent bouts of illness made it impossible for her to travel or to concentrate on any successor to her *Native Administration in Nigeria,* which had appeared in 1937, started to revise her diary of the Rhodes Trust Travelling Fellowship years. Then, when in the early 1970s she turned again to the text, she took the opportunity to amend some passages, delete – or at least disguise – many names, and generally tidy it up for imminent publication. While I have been given permission to examine Margery's original diaries and notebooks for 1929, and to consult the pre-1972 drafts of the present diary, what is now being offered is the final version of the diary for those three months of 1929 as Margery herself had re-revised and prepared it in about 1972. In short, this is the text which, when retrieved from among her papers in 1985, had attached to the typescript a note in her handwriting: 'A1 importance . . . awaiting publication!'. That moment has now come.

Margery Perham spent only three weeks of 1929 in the United States, principally in New York, Washington, DC, Virginia, Chicago and San Francisco; a month island-hopping across the Pacific, mainly divided between Pago Pago and Western Samoa, with stopovers in Hawaii and Fiji; and three weeks in New Zealand, followed by a week in Australia before she embarked on the long voyage across the Indian Ocean to Durban and Cape Town ('Four weeks without sight of land between Western Australia and South Africa!' – *AA*, p. 29), which she reached at the end of October.

Margery Perham's particular interests on this Pacific and Australian journey were twofold. One was race relations, in their full Atlantic and Pacific range: Amerindians and Negroes in the United States, Polynesians in Hawaii and, along with half-castes, in Samoa too; Indians in Fiji, Maoris and Pakehas in New Zealand, Aborigines and their white colonials in Australia – what she thought of, in the last two countries, as 'the attitude to the original inhabitants of the continent'. The other interest was the system of colonial administration as practised on the ground in Western Samoa (and, as an addendum if not an afterthought, in American Samoa, too), for the Government of which territory a League of Nations mandate had been granted to New Zealand in 1920. If J.M. Ward (writing in R.W. Winks, ed., *The Historiography of the British Empire,* 1966) is correct in his complaint that British historians have shown remarkably little interest in writing on 'the history of the distant, scattered islands which comprise Britain's Pacific empire', Margery's hitherto unpublished observations on the Mau rebellion and on the conduct of New Zealand's mandate over one part of what Paul Kennedy, quoting Sir Thomas Sanderson, has referred to as 'the miserable archipelago' of Samoa (*The Samoan Tangle*, 1974, p. xiii) or what Deryck Scarr has aptly described as Britain's 'Fragments of Empire' (1967) littering the Western Pacific, may offer some redress. Furthermore, because of the richness of the race relations material derived from six such classic contexts; because of the detail of the 'native administration' so closely studied *in situ* by Margery in the two Samoas and so doggedly pursued, in the case of Western Samoa, with the authorities in New Zealand, as well as its practice in colonial Fiji and the dominion Australia; and because of the sheer number of countries visited, *Pacific Prelude* could have a far wider appeal than the author's accounts of her journeys in Africa.

Apart from the intrinsic merit of the themes of race relations and colonial administration explored here in such depth and detail, the diary itself is written with Margery's characteristic descriptive vividness and wit, the whole enhanced by numerous, memorable pen-portraits of this Cabinet minister, governor or senior civil servant and that professor, politician, agitator or fellow passenger. Her literary talents render the text valuable not only for students of interracial relations and of colonial government but for anyone interested in seeing America, Western Pacific or Australasia through the critical eye of a young but highly perceptive and intelligent female observer. The light thrown by this diary illuminates a number of aspects of Margery Perham, both professional and personal. To start with the professional side of the journey, as well as the nature and manner of Margery Perham's prestigious Rhodes Trust Travelling Fellowship award, require further explanation. Margery herself dismissed it as 'a great surprise' (*AA*, p. 11) and 'an utterly unexpected intervention of fate' (ibid., p. 27). In one of her notes intended to serve as a possible foreword to the present diary she added the gloss: 'I still do not know what led the Trust to give me this exciting opportunity.' All she could think of was that the Fellowships were awarded to enable Oxford dons (exclusively) to 'spend a year away from the University seeing the world' (*AA*, p. 11). In those pre-air travel days, when Third World conferences, overseas consultancies or secondment, and external examining abroad were not so easy or so common, the life of an Oxbridge don could indeed run the risk of being a cloistered and bounded one. However, research into the Rhodes Trust files* now enables us to clarify much of Margery's mystification about the award of her Travelling Fellowship.

Following her appointment to Oxford in 1924 as Fellow and Tutor

---

* File 2695, vols I–III (1926–32). The files bear no folios.

in Modern History and Modern Greats at her former college, St Hugh's* in 1927 Margery, perhaps with the faint hope of one day returning to Africa where five years earlier she had spent a long period of convalescence with her sister and brother-in-law, decided to 'indulge' herself preparing two series of lectures for the new Imperial History syllabus. These Modern History School reforms had been initiated by the Beit Professor, R.T. (later Sir Reginald) Coupland, following his appointment to the Chair in 1920. One course was on British native policy, the other on the working of the mandates system under the League of Nations. Perfectionist that she already was, Margery not only worked her way through the extensive annual *Reports* of the mandatory powers and the 'voluminous records' of the League's Permanent Mandates Commission (PMC), but proceeded in the vacations to travel to Geneva so as to observe the PMC in action and to interview some of its members. It was from this period – now identifiably April 1929 – that her close relationship with Lord Lugard, the British Permanent Representative on the PMC from 1922 to 1936, dates. By the time of her Travelling Fellowship she was engaged in a steady correspondence with him on her travels (e.g. *AA*, p. 238; *WAP*, pp. 65, 151, 181), and within less than two years she was able to confide to her diary that Lugard was 'to me no longer just a famous name but a friend' (*WAP*, p. 53 and especially p. 214). Over the ensuing years until his death in 1945 the friendship was to evolve into a great and mutually gratifying association of minds, and she was to become his biographer and the custodian of his private papers.† By the time Margery submitted her application to the newly established (1926) Rhodes Trust Travelling Fund, she was able to frame her proposal in what a post-Second World War generation would broadly identify as the study of race relations. She has given the impression that, when the Trust gave her the award, its terms were minimal. 'There were no precise instructions', she recalls, 'as to the use to be made of the opportunity' (*AA*, p. 11), and, as she tells it, when she asked the two Trustees who interviewed her (probably H.A.L. Fisher and Geoffrey Dawson) for guidance, all she remembered receiving was 'vague replies' (ibid.). One suggested that she should simply take the chance to broaden her mind; the other encouraged her to go wherever

---

*How she succeeded Cecilia Ady in this controversial post has been discussed by Rachel Trickett, Principal of St Hugh's College (1973–   ), in her chapter 'The Row' in the centenary history of the College, *St Hugh's: One Hundred Years of Women's Education in Oxford* (1986), pp. 48–61.

† The Perham papers recently deposited in Rhodes House Library contain substantial additions to the Lugard papers.

she liked, as long as it was in pursuit of what he called 'colour problems'. And that, as she was to note as soon as she embarked on the topic in earnest, was in 1930 'an almost unknown subject of academic study' (*AA*, p. 27). All that remained in her mind at the end of the interview was the Secretary's admonition that she must never forget she would be regarded by others as 'an ambassador for Oxford' (*AA*, p. 11).

From perusal of the Rhodes Trust files sixty years later we can learn a lot more. Margery was the sixth recipient of the award; and, remarkably enough, she was not the first woman recipient, Charlotte Young of Somerville College claiming that distinction in 1927. The scheme ended in 1932: after the fifteenth award, to J.P.R. Maud (later Lord Redcliffe-Maud) of New College, also for travelling to Africa, a combination of dissatisfaction by an American university president over the conduct of one such Fellow and general economic austerity at home persuaded the Rhodes Trust that its resources might be better utilized for other purposes. Paid at the generous rate of £100 per month (at that time the Beit Professor of Imperial History at Oxford University enjoyed an annual salary of £1,200), and tenable for anything from six to twelve months, the Rhodes Travelling Fellowships were aimed at enabling 'Fellows, Tutors and Lecturers in residence at Oxford to travel and study and conduct research overseas, particularly in the countries from which Rhodes Scholars are derived'. Emphasis was placed on travel in the British Dominions and the United States. While there was no age limit, it was stated that preference would be given to those under forty-five who had held a teaching appointment at Oxford for at least five years.

When Margery applied for 'full particulars' on October 16, 1928, she was told that it was by no means certain that any awards would be made for 1929. The Trust was worried by the 'very inadequate number' of applicants, and indeed had not proceeded to make the full number of awards authorized. Margery seems to have lost either the form or heart, since we find her writing for another form on December 6; or maybe, as her two letters fall neatly into the first and final weeks of Michaelmas term, she had simply been too busy in College. But now she would have to move quickly, for applications had to be in by January 1. She did: four days later her application went off to the Rhodes Trust.

The Committee, representing the University (the Vice-Chancellor, the Principal of Hertford College, and Dr J. Wells of Wadham College in 1929), and the Trustees (in this case, the Warden of New College and Geoffrey Dawson of *The Times*), set considerable store by the acceptability of the proposed itinerary as well as the value of the envisaged research. Margery's proposal was for a nine-month visit to West, South and East Africa, to be followed by a three-month journey home from the Sudan and Egypt via India and the United States. Her object was that of 'specialising and writing on British Native Policy and increasing knowledge of the English-speaking world'. She had, she wrote, 'always hoped to concentrate on Colonial History' but only in the last eighteen months had she found the time to start. In the past year she had lectured on 'Colonial Policy in the 19th Century' and 'British Policy towards Native Races', focusing on imperial administration of the Indians before the American Revolution. She had also started 'at the other end of my subject' by studying the League of Nations mandates system and actually visiting the League in session in Geneva. In forwarding the application on December 19 to the Warden of New College, H.A.L. Fisher, the Secretary of the Rhodes Trust (1925–39), Philip Kerr (later Lord Lothian) thought it necessary to point out that 'it is not the object of the Trustees to give people a mere hurried joy ride' but rather to make sure they spent enough time in a country 'to acquire real knowledge'. He accepted that Margery proposed to 'do some real work in Africa' but felt that the last three months had the makings of 'a hurried rush'. A shorter tour or a better thought-out itinerary would, he believed, be in order.

A combination of Margery's proposal and the support of her referees, Sir Charles Grant Robertson, Fellow of All Souls and Principal of Birmingham University, and Professor Coupland, proved enough. Her award (one of three) was announced in the *University Gazette* at the beginning of Hilary term, 1929. However, not until she had met the wish of Trustees by reconstructing and shortening her itinerary – finally she reversed the whole direction of travel, to end instead of starting with Africa! – and had entered a spirited defence of her plans in an eleven-page letter dated January 17 and in an interview with Fisher, were they ready to confirm the details of the award.

Margery had heeded (and was not to forget) the warning that, to quote Kerr's letter of January 16, 1929 to her, 'The Trustees are definitely against a Fellowship being awarded for purposes which merge into globe trotting'. She had also taken Kerr's advice to write and seek the views of leading authorities in Britain on Africa. Kerr still thought America should come after Africa, on the grounds that it would be better to observe where 'primitive man' had got to in America after rather then before seeing him in his original state. But following her improved itinerary, her interviews with such eminent persons as Sir Donald Cameron, Dr J.H. Oldham, Sir Hesketh Bell, Professor

Macmillan, and Lord Lugard himself, and her obvious blend of enthusiasm, competence and determination, Kerr no longer entertained any doubts about the viability of her revised programme. The Trustees endorsed his opinion, and on May 5 the details of the Rhodes Travelling Fellowships were confirmed by a monthly grant of £100 for a period of a year, as from July 1929. She spent the last two months before her departure in yet further rethinking her itinerary, even altering her sailing from Liverpool to Southampton (curiously, in one letter, April 16, she gives the Trustees the date of July 25 for her departure, although she meant June 25, as on the next line she notes that she is due to arrive in New York on July 2), and in obtaining letters of introduction from the Dominions and Colonial Office, and making banking arrangements for letters of credit based on her £500 advance from the Trust. It was all a tight squeeze for the Trust, and the last batch of letters of introduction had to be delivered to Margery on board ship in Southampton, on the eve of sailing.

The Fellowships were discontinued a few years later. Margery believed this was because the experience was regarded as 'unfruitful'. The term is wide enough to embrace fact as well as speculation. It was part dissatisfaction, part disappointment, and part economy. She also picked up on the Oxford alumni grapevine in South Africa, home of so many Rhodes Scholars, echoes of the acerbic comment, repeated in some donnish conversation back in Oxford, that she seemed to be having rather a good time globe-trotting. 'That quoted remark . . . still stings,' she noted. 'I never worked harder in my life' (*AA*, p. 264). The insensitive Senior Common Room gibe notwithstanding, the Trust was to show sufficient confidence in her performance to offer to finance a further year's research in Africa before the first year had expired and without her asking for it. The correspondence on this arrangement, revealing the strong and sympathetic support of her college, her own hopes for being appointed to the Beit Lectureship, and the Trust's agreement to fund her second year but, because of the danger of precedent, not to look on it as an extension of her Travelling Fellowship, is contained in detail in the Rhodes Trust files. While Lord Lothian had received 'golden opinions' of her work, there was, however, one fly in the ointment. This was the coded telegram (June 28, 1930) from the Governor of Kenya, Sir Edward Grigg, who expressed his opinion that Margery was neither detached nor competent and that she was wasting his time and that of his staff. Lothian knew how to handle Grigg's grumble about 'ready made opinion' and what he subsequently described to the Trustees as the 'absurd' assumption of a need to test a candidate's political colouring (letter, September 14,

1931). To his credit, Grigg promptly asked Margery to stay at Government House.

Two important questions emerge from this Rhodes Trust award. First, how was it that Margery could spend at least one-tenth of her approved time and grant on research into a topic and in a place neither of which, according to her, was spelled out in her original application or in the award, and yet one whose central importance is underlined by the fact that it occupies nearly half of the present diary? This was the Mau uprising in Samoa. Second, how is it that, after working for several years on the copious documentation of the League of Nations Permanent Mandates Commission, and then having, unusually, been enabled to study the proceedings 'live' in Geneva along with the system *in situ* in Samoa, as well as observe Government policies on race relations in the United States, Fiji, New Zealand and Australia, Margery Perham suddenly distanced herself from this sizeable and at the time possibly unique accumulation of knowledge and experience, and turned instead to the as yet untried academic area of Africa as henceforward her principal field of interest and expertise? Reading now in the diary the inside story for the first time of how she did spend (in all senses) the first quarter of her Travelling Fellowship, one cannot but be struck by the abruptness of the fact that, apart from two Samoan articles in *The Times* in the middle of her travels, Margery never published anything at all on the Amerindian, Negro, Polynesian, Maori or Aboriginal problems which she had set out and been funded to study and on which, under the rubric of British policy towards native races other than in Africa and with special reference to the Maoris, she had already been lecturing at Oxford. And this despite the fact, as she makes clear to all, that Samoa had 'long fascinated' her. This unique opportunity provided by the Rhodes Trust to study colonial administration under the mandates system at first hand, and to write about it, must have been irresistible to an up-and-coming academic. Yet she never did. So, why this switch of fields in mid-research?

On the first query, we have Margery's own testimony. According to this, the idea of making Samoa the ultimate centre-piece of her trip to Africa via the Pacific came to her quite by chance. Shortly after her arrival in Washington, DC, in late July, Margery tells how she happened to come across a short report in a local newspaper about trouble in Pago Pago on Tutuila in American Samoa. She already had a 'vague' idea (no more, she insists) about stopping over at Upolu and Savaii in Western Samoa. So, having 'only very general ideas about where I should go next [after the United States]' and being rather 'attracted to [both the Samoan Island groups] by the report that . . . they were in a state of unrest' (*EAJ*, p. 12), what, she now casually asked herself, 'could be more attractive after glancing – no more – at some of the racial problems of a huge half-continent than to go to a tiny and certainly beautiful and romantic island and see America's "race relations" in tropical minuscule?' As to the legitimacy of this 'beautiful idea' of such a side-trip to paradise – an enterprise which Margery, being Margery, needed to settle with her conscience as well as reconcile with the terms of her Travelling Fellowship – why, she concluded her self-argument, she really had no terms! After all, had she not right from the start looked on the Travelling Fellowship as an 'indefinite commission'? Later, as we have seen, she was to show understandable sensitivity about the rumour going round Oxford's Senior Common Rooms that all she was doing was 'merely globe-trotting' (*AA*, p. 264). To her diary, at the time, however, she was to confide the admission that her inclusion of Samoa was 'more for pleasure than intellectual duty', and fifty years later she could still look back on that Pacific interlude as 'idyllic days living with the beautiful Polynesians' (*EAJ*, p.12). But she did find it necessary to defend her decision to the Principal of St Hugh's College, Barbara Gwyer, who had teasingly asked her about this ambition to see for herself 'the strangeness of the world' when it could be understood better and more widely by reading travellers' tales and letting them paint pictures on the mind. 'But then,' Margery had quipped, 'there must be travellers to do the painting' (*EAJ*, p. 178).

However, the Rhodes Trust files suggest that the Samoan experience was not quite as neat or vague as this. Far from Samoa being, in Margery's words, 'a sheer accident . . . never heard of the place before I reached America', the idea of Samoa first appeared, merely as 'New Zealand or Samoa', in a letter written to Philip Kerr dated January 17, 1929. And it unmistakably appeared in the revised itinerary submitted on February 27 to the Trustees: 'July 25: Sail for Samoa; Aug. 23, leave Samoa.' In this she had been encouraged by a talk in February with Sir James Parr, the New Zealand High Commissioner in London. It is possible that the idea of visiting the United States as well as Western Samoa did not take hold of her until she reached Washington, though perhaps not as much 'by chance' as she declares. It is also arguable that Lugard, given his profound disquiet over the calibre of New Zealand's administration of Samoa and his specialized knowledge of the mandate there (subsequently vouched for in Margery's biography, vol. II, 1960, p. 653), may well have sown the vigorous seed of comparative administration in her mind when she had that fateful first meeting with him at the Athenaeum Club in April 1929 (MSS 79/20).

At any rate, Samoa it was. Today we are the beneficiaries of this *soi-disant*, out-of-the-blue decision, made 'largely because I thought it would be interesting to investigate the troubles'. For we now have available for the first time a personal, substantial and detailed examination of American rule in Samoa, the Mau rebellion in Western Samoa, the responses and attitudes of both the American and New Zealand administrations, and much information on the character and roles of the chief protagonists in Apia, General G.S. Richardson and Mr O.F. Nelson.

When we turn to the second question, why Margery abandoned her personal research into race relations and the mandates system as operated in the Pacific, and half-way through her Rhodes Travelling Fellowship decided instead to make Africa her field of specialization, we are on perhaps less sure ground. True, we know from the concluding entries in her present diary, supported by various entries in the follow-up pages of her African diaries, that the idea had begun to assume shape the moment she left Polynesia and Australasia behind and sensed the African continent approaching. Certainly there was the latent attraction of Africa itself, to whose allure Margery had succumbed – heart, mind and soul – when she had lived in British Somaliland with her sister, Ethel, and brother-in-law, Major Harry Rayne, now a District Commissioner, nearly ten years before. Just what an impression that had made on her is emphasized by her contemplating, fifty years after the event and at the time when she was turning to revise all her diary-letters with a possible eye to publication, the idea of including as a prologue to her putative two-volume Rhodes Travelling Fellowship diary the talk on that protectorate which she had given on the BBC Radio 4 programme in January 1970. In the end, with no Pacific diary accepted for publication, it was to her *African Apprenticeship* that she added the text of that talk from the BBC's *The Time of My Life* series. As she was impatiently to exclaim, recalling how lost and lonely she felt in the drab atmosphere of Sheffield after the excitement of Somaliland, 'I wanted to *do* something about Africa – about the problems of what is now called colonialism which were thrashing about aimlessly in my mind' (*AA*, p. 26). There is no doubt that her Somaliland experience generated in Margery a lasting interest in the work and character of the British Colonial Service (witness the choice of hero in the consequent novel), an institution which she could, already on her Pacific journey, keep on using as a model despite her still limited personal knowledge of its men and methods. In the end, the Colonial Service was the institution on which Margery was destined to become as much an influence as an authority.

Now, almost ten years after her African initiation in Berbera and Hargeisa, the closer Margery came to Africa, the more positively the African idea took hold of her imagination. This was the great laboratory for the study of race relations: not Negroes or Amerindians, not Polynesians or Maoris or Aborigines, but black and white in Africa. As the stark silhouette of Cape Town's Table Mountain and Lion's Head came unforgettably into sight, Margery imagined beckoning to her 'a thousand miles of racial problems deeper and more complex than any I had yet surveyed' (*AA*, p. 34). Here, then, was 'the continent I mean to make my main study' (*AA*, p. 29). Having found earlier in Somaliland the 'guiding purpose for my life and work' (*AA*, p. 28), that dedication was renewed and reinforced as she now selected Africa as 'the most serious subject of my future work'.

But if this emotional rationalization takes care of part of the answer, it still leaves unexplained why Margery should have abandoned all the intellectual time and effort she had already devoted to studying the mandates system without – and she was to prove herself no sluggard when it came to publishing – ever putting a word to print beyond two short pieces in *The Times*. Two years of thorough homework on the League's Permanent Mandates Commission in Oxford and Geneva, determined field-work in Western Samoa and its follow-up in New Zealand, privileged introductions to and interviews with members of the PMC as well as with officials and parliamentarians, and the strong support of and close co-operation with the legendary Lord Lugard: what would compel a young academic, as yet unpublished and still very much in the making, to give up this substantial resource investment and never spend another penny of the accumulated capital? It is my argument that, as now and again happens with academic projects, it was largely a matter of bad luck. For if Margery's research topic was unusual, it was not unique. During the very tenure of her Rhodes Travelling Fellowship, no less then two unchallengeably important books on the League of Nations Mandates system appeared. One was Elizabeth van Maanen-Helmer's geographical case study, *The Mandates System in Relation to Africa and the Pacific Islands*, published under the auspices of the League of Nations Union in 1929; the other was Philip Quincy Wright's magisterial (and still authoritative) *Mandates under the League of Nations*, published in Chicago in 1930. And so, perhaps making the most of a stroke of damnable misfortune, partly conscious that, within the limited time of barely two months, she had merely '*surveyed* rather than *studied*' (*AA*, p. 29) race relations across half the world and had only succeeded in 'looking – *it could be no more* – at the Negro problem in the United States, with a *glance* at the Amerindians – in American Samoa *spent some idyllic days* living with the beautiful Polynesians . . . in New Zealand *plunged rather rashly* into politics concerning that country's League of Nations mandate in Samoa . . . *took a quick look* at the Maoris . . . and went on to traverse Australia *without learning much* about Aborigines' (*EAJ*, p. 12, my italics), and partly succumbing to the charms of that first and unforgettable love affair with Africa, Margery now set about reshaping her instincts and ideas. With almost missionary fervour, she rededicated herself and redesigned her energies into a positive, fresh goal: 'To devote myself entirely to the study of the government of "native" races, especially in the African regions administered by Britain' (*AA*, p. 263).

This African daydream seems to have been quickly converted into a blueprint, for within a few months of landing in Africa Margery took the irrevocable – and not uncourageous – step of resigning her College Fellowship so as to be able to accept the Rhodes Trust's telegraphed offer of a second year. This she was to spend wholly in Africa.

Her own chronology of this crossroads event undergoes a slight hiccup here. In her draft foreword to the present diary she maintains that she received the two cables calling on her to make up her mind, one from the College and one from the Trust, when she reached Northern Rhodesia. That would have been in February 1930. But this would rule out her belief that the Rhodes Trust offer of an extension was encouraged, if not motivated, by the appearance of her two articles in *The Times*, publication of which did not take place until April 1930. It would also make nonsense of the separate note inserted into her East African diary (*EAJ*, p. 53), where the cables are said to have arrived 'at this time' – that is late April (*EAJ*, p. 52) – or of the entry 'Suddenly . . . as I began to travel in Tanganyika, two cables reached me' (*EAJ*, p. 13). The confused chronology can now be straightened out, since the Rhodes Trust files makes two things clear. One is that the cables were not dispatched from Oxford until the middle of May. The other is that Margery's pardonable poetic licence about her historic telegraphic reply was, at least in the case of the Rhodes Trust cable, not as succinct as she would subsequently have it. Lothian's cable, confirmed in his letter of May 23, read: TRUSTEES WILLING FINANCE FURTHER YEAR'S AFRICAN RESEARCH IF YOU WANT IT STOP WOULD YOU PREFER RETURN TO ENGLAND SOON RETURNING AFRICA LATER OR PROLONG PRESENT

AFRICAN TOUR STOP WHERE WILL LETTER REACH YOU. Her reply consisted of fifteen words rather than the one (see below) she has had us all treasuring: ACCEPT WARMEST THANKS AND APPRECIATION STOP PREFER PROLONG AT LEAST SOME MONTHS STOP WRITING STOP NYASALAND CREDENTIALS NEEDED.

The confusion may lie in the fact that among the private papers of Barbara Gwyer is a letter that Margery had written from Salisbury on February 24, 1930. In this she first opened up to her head of house the idea of devoting herself to writing a book on native administration in Africa, possibly under the aegis of the Centre of African Studies that H.A.L. Fisher had in mind as the proper role for Oxford's new institution of Rhodes House* – indeed, already described by her in October 1929 as 'my own place of work' (*AA*, p. 37). In this case, Margery conceded, she would probably have to give up her College Fellowship, 'to leave and try and manage on my own resources', despite the palpable loss of Oxford privilege and status that this would involve. In the end, by the time she received the two cables some months after writing her letter, Margery had sufficiently made up her mind about Africa to be able to send what she liked to describe as her two one-word telegrams: 'Accept' to Philip Kerr at the Rhodes Trust, and 'Resign' to Barbara Gwyer at St Hugh's. In return for the loss of her prestigious College Fellowship, she now had the academic's rare privilege, 'the glorious gift of time' (*EAJ*, p. 13). Margery, who right from her early days as a lecturer at Oxford had properly identified race relations as an integral element of colonial administration† and whose skilful intertwining of the two had helped her secure the Rhodes Trust Travelling Fellowship, had now decided not so much to abandon her chosen topic of study but to restructure its context. From now on, it was to be Africa as the exemplification of race relations in colonial administration that was to become the central focus of her research and the primary basis of her reputation.

When one reads the present diary, one cannot help being struck by several facets of the young Margery Perham's *modus operandi*. Progressively recognizable as they become through her cumulative diary-letters, they claim a special interest in the pages that follow

---

* On the several alternative roles envisaged for Rhodes House, see Richard Symonds, 'Powerhouse of Imperial Studies: The Early Search for a Role for Rhodes House', *Round Table* (1983), 288.
† Cf. A.H.M. Kirk-Greene, 'Colonial Administration and Race Relations', *Ethnic and Racial Studies* 9, 3 (1986), 275–87.

because here we perceive the outline of incipient traits and tactics which over the years were to become her established mannerisms and characteristics, some personal, others professional.

A typical example is her interaction with officialdom. Bearing in mind the ways of bureaucratic hierarchy, above all within the artificially heightened colonial context, the reader will be impressed by the seeming ease with which this youngish and unknown don gained access to and earned respect from the top echelons of the Service. The Governor of American Samoa, whom she had sketched in her imagination as a tyrant and an ogre, 'one of the most complete despots in the world', readily takes her under his protective wing. Nor is His Excellency at all put out when she telephones him early one morning, while he and his wife are still in bed, to let them know that she is waiting on the quayside and would greatly appreciate a bite of breakfast. The Governor of Western Samoa calls on her, invites her to tea and thereafter frequently to dinner for long talks, as well as taking her out on tour with him. The Governor of Fiji sets aside a desk for her in the Secretariat and instructs his staff to make papers available to her, just as his opposite number in Pago Pago had done, to the point of not excluding confidential dispatches to the Naval Department. In New Zealand Margery interviews the Prime Minister, is very generously entertained by his predecessor, and has a supper-party given in Parliament in her honour. In Australia she is invited to stay at Government House, Canberra, and again to spend the day at Government House in Adelaide and Perth. And, for good measure, she ends up as the house guest of the British Ambassador to the United States of America, besides being entertained to a series of parties and picnics by Britain's diplomatic and consular representatives all the way from Chicago and San Francisco to Honolulu and Wellington.

But life is not all well-oiled and polished diplomacy. Margery is discourteously late for a meeting with one prime minister, whose invitation to come at 11.30 a.m. she had answered by saying she would if she could; presumingly queries another for not having answered a letter she had written to him; and brusquely declines an invitation to take tea with the wife of the officer administering the Government of Fiji. She moves straight into the attack when calling on the Civil Service Commissioner of New Zealand, with whose report (which she had come to discuss) she profoundly disagreed; tells members of Fiji's administration that she finds them complacent; and quickly arrives at the conclusion that, despite the perils of intellectual priggishness, she had a better brain than that of the Prime Minister of New Zealand. She is seldom slow to criticize or disagree with officialdom, 'hotly' or 'emphatically', whenever she thinks they have got their policies wrong. Even in seeking uniquely important interviews such as that with General Richardson, Margery saw no point in concealing, in her letter of self-introduction, the fact that she was no admirer of the man or his achievements. Throughout, she gives the impression of being in her element and at her best when talking shop; challenged by the obligations of social small talk or having to meet people in whom she could discern no professional interest (for instance, the international tennis player Norman Brookes, who appeared to her as dull as Melbourne itself), Margery seems, then as often later in her life, wont to dismiss them as quickly as possible in order to get back to quizzing and provoking politicians, public servants and professors alike.

One interesting consideration arises out of Margery's capacity for hobnobbing with her hosts while investigating their performance. They were fully aware of her mission (only the Governor of American Samoa later rather than sooner). She was often critical of them and had come to discover the seamy side of their policies. Her vigorous condemnation of the handling by New Zealand of the Mau rebellion, of the general conduct of her Samoan mandate and of the inadequate calibre of her island administrators, constitutes the central and most conspicuous example of Margery's inquiries narrated in this diary, without in any way being her sole public exposures of maladministration. Yet these officials, the target of Margery's investigations, not only received her courteously but spared no pains to accommodate and help her, by providing an office in the Secretariat or a table in the parliamentary library, and making available to her numerous official – frequently confidential – papers, even when they knew she did not exactly see eye to eye with them. As her potential arch-enemy in Wellington disarmingly greeted her, 'Ah-ha, Miss Perham, we know all about you. This department is entirely at your service. Anything you like to ask – information, papers – just say what you want'. It was to be the same wherever she went on this apprentice journey, whether it was the could-not-do-enough Mr Barrett of the Transkei administration (*AA*, pp. 72–3) or the Chief Secretary of Nigeria, who sat her down to write in the Governor's chair in the Legislative Council 'with the arms of England emblazoned above my head' (*WAP*, pp. 24–5). For all her self-deprecatory status of a 'young and unknown female investigator', Margery was already beginning to elicit the kind of respect which in later years she expected if, only rarely, it was not offered automatically. But the situation did contain a moral dilemma, one which, characteristically, she at once faced up to. 'I can already see', she noted in Samoa, 'that it is going to be difficult to criticize governors who are, in a sense, my hosts and upon whose goodwill I am dependent.'

There was one lesson in official relations that Margery learned early in her career and was never to forget in her years as a relentless researcher. It consisted of two interwoven strands. The first, which she worked out in Wellington, was the imperative of going at once to the top. She had no patience in waiting for the chance 'to gather a few crumbs' from some underling, 'looking with awe at the titles on the doors behind which the supermen of administration direct the world's affairs at high pressure'. The art, of course, was to go straight to the top man, 'never to the junior man first'. This tactic was supremely symbolized on the next leg of this trip, in Kenya. There she scandalized the ADC to the Governor by asking His Excellency, as he ceremonially left the Legislative Assembly, whether she might have a lift in his chauffeur-driven car: otherwise, she winningly assured him, she would be unpardonably late for HE's command to luncheon at Government House! The other strand to the secret of her success in getting the most out of those she wanted to meet, over and above her own capacity to charm when she wanted to, is best defined in her own words:

> No official . . . seems ever too busy to talk about his own work. The difficulty is not to get in to him, not to start, but to stop him. . . . This may sound rather cynical, and I do believe that the many officials I have met have been actuated by kindness and courtesy, but that alone could not explain the time and talk that has been showered upon me, especially as the point has sometimes been reached when kindness and courtesy should have prompted my release.

Yet, as again emerges from the pages of her Pacific diary, even more unambiguously than from those of its companion volumes, Margery was no strait-laced, purse-lipped bluestocking. Work, and then more work, may have been her first priorities, but this regime could still leave time for a young, attractive, energetic and ebullient, single woman to have fun. We find her enjoying picnics and midnight drives in the starlit hills behind San Francisco, swimming parties in Hawaii and Pago Pago, relaxing in riding or a game of tennis, bridge and even – perhaps rashly recalling her glories on the hockey field at Oxford – playing (or rather, trying to play) a shaming round of golf or, even more disastrously, a game of shipboard cricket. Above all, of course, was her sheer joy in meeting other young people with whom she could interact, relax and for a while forget she was that somewhat awe-inspiring creature, an Oxford female don breaking into a predominantly male, colonial, bush or outback society. In nine cases out of ten, when Margery could bring herself to relax, she could do so in full enjoyment with the best of them. The sense of warmth, acceptance, affection, even of relief, generated by such passing friendships is almost tangible in these diaries: Nichols the paragon in New Zealand, 'brains, games and breeding . . . an aesthete as well . . . most interesting, civilized and attractive to meet', and 'Petronius' on the voyage to Fiji, 'strikingly handsome, tall and slim . . . well-set grey-blue eyes, a fine nose and a rather scornful mouth'; the unnamed (but not anonymous) Assistant Commissioner in Basutoland, Hugh Ashton, 'good trek-comrade' (*AA*, p. 128), 'fair . . . slender . . . immaculate' (*AA*, p. 87); Graham de Courcy Ireland in Tanganyika, the 'handsome, long-lashed, lustrous-eyed cadet' (*EAJ*, p. 48); and more than one eminently personable District Commissioner in the Sudan, possibly including the empathetic, slightly younger, Civil Secretary himself, Douglas Newbold.

Two more aspects of Margery Perham in her first, formative years as an academic authority emerge from this diary, though these were to become distinctly less rather than patently more apparent as her career advanced. The first is her almost unbelievable capacity for being late for appointments throughout these three months. For example, not only did she cut an interview in Wellington generously set up by the Prime Minister himself and in Apia commit the colonial solecism of neglecting to sign the Governor's book on arrival, but frequently kept other hosts waiting unpardonably, such as her kindly cicerone on the Berkeley campus or the New Zealand women's luncheon club which she had promised to address. On more than one occasion Margery almost missed the boat – literally. As if she had not learned from her horrifying experience of having to run for the ship at Pago Pago ('I had a bit of a crisis getting away from the island'), and 'flung myself on to the boat at the last possible moment' in Wellington, her departure from Perth was even more dramatic– 'a humane second officer was desperately trying to hold the boat back for me, with all the passengers hanging over the taffrail to see the fun. I raced up the gangway in great embarrassment'. The same thing happened in Sydney, though this time it was a train. Yet nobody could accuse Margery Perham of being careless of the importance of time. She needed it too much to waste or undervalue it. The more probable explanation of her unpunctuality was that she tried to crowd too many minutes into a limited working hour. 'Nearly always twenty minutes behind time,' she records, 'because the breakaway was always so hard to make.' Not allowing enough time for all she took on was a habit that Margary never entirely lost, according to those of her research assistants who worked closely with her in the 1960s like Mary Bull, Patience Empson and Kathleen Stahl.

The other unexpected sidelight, which comes out more clearly in this Pacific diary than when Margery reaches Africa, is her remarkably casual attitude towards fixing up accommodation in advance. This is as true of her arrival in the big cities as it is of her experiences in more outlandish places. By the time she reaches Africa, she is – has had to be – more circumspect. Yet the image of Margery trudging along the upstate New York turnpike on a public holiday carrying her suitcase, or of sitting forlornly on the quayside in friendless Pago Pago watching the ship sail away, is as unforgettable as it is unexpected in a person of her administrative ability.

So sanguine an indifference to the basic planning of a journey – let alone a well-paid Rhodes Trust Travelling Fellowship – is perhaps no more than a reflection of the optimism of youth. Right from the dramatic opening entry ('I seemed aware of a great weight sitting upon my chest . . .') Margery evinces a profound anxiousness about her grand tour: 'Both physically and intellectually I shall have to make my way. I have no clear itinerary. . . . I have little experience in travel. . . . I could foresee it all, the tiredness and loneliness, the rebuffs in my work . . . gaffes in face of strange customs and currencies.' She sensed, too, the disadvantage of her gender: '. . . the prejudice against my sex in this context . . . the unpacking of crushed dresses and struggling with untidy hair minutes before some important occasion. How much easier all this is for men!'

That *cri de coeur* of feminism is poignantly echoed in her first impression of the Governor of American Samoa: 'I envied him his job – and his sex.' The anxiety persists all the way to Australasia. Only then, 20,000 miles, three continents and two months later, can she face up to the fact that she is no longer afraid of prime ministers and governors-general. And within six months we find her accepting a telephoned last-minute invitation from Princess Alice in Government House, Cape Town, with calm and considered appraisal: 'I thought this a good effort in informality for G.H. – and Royalty, too. . . . I have almost got over worrying about that sort of thing' (*AA*, pp. 157–8).

There need be nothing surprising in these reactions of a young, single female traveller setting out, sixty years ago, on a fifteen months' tour round the world. 'I was by no means', she notes in one of her successor diaries, 'what is called a woman of the world' (*AA*, p. 12).

Even the most sophisticated of today's jet-set is likely to be susceptible to an uncontrollable surge of adrenalin in the bloodstream as she or he steps aboard Concorde or sets out overland for Katmandu. What is surprising, not to Margery Perham as she embarked at Southampton but to the reader who arrives at the end of the diary, is either how needless was Margery's worry about having to make her way and hold her own socially and intellectually, or else how superbly she overcame her suspected lack of a 'brazen exterior behind which to cover the fears and embarrassments which are already tormenting me in prospect'. Yet think how triumphantly she succeeded in tracking down the Governor of American Samoa and fixing a passage on the same ship, in integrating herself with the top parliamentarians of New Zealand and in being personally welcomed by the sovereign's representatives in Australia, or in unswervingly seeking out notorious anti-Government agitators in San Francisco, Auckland and Apia.

Besides this worry about whether she was taking on more than she could handle, there was another anxiety that may have been lurking at the back of her mind that July morning as she lay in bed and faced up to the harsh realities of the journey which was about to begin. This was the matter of money. Nowhere does she actually spell this out. Indeed, we know that the Rhodes Trust was as typically generous with its travel grants as it has proverbially been in financing its Rhodes scholarships, chairs and lectureships at Oxford University. Yet throughout the diary the reader will come across incidental remarks signalling the fear that Margery, like virtually any other British academic (and her annual salary when she left Sheffield University to take up her post at Oxford was no more than £100), needed to keep a careful eye on her expenses. Thus we find her recording, 'with awe' that the tariff at the Royal Hawaiian Hotel was all of six guineas a day; that she found the price of clothes in Wellington 'simply appalling' when she spent on a dress (reduced at that) two or three times what she would have paid at Harrods; that she grudged paying 15s. 6d. for the hotel in Apia and half a crown for an American musical at the cinema in Wellington. In Sydney she alleged that she was defrauded three times in succession, once by a porter who cursed her for the meagreness of the tip, once by a taxi-driver, and finally by a newspaper boy who took a shilling for a penny-halfpenny paper and then 'walked off without so much as a thank-you for the enforced tip'. Margery reckoned Auckland to be the most expensive city in the world, yet she was quite ready to play bridge in Fiji at a shilling a hundred! Maybe all this was prudence rather than anxiety, for despite her prosperous upbringing in Harrogate, one cannot quite imagine the young Margery ever being wantonly extravagant. As it transpired, Margery had husbanded her Rhodes Trust grant so adroitly that she was able to show an unspent balance and put it towards financing the best part of yet a third year, visiting West Africa.

The final item for comment on Margery Perham's persona as it emerges from the pages of her very first 'public' diary is her appreciation, instant and enthusiastic, of beauty. At the scenic level, of course, descriptions of natural beauty are to be expected from the pen of this gifted and graceful writer. Accordingly she enthuses over the idyllic splendour of Samoa, the special quality of green in the Pacific, the mountainous magnificence of New Zealand.

But in the present diary more strikingly than in any of the other three it is Margery's continual allusion to personal good looks – mostly in males – that catches the reader's attention. Her porter at Grand Central Station is 'an enormous and handsome black man. . . . Massive, intelligent, smiling'. The Maoris she sees as 'very vigorous and healthy . . . so attractive and clean that one is not surprised that they can win white women'; Lady Pomare is 'so jolly and attractive that I can well picture her managing a white man'; her youngest son seemed 'just a very good-looking, dark-haired English boy'; and the Maori schoolteacher at Otaki was 'extraordinary attractive'. A shipboard passenger, an eccentric British MP, on the Wellington–Sydney voyage she found 'Byronic in appearance'; the Scottish pastor in New Zealand's rural North Island catches her attention – 'young, good-looking, full of force'; and, textbook-like, the Governor's ADC at Canberra turned out to be 'a very good-looking young man' and, only two lines later, 'dark and good-looking'. Her guide in Eastern Samoa, Kalamete, she described as 'a very beautiful boy of fifteen or sixteen', while on a visit to a school in Fiji Margery spots 'one of the most beautiful human beings I ever saw, a young, slender Fijian . . . dressed in a spotless white *lava-lava* and shirt open at the neck. . . . I walked round to get his profile – he was equally beautiful that way'. Of her swept-off-her-feet reaction to the elegant and sophisticated Philip Nichols of the Foreign Office mention has been made earlier.

Margery Perham consistently describes her writing home as a 'diary-letter'. She believed that by sending instalments of her travel diary to friends in England she received in return their 'deep encouragement' from this way of 'sharing my experiences and ideas' (unpublished note to the present diary). What this meant in practice she has described thus: 'Written day by day, and often wearily at night [the diary] was sent out at intervals to England, where it was typed and distributed to members of my family and a few intimate friends' (ditto,

MS: on who the 'five favoured' recipients were in 1931, see *WAP*, p. 16).

In the event, there is overwhelming internal evidence to challenge this image of a regular and devoted diarist. We even have Margery's own testimony, again in a manuscript note, stating that 'I wrote it at occasional intervals of leisure' (ditto, MS). On another occasion she probably came nearer the truth when she declared of her diary-letters that 'They were written in such hours and half hours as I could snatch from the assiduous round of travel and interviewing, and were often jotted down in weariness and discomfort late at night' (*EAJ*, p. 18). At the same time, she collected a huge amount of official documents and kept separate notebooks for her interviews and her research data. Margery herself has given us a useful guide-line on the division of content: 'As my more serious investigations – and travelling at speed even these could not be very serious – went into my notebooks, the diary contained the more general impressions and personal experiences which might interest my friends, but often ran on to deal with politics and public figures' (ditto, MS.).

In the present diary, tidied up (rather than revised) and purged of 'a few of the grosser errors of style' by Margery herself in the early 1970s for possible publication, Margery was far less heedful about giving dates than in any of the other diaries. In a note included in the first reorganization of the original 1929 diary, undertaken in the summer of 1939 when she did not feel up to travelling to Africa, she remarks, somewhat cavalierly to and for a scholar, 'I have decided *not* to put the exact date – the journey began several years ago' MSS 35/3, 2)! Specific dates are mentioned less than half a dozen times in the whole diary. For instance, she tells us she reached Fiji on August 25, 1929, but (surprisingly) not when she sailed from Southampton (June 25); we can calculate from an earlier reference to September 28 which day she landed in Australia; and we have a reference to the date that she was due to sail for South Africa, her ship leaving Adelaide on October 5. We can also deduce on which date she set off on her uncomfortable journey to Rotorua, because she ruefully mentions it took place on her birthday! On the other hand, one of the few dates she has entered is wrong by ten years: 'August 1919' as a heading for entering the harbour at Apia is surely a slip of the pen. Whereas this kind of omission is no more than an irritant to the historian, who all too often has other means of dating events, a second problem in the Pacific diary, unlike the African ones, is created by her deliberate effort to disguise the names of some of the persons she met. Wherever possible I have dealt with this in my editorial Notes, but the detective work still has a long way to go; nor is it helped by Margery's own inconsistencies – for example, a character is called D. on one page, A.D. a little later, and given a pseudonym elsewhere! While a scrutiny of the original diaries, along with an examination of the 1939 textual fragments, has revealed some identities, a notable lacuna remains in the research into the Australian pseudonyms and anonymities, for regrettably there are no notebooks or manuscript diaries for that part of her 1929 journey (the relevant 'Notebooks and Ring-Files' series comes to an end with Box 81/27, on Western Samoa and New Zealand).

In my editing of the manuscript my aim has been to present the original text in a coherent way without interfering with Margery's own prose. Here is the version of the diary she favoured. The few necessary textual alterations, other than shortening, consist – apart from two major deletions, clearly indicated in the text – of standard editorial tidying up, especially in the spelling of proper names and the unexpectedly necessary substitution *passim* of 'kangaroo' for 'kangeroo' and 'coconut' for 'cocoanut'. Her own draft foreword has been eliminated: apart from the excerpts reproduced above, essentially it repeated what eventually appeared in the forewords to *African Apprenticeship* and *East African Journey*. I have also regularized her use of Samoan and Maori vernacular terms. In respect of a number of Maori names and place-names, I have made use of a list of corrections suggested by W.B. Sutch of New Zealand when Margery sent him a copy of the New Zealand draft in case it was of help to him in his work on Coates (MSS 37/9, 71-2). In sum, very little has been omitted from the diary and nothing has been added to it. Throughout I have sought to be faithful to Margery's own claim (here and there denied by her frequent and occasionally cavalier selection from the multiple versions at her disposal) made in her draft introduction to one of the 1972 revisions: 'The material is published here word for word almost exactly as it was written, generally very hurriedly, forty-three years ago' MSS 38/8, 3). The truth is that Margery was too good a scholar not to indulge in the revisions enabled and encouraged by rereading. As with *West African Passage*, the original had no title, and the present choice I made with my wife and publishers.

Working in a field far wider than my shared interest in Margery Perham's African and Colonial Service history – in those areas much of my expertise was learned from her – I have an unavoidably long list of those to whose writings a special acknowledgement is in order. Besides the specific bibliographical sources cited in the Notes for the guidance of readers wishing to take the story further, I have derived considerable inspiration and benefit from generally consulting a number of standard sources on the Pacific and Australasian culture area, namely:

Southwest Pacific

C. Hartley Grattan, *The Southwest Pacific Since 1900* (1963).
Linden A. Mander, *Some Dependent Peoples of the South Pacific* (1954).
W.P. Morrell, *Britain in the Pacific Islands* [1830–1900] (1960).

Samoa

J.W. Davidson, *Samoa mo Samoa* (1967).
F.M. Keesing, *Modern Samoa: Its Government and Changing Life* (1934).
Paul Kennedy, *The Samoan Tangle* [1878–1900] (1974).
I have also profited from reading Sir Harry Luke's *From a South Seas Diary, 1938–1942* (1945).

New Zealand

Mary Boyd's chapters on Western Samoa in Angus Ross (ed.), *New Zealand's Record in the Pacific Islands in the Twentieth Century* (1969).
Keith Sinclair, *A History of New Zealand* (rev. ed., 1980).
W.H. Oliver and B.R. Williams, *The Oxford History of New Zealand* (1981).

Australia

W. Keith Hancock, *Australia* (1930).
O.H.K. Spate, *Australia* (1968).

On the Mandates system under the League of Nations, I have leaned heavily on such time-tested stalwarts as Freda White, *Mandates* (1926); Quincy Wright, *Mandates under the League of Nations* (Chicago, 1930); and H.D. Hall, *Mandates, Dependencies and Trusteeship* (Washington, DC, 1948).

Following Margery's footsteps, I too have been able to consult, more easily than she, the Minutes of the Permanent Mandates Commission – her 'vast documentation' – and have also been able to consult the relevant annual volumes of the *Survey of International Affairs*, notably those edited by Arnold Toynbee for the crucial (in the context of this diary) years of 1926–9, as well as the extensive United

Nations documentation on the transfer of power in Western Samoa between 1947 and 1961.

Finally, I should like to offer my sincere thanks to Margery Perham's Executors for permission to publish this manuscript and for their generous help and encouragement; to Dr Robin Fletcher, Warden, and Mr. Alan S. Bell, Librarian of Rhodes House, for permission to consult the Rhodes Trust Travelling Fellowship files; to Mrs Patricia Pugh, archivist, currently engaged on cataloguing the Perham papers, and an encyclopaedia of Perhamana; the Head of the Library and Records Department, Foreign and Commonwealth Office, for valuable help in identifying the several holders of consular and diplomatic appointments in 1929; to Mr Philip A. Snow, OBE, for sharing his profound knowledge of the Colonial Service in Fiji; Mr Michael Levien, my editor at Peter Owen; and to the Chairman and members of the Department of History in the University of Calgary, whose invitation as Visiting Professor during the fall semester of 1985 furnished me with the opportunity to edit this diary.

St Antony's College   *A.H.M. KIRK-GREENE*
Oxford

1

The United States

I woke up this morning lying not only in perfect physical ease but contained also within that blessed moment of unconsciousness of what the new day might hold. Then, suddenly, I seemed aware of a great weight sitting upon my chest. For a few seconds I could not identify it. Then I knew that in an hour or two I was to start alone on a fifteen months' tour round the world.[1] My luggage lay locked up and labelled in the study leading out of my bedroom, the room which held my books and papers, such *objets* as I had collected, and in which for some years I have been trying to help the young to study history.[2] My sudden sense of fear, almost of panic, which has still not quite left me as I write on my first night on board this Atlantic liner,[3] was due to the sense of my incompetence in getting around the world and achieving some kind of success in carrying out my large and indefinite commission.[4] Both physically and intellectually I shall have to make my own way. I have no clear itinerary beyond New York. I have little experience in travel, no brazen exterior behind which to cover the fears and embarrassments which are already tormenting me in prospect. I could foresee it all, the tiredness and loneliness, the rebuffs in my work, the prejudice against my sex in this context, gaffes in face of strange customs and currencies, the unpacking of crushed dresses and struggling with untidy hair minutes before some important occasion. How much easier all this is for men! And for the brazen – if indeed there are such, rather than persons who know better than I know how to act the necessary part.[5]

I boarded this ugly great liner at Southampton and watched the diminishing figure of my sister[6] waving to me from the quay. Then we edged out into a grey sea. The first contact has been with the men sitting on each side of me tonight at dinner. One was a young Norwegian, appropriately blue-eyed and golden haired. He expounded to me the problems of his profession, the ocean transport of very heavy

35

machines, such as railway engines. On the other side was a fat-necked German-American who, without any encouragement, contributed the history and philosophy of his life. His father had brought him to the United States as a child. Both his sons had fought against Germany in the war. He had just achieved his first visit to Germany to look up his family background. He was very clear that his first visit would be his last. He was bored and disgusted with what he saw, a small town on a wooded hill, a background of agricultural simplicity – a living burial compared with the suburbs of New York where he had built himself a house with every conceivable modern gadget, for all of which he explained their cost and specifications.

New York

No more about the voyage. I was neither physically nor mentally in the mood to enjoy traversing a rather sulky Atlantic. This evening, at the climax, I stood with the row at the taffrail, prepared, a little self-consciously, to take my first impression of America. As an alien among a group of natives I saw that I was expected to register an adequate reaction. I certainly offered them a genuine gasp of astonishment when I first realized that those odd-shaped crags forming themselves on the horizon were man-made. The Statue of Liberty had every chance to impress. I saw her suddenly, standing over our bows, cut black against a gaudy sunset. I expect she gives some English people a slight sense of embarrassment, a feeling as if a young relative had made some rather naïve pretension.

We ran alongside the city through the ferries and tugs which were darting over the water like phosphorescent water-spiders toward the docks where, by contrast, the big ships lay motionless like larvae in their cells. As we drew closer, with so many smaller buildings crouching round the base of the larger, the effect of height was diminished. They seemed like children's bricks piled aimlessly one on top of another to the point of collapse. But as we drew in New York switched on its lights. In some the illumination was constant as with perforated tiers full of fire. In some of the larger buildings the lights going on and off gave a ripple of movement as with a sequin dress.

As the tugs pushed our 40,000 tons into its dock a galleryful of people burst into sound, shrill screams, concerted roars and antics of welcome, all answered from the ship and rising to a crescendo as we were nudged alongside. Like most of my nation I felt at once half critical, half envious of such uninhibited spontaneity. But I was mainly concerned as to whether anyone in that crowd had come to meet me in response to such notice as the Rhodes Trust had sent of my unimportant arrival. After fifteen anxious minutes a quiet-spoken dignified man asked my name, and announced himself as Dr Abraham Flexner,[7] a scholar of high international repute and author of a great book on European universities. He conducted me, entranced as I was with relief and gratitude, through the various processes of disembarkation. When I saw my luggage shot downwards to a point a few feet from the foremost taxi in the rank, he smiled at my astonished admiration like the uncle at a party when a conjuror amuses the children and remarked 'We are full of tricks like that.'

Arrived at my hotel, thirty storeys high, Dr Flexner, whose kindness is, I hope, a foretaste of all that is to meet me in America, insisted upon coming to my room to see that it was comfortable and quiet. Quietness here is relative. New York must be the noisiest city in the world, as well as among the hottest in midsummer. Since New Yorkers can have all they want, presumably they like noise including that of their fiendish elevated railway which hurls roaring trains day and night a few feet above the streets.[8]

All the next few days, with senses bruised by speed, noise and the intimidating proportions of the city, I found my way around to make contacts with administrators, academics and others in my field – kind people and an unkind city, which seems to dwarf human dignity.

Upstate New York

I have escaped from New York to go up by train along the Hudson River to Albany. This journey will not be intelligible unless I explain its background.

During the last two years at Oxford I have begun studying British policy towards native races, excluding our vast and rather special relations with peoples in Africa.[9] Finding my way back to discover where 'native policy' could be said to begin, dismissing the possible inclusion of our dealings with Ireland, I found a strenuous figure rising out of the past, Sir William Johnson,[10] an Irish pioneer who thrust himself in the mid-eighteenth century into the forested region some 150 miles north of New York, the country leading up to Lake Ontario and the French colony of Canada. This was the home and hunting ground of the strong group of Amerindian tribes known as the Six

Nations. Unlike most colonists, Johnson did not regard the Indians as vermin to be cleared from their desirable lands. He admired the more humane and intelligent methods of the French. In any case, while the struggle with France for North America was undecided, the alliance of the tribes was needed, especially in this frontier region. He therefore entered into close relations with them, learned their language, took an Indian wife and spent much of his time in conference with them on the lawn of the fine house he built on the banks of the Mohawk River.

I had spent long, absorbing hours in the Record Office[11] reading the letters addressed by this man to the shifting ministers of George III, advocating recognition of Indian rights and an orderly system or relationships with them. The Seven Years' War, ending in 1763, opened the whole of North America to British occupation. Johnson saw in it a chance to build up a really constructive and protective administration for the Indians. I found his letters outlining these plans enthralling. In many ways he seemed to anticipate ideas later employed by the Colonial Service in Africa.[12] Johnson was given the title of Colonel of the Six Nations. Unfortunately the white colonists had purposes exactly opposite to his. They meant to exploit the end of French rivalry by a sweeping westward advance in which Indians and their rights would be trampled underfoot. The attempt to control the expansion and to tax the colonists for a continuing British administration was, of course, the main reason for the American Revolution. So the white men pioneered across the continent and the red men were exterminated or thrust aside to rot in reservations. I hope to write about this man and for this reason I wanted to visit the country and the house where he worked, all vividly in my mind from the reports written in his own firm clear hand.[13]

My train left the Grand Central Station and soon crossed the Harlem River which once, but no longer, bounded the negro[14] quarter. It ran for three hours up the Hudson Valley through low wooded hills, clinging to the edge of the river. I realized too late that I was on a very dubious enterprise. It was the only time I could spare for the journey and, being British, I had quite forgotten the meaning of the next day, the Fourth of July, though, as a student of history, I ought to have remembered it. It meant that on this public holiday all the people I wanted to see would almost certainly be away, the State library closed and the State historian, editor of Johnson's papers, inaccessible. I got off at Albany, found a hotel[15] and was told that it would be practically impossible to reach Johnson country next day.

I went to bed feeling rather wretched. My first enterprise seemed a complete failure. In such a mood it was not easy to share the jubilation of a people all going mad because they had thrown off the British 159 years ago.[16] But at least, I thought, I could sleep. It was already twelve o'clock and I turned in hopefully. It was a false hope. My window faced on the public square of Albany. A roar of motor traffic, and of trams, all hooting and ringing for the crossroads, came through my window. About midnight started the fireworks. And such fireworks! Not lovely showers of coloured fire, but simply things that banged, louder and bigger as the night went on until the noise was like a bombardment. Then, as if that were not enough, all the fire-engines came out and, just for fun, raced round and round the square. Each American fire-engine is equipped not only with clashing bells as in England, but with its own fog-horn. I shut my window, plugged my ears with cotton wool, hid under the bedclothes. It was all of no avail. So I lay awake for all night, thinking ever more bitterly of the Adams and even of George Washington and ever more kindly of Grenville and Lord North.

This morning I rose early and paid my bill and went to the station, determined to push through as far as I could. I took a train thirty miles up the Mohawk River to Amsterdam, thence to Fonda. At Fonda I found a trolley-car, an antediluvian machine I had not expected to meet in America, and this took me ten miles to Johnston, the valley settlement which Johnson had built up in the sixties of the eighteenth century, and which his loyalist son and the Indians slipping down from Canada ravaged in the revolutionary wars. I won't here describe my long walk to find the solid house, so familiar to me from his letters, my pushing wearily through holiday crowds, which on all sides were waving flags and exploding crackers. But Johnston was pretty quick in getting on to me. A man of whom I had asked the way followed me afterwards in his car, and spent an hour motoring me all round to show me the sights, though it was a little difficult to make him understand that it was old and not new Johnston that interested me. Later he ran me to earth in the restaurant, bearing a great bundle of local papers issued in 1922, when there had been civic celebrations.[17] Then a policeman . . . told the editor of the local paper about me and he ran after me in the street with a notebook and said, 'Now, I want your story.'

Hardly could I escape Johnston, going in another local tram-train in search of Fort Johnson, where Sir William had earlier built himself a plain stone house on the edge of the Mohawk River. This also I found and, having induced the old Irish caretaker to let me in, I pondered over the Georgian furniture and fittings which Johnson had so eagerly and minutely ordered from England and had awaited with such impatience on their long, slow voyage. I saw, too, the old red brick court-house where Johnson had worked as a Justice of the Peace.

I was now a few miles from Amsterdam and the railway, and the afternoon was getting on. There was nothing for it but to walk, carrying my suitcase.[18] It was a wet day on and off but this had not kept in the holiday-makers. The cars in America have to be seen to be believed. All along the road, at intervals of a few feet, a double row of Fords passed me, full of joyous Americans, mostly sitting all on top of one another. As there is no provision for pedestrians, I had to stumble along in the ditch as best I could. I never saw anyone else except on wheels, and there was hardly a car from which I was not pointed out with obvious exclamations of amazement. At Amsterdam I managed to get a train to Albany, and after waiting there two hours, got one to New York, and so to bed, very, very tired, about half past one.

During my travels in the Albany district, I had one strong impression, that of the strangeness of a country owned – exploited one might say – by a people which has not been bred there, whose associations are of yesterday. There is none of that impression of spiritual affinity between the people and the country that comes from many centuries of mutual moulding. The country, in spite of occasional beauty, seems unloved, neglected. I look back upon the cheap buildings, the ugly fringes of towns where they link with country, tangled woods straggling into shabby fields, the endless façade of shouting hoardings, the glades defiled by great heaps of the rusting carcases of motor cars, the farm buildings painted with the giant letters of some 'boost'. There may, there must be, much that is better than this, but this is true and distressing. All the time one thinks 'What a continent to use – what a continent to play with!' Have the people been worthy of the opportunity?

And of course I could not help having often in my mind the people to whom the continent once belonged. They belonged to it, wild, cruel and yet beautiful in some ways. When you see the rivers and hills, with the forest still only partly hacked away, you imagine the long canoes mirrored in the water, the camp-fire, the wigwams. I remembered how the leader of one of the tribes in these areas declared, 'We are not slaves. These forests, these lakes and rivers are ours and before we will part with them we will spatter the leaves with their blood or die every man in the attempt.'[19] President Theodore Roosevelt's comment was that this great continent could not have been left as nothing but a game preserve for squalid savages. Was no compromise possible? As it is, I found that in the country of the Six Nations there is not one Indian to be seen.

On the human side New York was all ungrudging hospitality and help from men and women distinguished in my sphere of work. But I feel battered by the physical setting. First there is the congestion in the streets whose single surface has to carry the traffic and population of a city which reaches so far into the air above them, and so deep into the rock below. My first view from the top of a building showed how the skyscrapers were advancing in monstrous formation from the West upon what remained of the older city. Far away in the hot mist loomed the mammoths of Battery Point, Woolworth and the rest. Nearer were some newer towers, some absurdly topped by Gothic ornament only visible from our equal level, some gilded and domed, others just block. Right below us, an aspect hardly tolerable, I could see a church, built long ago to the human proportions of another age and looking like a child's toy. There were rows of little two- or three-storey houses, with filthy chicken-ravaged gardens and even trees, all doomed. Already the wrecker was busy not far away destroying the skyscrapers of yesterday while those of tomorrow were mounting almost visibly in a mist of scaffolding.

Will the final effect be beautiful? No. I was disappointed in the skyscraper. At close range it simply cannot be seen without craning the neck until vision is distorted; at a distance the effect must depend entirely upon general proportions and upon the relation of one block to another. And this is where the disappointment comes in. The blocks are built quite haphazard; some of them, just to fit in, are lopsided, and there seems little or no attempt to relate one to the other. Mere size can have no beauty: after the first shock it ceases to impress. There is only a jagged group of rectangles, broad or narrow, taller, shorter, new and white, or old and grey. Not only is co-ordination and harmony needed for the group. New York has not learned how to shape nor how to decorate each of these giant masses. Gothic turrets are merely absurd, cathedrals on stilts. Rows of columns, abruptly appliquéd on the side without any function, are insignificant. It is with relief that one turns to the unrelieved block, for its negative quality of being steel frame and concrete, naked and unashamed. There is room for some architect to make the great discovery, the ideal shape and the significant siting and decoration, above all the relativity, for these crags of masonry.

Night helps the skyscraper. Decoration lost and shape dim, it rears up against the sunset or stars, itself glittering with lights, perhaps its crest rimmed with electric fire, or the surface flushed with a play of light, yellow, rose or silver, thrown up from below. This brings an element of fantasy, so utterly lacking in the American daytime city. And this effect is enhanced where there is water below to double, rippling, the lighted towers.

Washington, DC

Now back to my train and the journey to Washington. The station is the central Terminus. Compared with our dingy Victorian erections these main-line stations are most impressive – almost the cathedrals of America.

I now had to turn my back upon the unfortunate Amerindians and face up to the negroes, unfortunate perhaps, who show no signs of vanishing. And there they were at the station, represented by a crowd of porters. From among these an enormous and handsome black man, who had at once caught my eye, came forward. The ways of American stations and trains being new to me, I knew I should be very dependent upon my porter. Massive, intelligent, smiling, this one assured me I need not worry. He would look after me. To my surprise he spoke not American but English, the soft, drawling English of the gentleman. On the way to the train, I got his story out of him. He was from the West Indies – I forget where – had been at college there and was now working for his medical degree at Columbia University. To make this possible, his wife worked all day, charring, and he worked at night. He did not like New York but the educational opportunities were great. He was only amazed that the American negroes made so little use of their chances. He could not get on with them: there seemed to be an antagonism towards West Indians. His hope was to return and practise at home, where the chances of advance were so much greater.

There was still fifteen minutes for the train to go. It was a very famous train, he told me, the Congressional Limited, full of America's successes in business and politics. I stood at the door of the Pullman after checking my seat. I asked the man to stay and talk until the train went. He talked well, flowing sentences, great command of language. Had I shut my eyes I might have believed it was anyone talking – an Oxford don. In my momentary vignette I could find no fault with the man, intelligence, appearance, manner to me, respectful without being servile, accepting with pleasure the chance of talking on the level with an English stranger, much interested in my own expedition. The white conductor eyed us curiously, so did the inhabitants of the Pullman. Time to go. I gave him a good tip for the sake of his studies, and with mutual good wishes for success in our intellectual enterprises, we parted.

In my seat I pondered this race business.[20] Was I deceived by my sentimentality, my readiness to be prejudiced in favour of the negro, into thinking that man my equal, into thinking the race that can produce such types, given time and opportunity, is potentially the equal of the white? My attitude, my thoughts, would be violently condemned by most South Africans, and in this country by nearly all Southerners, and most Northerners. 'They are not to be trusted; some of them are plausible enough. They know how to talk, but as a race they are permanently inferior and must be kept in their place.'

To the innocence of my impartiality, my lack of permanent involvement, the issue does not present itself in those terms. Here is a people, brutally torn from their primitive environment for a century or two of slavery, and then living, through three difficult generations, as only half citizens and still socially outlawed. What they have achieved – what I hoped I was soon to see at the negro colleges – is surely a marvel. Many of the negroes may, by our standards, be untrustworthy, dirty, immoral: that is inevitable from their past and their present. We must ask ourselves what is it in us that makes for our social virtues? We must make that difficult effort of imagination to put ourselves into the position of a person, never able to stand up to his full stature, nor to feel a full stake in the country in which he lives, hardly able by any effort to earn respect and so finding self-respect difficult to achieve. Is the only answer to this 'Keep them in their place'? But I should not have blundered prematurely into the negro question. It will recur again; it must be the main theme of all my thoughts while I am in America.

Our train travelled deep into the rock of Manhattan Island and emerged again where New York stops – abruptly and hideously – in swamps. It is an ugly run from New York to Washington. Nature is plain and man's efforts, though large, are not beautiful, except for those with a taste for the diabolic beauty of heavy industry. I think I know as well as any layman the look of factories, textile works, iron foundries, steel and chemical plants. Living in England, working in Sheffield, I have moved about from there to Leeds, and to Manchester, taking in Bradford, Newcastle, the Five Towns. It is impossible not to notice a difference between American and English industry, but one hard for the inexpert to describe. It is not only that there are more smokeless chimneys: it is in the look of the buildings. The very machinery seems more lusty, more versatile: the cranes, the chimneys, the foundries, the overhead trolleys, appear to have a strength and size lacking in England. Above all, the endless regiments of goods wagons, enormous in size and built with careful adaptation to their different freights, give an impression of prosperity and efficiency.

I am told there are bad slums in New York, but I never saw anything like ours. The nearest approach to slums that I saw was the spawn of little wooden shacks that breed on the outskirts of every city, among semi-swamps, and those hecatombs of mouldering automobile carcases that are among the most striking sights in America.

The train was marvellous for comfort and elegance. They served a dollar and a half dinner with delicious chicken, fresh green corn, crisp lettuce hearts. My companion at table, Miss Fishback,[21] elegantly marcelled, manicured and attired in pretty chiffon, told me that she was in the advertising department of a big store, but that she always came back to Washington for the week-end. With the usual American kindness she promised me that her brother, who would meet her, would motor me to my hotel.

Back in the observation car, sitting out at the end, I decided to 'turn on' one of my neighbours. By this I mean releasing the flow of friendly American talk, which had hitherto always been ready to respond with information and welcome for the visitor. For the first time the tap did not flow. I said, 'Can you tell me what city this is?' He answered, 'I'm afraid I can't', and returned to his book. Such a thing was without precedent. Could he be English? The voice was very suspicious. I turned to look at him. He was a young man, indeed there were two young men, with pale, finely modelled faces. They did not look English – more French or Italian. I held my peace.

The mystery was solved at Washington. The young man and his brother alighted into the arms of a middle-aged couple, an impressive grey lady and a neat, square, obvious Englishman. I turned to follow Miss Fishback. The older man called me, asked my name and introduced himself as Sir Esmé Howard.[22] In another minute I was in the Embassy car, sweeping through the streets of Washington, and soon in a house without elevators, in a nice, quiet 'English' bedroom, with a French maid unpacking my ravaged clothes and promising to iron them.

Oh, this is civilization! Away from the click and whirr of machines, away from boost and skyscrapers, in the dignity of an old house, with its orderly jumble of precious furniture, its quiet Italian servants – Lady Howard is Italian –, the soft voices, the restraint and dignity, and conversation in which so much can be taken for granted. I sat through dinner watching the family and resting myself in the delicious cool, dry, mental and spiritual atmosphere. Then – for the 'boys' were only just home from England and I broke the newly formed family circle –, I went early to bed to a long, lovely night and a tray bringing a late breakfast with heavy old English silver and china. I felt a snob and a sybarite and revelled in it.[23]

I have had a busy day. First I rang up the Department of Agriculture to see if the letters introducing me had arrived. They had not but the head of the Department told me to come along at once. So I taxied off to the great blocks of government offices lying near the Capitol.

My reception was certainly a credit to the American people and Government. It was the middle of Saturday morning, stifling, indescribable heat that made the perspiration pour incessantly down one's face. Yet here I was, an entirely unknown foreigner, inquiring about the extension demonstration work among the Southern negroes. Response? Instant, kindling enthusiasm, and all work put aside, while one official after another, men and women, took me to his or her office and explained, almost rapturously, the work being done. They produced literature and photographs, handed me from one to the other with complimentary speeches, bewailed my having so little time for them, urged me to come again, took my address, promised to send me more literature and to arrange contacts in the South. My visits to the Colonial Office make a stark contrast.

This is what they are doing. The Federal Government sends farm demonstrators on tour in the South. These find the negroes farming in primitive and slovenly style, ignorant of science and of marketing. Simply and tactfully, the agent makes suggestions; he asks permission to put fertilizer along a given number of cotton rows. Then he calls again when cotton harvest is on and draws attention to the quality of the fertilized cotton which, indeed, draws attention to itself. He then calls together the neighbouring farmers, explains results, hands out, fertilizer, tells them how it can be got. These methods are applied to all kinds of farming – poultry, hogs, corn, etc. Grading and marketing are facilitated. Attention is given to the condition of the farmhouses. Under the supervision of the agent a day or two is given to cleaning up, painting, reordering the homestead. The reformed farm sets a new standard in the district; others tend to approximate to it. Photographs were shown me, negroes crowding round the agent, a negro farm before and after improvement – miracles of transformation! I saw pictures of clean, friendly, modern homes; well-dressed, smiling negroes on the verandah; inside, views of respectability and the ordered American 'standard of life' expressed in oak furniture from the store, a sideboard and an aspidistra.

Wonderful work, as they told me, with human interest and spectacular results to show for it. How could it not go forward with such romantic bureaucrats behind it? How they shook my hand when I left! How hard they made it for me to get away! But – once away – I had to wonder whether it was not all a little too good to be all true. I hope I may go South to judge for myself.

So hard to get away that I was late for my next appointment. I hailed an expensive American taxi – no ride under a dollar – and told him to go quickly to Howard University.[24]

It was a long drive. The University crowns one of Washington's hills. To get to it we ran up a long slope with block after block of wooden houses, once built for whites, now inhabited by negroes. Crowds, too – dark faces in the windows, family groups on the steps of the verandah, always the old black grandmother and the children, many of them slightly pot-bellied, as in Africa. The houses on the whole look clean and bright: there are plants and gramophones and wireless, often a car standing at the door. Dresses are simple but clean and good. The houses are largely detached or semi-detached with a scrap of garden. An impression is given of a standard of life higher, more decent, more pleasurable, than that of many of our own working classes. And later, for I have failed to write this letter daily and am now being retrospective, down in Norfolk, Virginia, I saw some of the old slave-cabins, where such people as these had been living not so many decades ago.

Now the University! Through big gates, sweeping round the drives, and between the scattered buildings of an American campus. Having not then been introduced to the University standards of masonry in America, I was impressed by the vastness and variety of the buildings. At last the library, with huge columns and wide steps. Here were the President's offices. Up the steps and through passages, with quiet, well-dressed, intelligent-looking negroes everywhere, carrying books, reading them, sitting at desks in the President's Office, clicking typewriters. All strange to me, this university run entirely by, and for, negroes.

In the office I must wait and watch the two chief secretaries, a man and a woman, at their work at big, well-appointed desks. The woman is chic in a workmanlike way, clustering black hair tamed to the latest fashion, brown skin of lovely texture, serious, sensitive expression. The man, like so many of these so-called negroes, does not look negro at all. Lighter brown than the woman, he has a purely Hamitic cast of face, and would be handsome by our standards if his nose were not too thick.

At last the President is at liberty. I am ushered in to his spacious office. I had not been warned whether to expect a white or coloured president.[25] This is surely a white man, dark eyes, a little swarthy, but not a trace of Africa in his face. He eyes me keenly, puts himself at my service. Yes, he will answer any questions.

And he did! For a full hour, with nothing from me but monosyllables and nods of the head, he talked upon the racial question. I canot remember all he said. Much of it I already knew. The attitude of the South, the northward migration of the negro, the South's fear of losing him (or, rather, his labour), the awakening and education of the coloured people, the rise of a professional class serving the negro (doctors, dentists, bankers, lawyers, newspapermen and artists, insurance companies, teachers), the whole hierarchy of American business and educational life built up in thin blocks alongside the white man's structure.

At two things he was moved. Lynching. He told me of the investigation of lynching that proved that, of the total of nine thousand lynchings recorded, in only 13 per cent of them was the negro even *accused* of rape and in most of those cases he was most probably not guilty.[26] His eyes flashed even more when I spoke of Africa and Britain. Evidently there is a deep prejudice here (and one I have struck again since this meeting and have not yet fully analysed). It seems as though the ordinary American resentment of our imperialism is deepened among negroes by a sense that it is *their* people we have subjected in Africa.[27] Add to that, perhaps, rumours of conditions in

South Africa which they do not distinguish from imperial territory. I say rumours advisedly: I found great ignorance about Africa and not much desire to know more than the one or two generalizations that are good weapons in their general armoury.

He spoke, however, with great feeling of the work of the early Northern philanthropists in the South and of the newer generation of Southern workers in the cause. He said that many of his negro friends were happier in the South than the North. In the South the negroes said, 'We know where we are. We belong to the order of things, and we are therefore able to make friends with the white men in a way that is impossible in the North, where, superficially, there is equality.' That, of course, is natural enough, and could be paralleled in England in the relations between the peasantry and the gentry in the south of England and the anomalous position in the more democratic industrial north.

It was only towards the end, when he spoke in qualified praise, or at least in defence, of the rather aggressive artistic group led by DuBois,[28] that I suspected that he was himself coloured. He spoke too, with some criticism, of Hampton Institute (which I am to visit),[29] for here the white staff find their position delicate in view of the increasing confidence and self-consciousness of the coloured students, and with the contrast of the all-black Tuskeegee flourishing not far away.

He walked me out on to the campus, gesturing with legitimate pride about the position and extent of his university buildings and totting up, in true American fashion, their dollar value and that of the yearly budget, plus that of the new buildings that were shortly to go up when the old ones were to be torn down.

Dr Mordecai Johnson is obviously efficient; his command of language is amazing. I hear he is one of the best speakers in America. He broods much, I imagine, and only wide knowledge and shrewdness saves him from corroding bitterness. There he is, President of a huge university – brilliant, responsible, cultured, and yet he is outlawed from nearly all social contact with his white equals and even inferiors.

Two last points. As we went out through the campus and saw the students sitting about in the shade of the trees, he said that with freedom and education a great change was going on in the very appearance of his race. It must be true. Here and again at Hampton I saw men and women students of great beauty, both of expression, face and figure. But I had no way of judging if this was a *new* manifestation.

The second point. I said I would look for a taxi as I went. He said they would order one. The taxi came - a black firm, a black driver. 'Support black Industries' is their slogan.

In the interval between this and my next engagement I wandered about Washington. I was quite unprepared for the heat. It was the kind of heat that made you wonder if you could walk for a hundred yards along the road, the heat that turns asphalt to jelly, that makes you pause a moment under the shade of each tree before you cross the sunlight to reach the next. The grey-white pavements and buildings radiate the burning heat and but for the abundance of trees and greens the city would be unbearable.

I am now doing my best in the absurdly brief time I have in America to learn what I can of the negro problem. I began today by going to see Canon Phelps-Stokes.[30] He belongs to the family of the famous Miss Phelps-Stokes who left her money to found a trust to promote negro education in the States and - this was remarkable - in Africa.[31] The Trustees have met this latter obligation by sending a commission to that continent to inquire and report.[32] It included the first African negro graduate to win an international status, Dr Aggrey. They toured round southern and western Africa and their report showed the paucity of anything that could be called higher education in Africa and also the degree to which education was, inevitably at that time, being specially adapted to meet the needs of black men as interpreted by whites. It also brought out that education in Africa was almost wholly due to the initiative of Christian missions and was still almost entirely in their hands. In spite of fundamental differences between the position of the negro in his own continent and that of his fellows forcibly transported to the new world, many of the conditions and the attitudes of mind of black and white seem to be common in both situations. Certainly the religious concern still seems to be a major element in negro education here in America. I am therefore fortunate that the Phelps-Stokes foundation are looking after my own education in their field while I am in America.

So I found my way to 3040 Massachusetts Avenue, a pleasant medium-sized house, crowded with books, family portraits and old furniture. This home of a church dignitary and scholar seemed hardly to belong to the surrounding modern America. We talked and talked - negroes, education, Africa. Then they motored me to a large park where we walked hard for some five miles, clambering up clayey slopes, leaping ditches, and creeping under branches. And all the time we continued to talk - negroes, of course, education, missions, Oxford.

I am too tired tonight to make notes on it but I suppose some sediment remains in the bottom of my mind.

After my Anglican, or rather Episcopalian church tea, I have just had an all-Roman dinner at the Embassy. I felt myself the only one at the table whose ultimate destination was uncertain. The priests looked ageless, chubby and shrewd, men of this world as well as of the next, somehow remorseless in their self-confidence. Though they had a slight American accent they seemed more Roman Catholic than American. I watched marvelling, as I always do, at their assurance. Does it spring from their belief that they have the monopoly of truth, as against us poor divided, groping Protestants? . . .

I wondered as I listened if it were easy for a Roman Catholic to be an ambassador for a Protestant nation and working in mainly Protestant countries where your conscience could be at least partly in the keeping of American or Irish priests. Well, it must be. Sir Esmé is regarded as a success. To me he and his wife are all kindness and charm.

After a delicious long night and breakfast in bed Sir Esmé took me out for a long drive around Washington, his son driving the car. But I cannot suppose you want paragraphs of ill-informed impressions of America's capital, with its great buildings, constructed to impress, and its river gloriously veiled in willow trees. Back to lunch with a number of apparently distinguished guests and talk about the Peace Conference and President Wilson. He was universally attacked – and this by some who knew him – as pedantic, impractical, egotistical, capricious. His extraordinary behaviour to Colonel House[33] was instanced – his obstinate commitment to one idea coupled with absolute sterility as to how it could be achieved. It seems he has now little honour in Washington. But I was fresh from books on the Peace Conference and I had lately contemplated the inscription outside the League of Nations building in Geneva,[34] 'To the Founder, Woodrow Wilson'. It seemed to me to speak the truth. We were talking so hard that I nearly forgot that my time in Washington was up and I should have missed the crowded train for Richmond, Virginia, if my hostess, kind Lady Isabella, had not rushed me to the station.

Virginia

There is a lot to be said against American trains. They burn what must be the foulest coal which earth disgorges; they are bad starters; they are expensive; and they rock on the metal so that I am bound to write late

at night, and late in time, what I could have written on my long
journeys. The gauze on the Pullman windows keeps out some of the
filth but in the few hours from Washington to Hampton I was so
befouled and blinded with grit that, on arrival, I had to go straight to a
bath and then wash all my clothes.

I was met at the station by Mr Jackson Davis, of the General
Education Board.[35] This is an unofficial board set up by the
Rockefeller millions to study and help education in the States. Owing
to the backwardness of the south, that part attracts most of its efforts
and benefactions. Mr Jackson Davis, with a roving commission to
watch the south, but especially negro education, and to dispense
Rockefeller millions as desired and deserved, is therefore a person of
the greatest importance. He is also one of those interesting 'new'
Southerners, who have been converted to the negro cause. They are, I
suspect, the best workers in this field. They are not tainted by the
suspicion of patronage, of officiousness that handicaps some Northern
philanthropists: they are known in the South, the South that is still
soaked in consciousness of 'The War': best of all, they know this South
and they know the negro.

In the evening, after depositing me at the best hotel called, of course,
the Jefferson, Davis and his wife motored me around the city. The two
great events of America's short life, the Revolution and the War (I
refer, of course, to the Civil War) are painted large upon the town. Here
is the church, an early eighteenth-century replica in wood of a Wren
church, like a dozen in London, where Patrick Henry[36] said 'Give me
liberty or give me death.' It is full of the graves of men famous and
obscure, of his time and group. Here is the Capitol planned by
Jefferson to reproduce the Maison Carrée of Nîmes; here the famous
statue of Washington, contemporary, or almost contemporary.

But larger and later is the print of 'The War'. Here is the Central
Avenue, punctuated by all the Confederate generals, grey stone
figures, each in his little plot of green; here are the ramparts
overlooking the Appomattox, with the sudden escarpment which
defied the Northerners throughout the war; here is Jefferson Davis's
house, the White House of the Confederation; here the hospital – and
so on.

I was called for early – Americans get to work about an hour earlier
than the English – by Mr Jackson Davis and Mr Gresham, the State
Superintendent of Negro Education for Virginia. The latter is in a
peculiar position. The General Board puts up the money to the

Southern States for this office, but the state appoints him. One can imagine this a position calculated to make for friction, but I understand it has worked well though it is still a new idea.

They took me into the state buildings of Virginia and there I met the State Superintendent of Education, and the Director of Agricultural Education, and we all talked. There was the usual keen spirit – the business zest put into government work. The agricultural man was especially intense: he quoted impressive facts and figures showing results.

Then there came one of the blackest negro women I have seen: a short, crab-like figure with hideous, wrinkled nostrils like a monkey. All the men treated her with politeness, spoke to her as Miss Randolph, and introduced her to me. I knew I was seeing something that could not have happened twenty, perhaps even ten years ago.

Miss or Virginia Randolph demands explanation. She is a Jeanes Teacher. The Jeanes Fund was started not many years ago and has been used to send out itinerant negro teachers to stimulate rather than to supervise the negro staff mostly in the rural schools, to extend their work into the community and correlate its activities. The Jeanes teacher has to be tactful and versatile; her mission is not only to the teacher of the school but, as far as she can extend it, to the parents and the community generally. She will clean up the school buildings, show them how to make the best of their resources and beg money for her little experiments. She then reports to her headquarters and the reports make very amusing reading. Of these Jeanes teachers Virginia was one of the first and most successful.[37]

The plan was for me to be driven out to one of the show rural schools while Virginia talked to me about her work. She *did* talk without stopping for nearly two hours, and I am afraid that only a small proportion penetrated my sleepy mind, especially as I was also taking in the countryside, the long, straight road, the sequence of ugly gasoline stations, the hoardings, certainly bigger and brighter than ours, the large placards announcing those battles of the Civil War that ringed the key position of Richmond.

One thing obvious about Virginia, through all her talk of flowers, of poultry, of curtains, dressmaking and paint, was that she knew her place. She said so, two or three times; her attitude was one of unmeasured appreciation and admiration for Mr and Mrs Jackson Davis and other white benefactors. Clearly she belonged to a generation that, with more education, must pass away. Her attitude, of course, made co-operation easy and personal relations happy. But will there always be a supply of Virginias?

The school was certainly better than most English village schools, and more building was contemplated. But I understood that it was an exceptional school in an exceptional state.

Back to Richmond for lunch, and after lunch another long drive, out to Petersburg, some thirty miles from Richmond. Another ugly road, gas pumps, hoardings, battle sites, scrubby land. Long, long talk from my companion, Jackson Davis, one of the most charming men I have ever met, gentle, modest, considerate, courteous. The dispensing of millions must be a job that often brings out the worst in the applicants. I wondered how anyone so sensitive could ever say no, condemning and disappointing at once the applicant and the institution concerned. These apparently soft men, with no hardness in them except of principle, are the best of all, but at great cost to themselves.

In his talk to me he revealed the power of a good and sound idea. He, like other Southern workers in this field, including Dr Flexner himself, told me how they were brought up, accepting the traditional view of the negro and soaked in the prejudiced memories of the war. Then, one day, they met one or other of the big men – a certain Dr Butterick figured much, creator of the General Board – who opened their eyes to an entirely new conception of the situation: that the solution to what they had not even regarded as a problem lay in raising the negro to their own level, instead of keeping him where he was. So, with doubt, but ever-increasing conviction, they embarked upon this difficult work, risking misunderstanding and isolation and violating their own nurtured instincts against consorting with negroes. This enterprise is now spreading of its own vitality, justified by its own results. Every white official set up as State Superintendent for negro education, or put in charge of demonstration work, becomes a convert, perhaps an enthusiast; the work is now *his* work. His conversation, his reports, his very existence, represent valuable propaganda.

We reached Petersburg. It was one of those surprise visits that Mr Davis must pay. The place already owes some of its buildings to his fund and it hopes to owe more. This is an all-black State University, a term which means something different in America from what it does in England, and even more different when applied to negro institutions.[38] Being vacation, only a summer course was being held.

The President was a very different type from Dr Mordecai Johnson. No mistaking the negro here, or rather the colour, for the man, though dark, was not very negroid in type. A strong, broad, keen, rather harsh face. There was none of the harshness for us, but he was not servile.

He rushed us round the classes. It was thrilling. Men and women of every shade of colour from black through bronze, olive, amber and ivory to pure white, faces of all kinds, from that most repellent to us which we associate with the prizefighter, to faces by our own best standards, handsome and intelligent. These people are earnest, amost breathless scholars. More than that, they are merry and natural. Our entrance caused no embarrassment; it was acknowledged by a smile and a bow from the teacher and a flash of response from the class.

I was much interested to see the work. Here is 'English Composition', and very disappointing. An old negro teacher called upon his pupils to read out theirs: they were schemes for composition under five general headings, and seemed to me a bit rule of thumb, educationally worthless. Perhaps I failed to understand.

The next class was elocution. A young man was called upon to deliver a speech about the bravery of some young sailor, and he did it beautifully. Public speaking shows them at their best. They have always talked; they have only just begun to write and to calculate. Their voices are beautiful, their eloquence overflowing.

Next class, geometry. This is fine. In front of the blackboard is a young girl, with lithe figure, freshly dressed in pleated organdie in the new high-waisted fashion, silk stockings to match her pretty rose-beige arms, refined face, merry, rather mocking eyes. She passed, poised on her dainty feet and ankles, from one board to another, working out her problems with dashing rapidity. Every now and then she would pause, and dart like a kingfisher at some staring man or woman and drag the next move out of her pupil. A beautiful woman, a mathematician, a born teacher – and a negress.

We moved on. The pupils – all are teachers – are being taught the teaching of writing. By a method of counting and writing together they will teach the rhythm of writing to unaccustomed hands. A different type of teacher this, a grave, thoughtful, tall woman, dressed with perfect taste and suitability, with the whole class in the hollow of her hand. The President told me she was the best teacher on the staff. I won't continue too long, but I must mention history, taught by a fair-haired, apparently white man, who was teaching, most intelligently, about the policy of Jefferson and getting very pointed opinions from his class. I could not believe he was negro: he could have 'passed' more easily than I could have myself. One guessed at some of the tragedy that may lie in such colouring. Cooking, hat-making, carpentry, tailoring, automobile shops, a laundry with rows of gleaming electric irons and washing machines; then, in the distance, the impressive-looking dairies and farm buildings of the agricultural college.

I was handed over to some of the girls and taken through their quarters. They compare very well with those at St Hugh's (Oxford) and are somewhat in that style. Here they draw to their own advantage upon the high American standard of living. Two girls to a room; a huge cupboard for each; upon their tables the little ornaments and the framed photographs of mother and father – just the room you find belonging to any girl student all the world over, perhaps rather better than many in England and on the Continent. Beautiful bathrooms and pantries, of course. And I interrupted one girl dressing, her underclothing as clean and pretty as most of their dresses. They enjoyed taking me round; the atmosphere was delightful: one realizes at these moments what we both lose by the almost universal racial repression and ostracism.

Then we went down and all had drinks together in the students' shop, where students served us, and we were very cheerful and paid each other compliments. Jackson Davis is marvellous – no shadow of difference in his gentle, courteous sympathetic manner towards the negroes.

We motored home, stopping to see the crater battlefield which, until the world war, was perhaps the place where most men were killed in a small area.[39] This was due to a huge mine made by the Confederates and inserted under the Northerners' camp. Six or seven thousand men were killed in some ridiculously small space. We can do much better than that now!

Taken to the station by the kind Mr Davis, I set out for Hampton, that is, South Hampton, named in the early seventeenth century. For now I was getting into the district of origins, when, earlier than the *Mayflower*, English gentlemen, adventurers and their servants found their way inland up the wide estuaries that break up the Virginian coast. Hampton Institution was founded just after 'The War' and is therefore hoary with traditions.[40] Many of its buildings are old, as age goes in America. It is beautifully placed on a promontory of Hampton Roads, opposite Norfolk, the great shipbuilding centre of America, and the tides run round its gardens.

I will not describe my time there in detail. The impression it made upon me was not altogether favourable. I soon felt a certain malaise in the air. The first member of the staff whom I hailed in the grounds, a white woman, criticized severely their President for not meeting me. (The poor man had just missed my train. And anyway, why *should* he meet me?) This woman, one of the few unpleasant Americans I have met, continued throughout my stay to take the bloom off Hampton for me. Nor did the staff table at lunch give an impression of cordiality or harmony, though it was many degrees higher than the atmosphere for a stranger upon some comparable occasions in Oxford. At least one had the satisfaction of expressing one's principles by eating at the same table with negroes, for the staff is mixed, half white, half negro.

In the course of my stay of two days at Hampton I guessed a little of the reasons for the malaise. Hampton is old; traditions of philanthropy, religious and Northern, are still dominant. Dominant but challenged. The famous, nearby all-black University of Tuskegee[41] has abundantly justified itself, and the new negro with his better position and so his resentment that it is not better still, is a little impatient of philanthropy. Moreover, he reads the newspapers, written and edited by his own race, which express the self-consciousness and the bitterness of the intellectuals. There is still another side. The founder and first president believed in a balanced education, which is to say that he had a distrust of the purely intellectual development and, knowing that the negro must build up as his foundation self-support and self-respect, he emphasized vocational training and mixed the arts with the technical. But now the negro begins to think he wants his college to be just like a white man's, and dislikes every mark of difference as one of inferiority. Moreover, the young white teachers coming in from other colleges, and negroes, perhaps from the North, bring in their ideas of what a college should be, with all the paraphernalia of American undergraduate life, and chafe against the older ones who remember the ideals and memory of the founder.

I do not mean by all this to belittle Hampton. These are growing pains. But they are symptomatic of what will come everywhere with backward peoples, especially in Africa. The white man says, 'What you want is vocational training. Intellectual development merely unsettles you for the life you must lead.' This means, to the subjected, 'We wish you to become more skilled in all ways that are useful to us. The government, that is your destiny, we keep in our hands.' But they reply, 'We mean to have all you have. We want to be educated as men, not as menials. These highest treasures of yours may bring conflict and suffering but we want them, at least for some of us, and we shall never be content until we have them.' In Africa, in the long run, this belief in inherent inequality must lead to Pan-African agitation, even, if mishandled, to war.[42] In America it will lead to discontent, striving and bitterness on the part of many of the most intelligent negroes, denied complete opportunity though conscious of deserving it; and it will maintain restlessness among all those who can read them or hear them. But even if real equality of opportunity were not the best way, and the only way, for a great nation to give of its best, it is too late to call a halt. Men such as those I have mentioned are already giving with both hands, going step by step in faith, perhaps unable or willing to see where the road leads. And though they are few, and the lynchers many, and the indifferent and the sceptical many more, time may prove them right.

One memory that stays vividly with me is the evening on the campus. Some of the girls showed off, playing silly games, to several hundred young men and women. Then they played hockey as played in the earliest days, in old-fashioned costumes, with hats and long skirts, with play and remarks to match. It was very clever and very funny, and one wondered how they did it, for *they* were not playing hockey in 1900, nor watching it to any extent. Then they played a game which I could not understand, but girls in knickers ran and scrambled between each other's legs. What struck me here was the refinement or restraint of the audience: no shout of laughter with a trace of vulgarity in it, such as would have been heard in any other crowd, greeted the fat girl when she rolled over in comical somersault.

Another thing struck me as I wandered among the audience, noticing their faces and manners and overhearing their chance conversations. This was an *American* audience, the same accent – though sweeter and softer – the same slang, interests, topics of conversation.[43] Had I closed my eyes I should have believed them white. Clothes, hair-dressing, manicure, motor cars – all American. And many of the women were very smart and pretty and many of the cars were quite expensive makes.

But they had not much use for me. I was, I think, the only white person in a crowd of several hundred. I naturally felt rather embarrassed. I made a few timid approaches. I was met politely but coldly. Not once did I succeed in starting a conversation, except with a farmer's wife here on a holiday course, who wanted to tell me that she had just lost her husband.

The Vice-Principal took me for a very long run in his car with three women on the staff. We covered nearly a hundred miles, all round the peninsula. First to the old, or rather the second, capital of Virginia, Williamsburg, where William and Mary College, a soft pink brick building of its period, has suddenly been caught up in the wave of educational progress, which means too often crude educational building. Alongside the street stand the quiet wooden or brick buildings which gentlemen built for themselves in the late seventeenth or eighteenth centuries, the most perfect form of architecture for the middle-sized house, flat, wide windowed, relieved by the delicate columns of the porch. It is sad that so many are in wood, for they must perish. We went into the old church where Jefferson and Dunmore and Washington worshipped, and where they had – surely a sign of advance in tolerance – draped the governor's box with crimson curtains and canopy and placed a leather cushion stamped with the arms of England.

On through flattish, wooded, uncultivated land to the little island, hardly separated, by a narrow weedy river, from the mainland. Here, contrary to instructions to avoid low marshy places, the first prospectors for the Virginia Company made their settlement and wasted away with malaria. For long the island lay neglected, and what was left of Jamestown was quietly settling down upon its foundations when the Daughters of the Revolution and other efficient people suddenly took hold of it. They have, thank Heaven, only just begun. But already in place of the eloquent emptiness of that first foothold, which this nation has left so far behind in its race four thousand miles across to the other ocean, there now stands a simpering statue of Pocahontas, inviting with both arms the murderers of her race, and a conventional John Smith gazing at the river. It was right to save the ruins of the church from the strangling ivy, wrong to start rebuilding it. The little altar marking the supposed site of America's first Holy Communion is inoffensively preserved.

On at full speed to Saratoga, which my American friends, who thought me rather aggressive, were determined that I should see. This, too, might be worse. A monumental column in the crudest possible taste – artistically not politically – stands on the river bank. But the actual spot of British surrender is marked by a modest tablet half hidden in fooliage. We stood in silence looking at it and then, being determined to exercise self-control, I contented myself with the remark that I thought it was all a great pity, not so much for us, but for them. They nearly lynched me, and it was with some difficulty that we got under way again.

Incidentally I drew some interesting views from them by the way. Of the three intelligent young white women in the car, two were summer teachers from negro colleges and one was Dean and had been for five years at Hampton. The man had been there nearly thirty years, having married General Armstrong's[44] daughter. One could take him for granted. But the women, two of whom were Southern, were quite startling by the liberalism of their views. They all agreed, thoughtfully and sympathetically, that there was no difference in the mental capacity of the coloured and whites, and that such backwardness and faults as they had could be accounted for entirely by their lack of education and of home background. They also confirmed my impression that the negroes feel very little interest in Africa, have no strong sense of having come from there, and feel they have earned their right to be full American citizens. No Liberian programme of emigration would be of the slightest interest to them today.[45] All the Pullman men I had talked to upon the trains confirmed this view. Some of them asked me if the natives were very wild in that country, as if they were speaking of chimpanzees. Even the New York medical student treated as quite new and extraordinary the idea that Africa might offer a field for him. It rather looks as though the possibility of the negro in the new world finding unlimited scope for his talents in the Africa of tomorrow is a mirage of my own. And with every decade of the intensive Americanization going on today, the gulf will widen between the 'American' African on one side and the 'British' and 'French' African on the other. Nor, as my meeting with Dr Mordecai suggested to me, would either colonial government exactly welcome waves of the American negro intelligentsia. However, it is a point which I must consider further.

They motored me down to historic Old Point Comfort where I took a very clean, sensible, flat-bottomed boat which clicked quietly through the night down Hampton Roads, turned away from the open sea to click north up the Chesapeake and then into the Potomac River, waking me to see the early morning throw its charming sideways glance upon the Capitol. So past the glorious, sorrowful willows of the Park to our moorings at 6 o'clock.

Chicago

A long day in Washington. Then on another first-class train, the Liberty Ltd, to Chicago.

At first view I thought Chicago beautiful. The half moon of skyscrapers along the shore of the lake get their effect far better than the huddled blocks of New York. There are some fine pseudo-Greek buildings, though Greek architecture, very much of one storey, does not mix with skyscrapers. Fortunately at the moment, they are well apart, and one can appreciate both. I thought the stadium and the new half-built Aquarium, both on the edge of the lake, were buildings of which the city might be proud. They may be proud, too, of the Field Museum, not so much for its architecture, which, vast though it is, is rather conventional, as for its exhibits. Nowhere have I seen game so beautifully mounted and set out. The collections, within their range, are marvellous, and it is the only museum I have been in where they give enough light and space. I met young millionaire Field[46] – Eton and Christ Church, a thoroughly Anglicized American on the outside – and he gave me some idea of the cost of the Museum and the rank of world experts who had been employed. The actual man-eaters of Tsavo are there, and all Carl Akeley's[47] collection. The two African elephants at the entrance are marvellous; it is said that they represent the best piece of mounting in the world. And against the glass cases are pressed the noses of Chicago's children, Italian, Scandinavian, Russian, Negro. I gather from my first day that America's contrasts reach a climax in Chicago – art, science, architecture, drink, dope, crime, and a raw mixture of races. Dr Flexner told me it was the greatest centre of crime and Chaucerian study in the world, and in a library we visited we found collection upon collection of old maps, old books, and Red Indian relics, being studied by gentle, dowdy, scholarly men and women, and crowded with students.

The British Consul,[48] with whom I had lunch and dinner, had a very low opinion of the city, and both he and his French wife spoke with abhorrence of the life of the young, especially the girls – the debs and the sub-debs, blasé, spoiled, sometimes dissolute. (I might insert here that the Consul I met later at San Francisco told the same story. Both kept their own daughters out of it, one by sending her to England to school, the other to Canada – although that, it seemed, was not much better.) The Chicago consul told me that his main work was to get British subjects of foreign extraction out of trouble.

He took me up to the top of one of the highest skyscrapers and we stood on the roof – forty-six storeys. Chicago ought to be good, it has so many elements of beauty. The lovely drive that curves round the edge of the bay is fringed with trees and gardens; everyone has a car in which to race along the drives or out to the country. Thousands of people were bathing on the shore, the women, a luxuriant mixture of races, exposing their limbs and backs in the new 'sun-tan' bathing dresses or lounging under the trees half-covered in vivid cloaks. Away at the back the slums do not look like our slums; the houses laid in their square blocks are small but decent; there are hardly any tenements of our kind. Why all this crime that makes Chicago's name infamous throughout the world? The mixture of races – prohibition – are these enough?[49] A young Englishman told me that seeing a crowd under an arc lamp he went up and saw them all watching a policeman bashing a man over and over again on the face with his fist, the man being held up for the purpose by two other policemen. This went on until some time after the men had become unconscious. And the crowd watched without comment and people were surprised at his surprise.

San Francisco

I do not think even the dullness of the great northern European plain is as dull as north-central America. Hour after hour of corn and wheat, and not in such big fields nor of such a fine quality as I had expected, with every here and there the hideous, haphazard little township, with its squared clumps of mean wooden houses, its gasoline station and oil-tanks and wheat elevator; very seldom much sign of a church; neglected roads patched with grass and lined each side, where once the horses were tied, with rather disreputable cars. Horses and Indians once gave some appearance of romance to these settlements; now they are just ugly and dull.

They have their own form of excitement, perhaps. North Platte,[50] through which we passed, had, according to the local newspaper I bought, a little flutter that very day. A policeman went to arrest a negro for some matrimonial offence; he resisted arrest and in the struggle shot and killed the policeman, a popular young man. A crowd gathered around and, as he would not come out, they threw in tins of gasoline and fired the wooden building. The negro hid in the cellar, and when they got in to him with more petrol he shot himself. The crowd, brandishing ropes, attacked the negro quarters and drove them all out of their houses and gave them just so long to disappear. On any vehicle they could get, or on foot, laden with what they could carry, they trooped off. Only the instalment salesmen were worried: they had hardly gone than all the houses were stripped bare. Military were sent for, rather late, but could – or would – do nothing. The next day the police said it was doubtful if the negroes would return, though they were promised protection.

We stopped at this North Platte and I got out and walked into it. The negro Pullman porters and waiters on our train knew all about it; they had listened to some joking references on the train. North Platte was like all the rest, a little bigger and a little uglier than most. But it had quite settled down. No sign of police or military; no sign of stragglers on the road. I took the trouble to discuss the incident with a number of people in the train – no one was much interested; no one began to see my point of view about it. It is this that is worse than the incident.

And so, on across the Nevada desert, Utah and Salt Lake, to California. San Francisco, with its arms all but meeting round one of the biggest harbours in the world, disappointed me a little. The city itself is made interesting by the way in which the straight roads suddenly stand up on end as they scale the rocky heights behind the city, and skyscrapers running up hill, out-topping their tallest fellows step by step, were a novelty. But the city itself is much like any other, even the Chinese quarter is squared in the usual fashion, with wide, well-lighted streets in which the traditional mystery of the Orient has hard work to express itself. And the weather was cold, with a piercing wind night and morning. And I, unwarned, had only the silken wear in which I had travelled through all the baked continent that lay behind me.

One shrinks a little from contact with a strange city. There is nothing serious to be apprehended any more than for a blind man in a strange house, groping, and every now and then running into something and barking his shins or skinning his knuckles. But that you must do, and you do it all the more because, thinking America is not quite a foreign country, you take risks. Also, you imagine you know the language. But, how are the streets numbered? How do you pay for your ticket? How stop the tram? How deal with your luggage? How conduct yourself in a cafeteria?

San Francisco was crowded. I tried one hotel after another. At last a little place took me in and I was able to wash away the horrible grime of the long journey.

I am having a good time here. The British Consul[51] had a party in the evening in his rooms, and a young Oxford man whom I picked up in his office gave me lunch at the St Francis Hotel, the best in the city.

To talk to that young man was like lying on a sofa and resting – the effortless conversation, all the familiar arrogance, the slightly pedantic humour, and the cynicism of the ex-undergraduate. Congruity depends entirely upon the number of things you both take for granted; ringed around by these, the subjects still open for argument can never give very much trouble.

This afternoon I wandered round the town. It was not difficult to get the impression of being on the fringe of one continent upon which a wave of peoples from another is lapping. This is also a big port, with an original layer of Spanish civilization. There is a medley of people in the streets and oriental influence is well to the front. I was much struck by the beauty and elegance of the women. I never saw women so expressive of all the most alluring qualities of sex as I did here. One after another they passed me, dressed in vivid and often lovely colour schemes, chic, original, often with low backs revealing smooth, golden-brown skin; some exotic dark types, nearly all lavishly made up; tropical flowers, gorgeous and rather overwhelming in the exhalation of sex appeal.

Last night, after the Consul's party – with intoxicating liquor, of course[52] – I saw all these racially motley people, nearly five thousand of them, stilled and dim in a vast auditorium, listening to the wonderful music of their own orchestra, the most reverent large audience during, between and after the music, that I have ever seen. Americans, Scandinavians, Japanese, Chinese, Negroes, Indians, Italians – I saw all these races represented in my part of the hall.

After the concert we all got into the Consul's big car and he drove and drove. Right up the mountains, until San Francisco and the bay looked like another but inverted sky of stars. Then the inevitable San Francisco mist floated across the hill and there was nothing left to be seen except our own car, and, at the summit of the Peaks, a row of cars, containing a long series of 'petting parties', a fashion of which I had heard much and, so far, seen nothing. We zigzagged down the slope again, hilarious in spite of the mist, and drove to a café where we indulged ourselves in an elaborate choice of sundaes, combinations of cream, syrup, fruit, nuts and ice of a variety and richness unknown in England. Then we started off again to see the sights of the city by starlight, and our car broke down, a thing I thought American cars incapable of. Another car, belonging to others of the party, was fetched, but the morning was two hours gone before I got to bed.

In the morning I tried shopping but failed to buy anything, partly because everything was so dear, partly because everything was too chic for my simple, English tastes. Shop-girls called me 'dearie'. . . .

I now had an appointment across the Bay in Berkeley with a man I picked up on the train, March[53] by name. I went across in one of the three lines of huge ferries that cross the bay. I marvelled again at the efficiency and speed of everything American. This ferry was like a floating hotel, with restaurant, two storeys, special section for ladies' stores, a beautiful cloakroom, and all spotlessly clean. I had my first involuntary spasm of racial antagonism at being pushed away from the wash-basin by a huge, blowsy negress. We stepped from ferry to electric train, where the same ticket took me through block after block of Californian homes, framed with flowers, to Berkeley University. I went into the enormous grounds of the campus and on to the main drive, and found my friend waiting for me. He had been waiting, poor man, for an hour. He had arranged a luncheon party at the men's club and then we went to find five or six professors or lecturers, anthropology, Spanish and Mexican history, politics and government. We talked hard, waited on by elegant young women earning their college fees. There was no one quite on my line, though some near it. It all went very well and Anglo-American relations had perceptibly improved by the end.

Then Mr March took me round the University and played heavily upon all my feelings of wonder, admiration, envy and despair. The buildings are endless, vast, palatial, and the setting, on a wooded slope, rich in glorious trees and brilliant with flowers, is superb. Here the soaring campanile, there the colossal stadium, the enormous library, with God knows how many books and two hundred librarians; here the pamphlet rooms; the seminar rooms; the graduate reading-rooms; here special and lighter collections with luxurious chairs and settees; there the women's clubs and dormitories, fraternity houses, all marvels of comfort and suitability and charming architecture; here street upon street of elaborate mansions, experiments in every design and bowered in shrubs and flowers. There is the vast Greek theatre, modelled on that of Orange,[54] wreathed with glades of pine and eucalyptus, and now filled with a vivid company. Students everywhere, mostly in cars, lovely American girls, Japanese, Chinese, Indian, Hawaiian, even Red Indian. The largest university in America, perhaps in the world – 25,000 students in all. And whatever may be said of its undergraduate work, it is putting out an immense amount of postgraduate work, and it sent me . . . a graduate student[55] who, in spite of being newly married, went to Oxford, London, Berlin and Geneva, to study the mandate system. Even to bring so many people and races and so many books together must be a good thing. Going about America as little as I have, I would risk the opinion that though one may meet fewer highly cultured, mature people yet the average of intelligence and knowledge is higher than in Britain. Men and women, met casually in a dozen occupations, are quicker on the uptake, have a wider range of knowledge, however superficial, and can handle a personal encounter better than the same types picked up in England. I never met one case of gaucherie or stupidity the whole time, and only one of rudeness, when I was without enough money to tip two porters. And, of course, on the positive side, my journey was one long story of people coming forward to meet me, people interested and interesting, helpful and kind, indeed almost too kind. What must American visitors think of the reception they get in England, I tremble to think. It must take a lot of cathedrals to make up for our churlishness – and bad plumbing.

I am not sure if I have ever clearly explained to those who read this diary that I went to the United States and travelled round it with only very general ideas about where I should go next, though the obvious direction would be westwards. But one day in Washington my eye fell upon a relatively small newspaper item about 'American Samoa'. It reminded me that America possessed a small colony or – more tactfully – a naval station, in the Samoan Islands in the Pacific Ocean. It was called, romantically, Pago Pago, on the island of Tutuila. It seemed that there was trouble on this island as, I already knew, there was on the other, larger, ex-German islands held under League of Nations mandate by New Zealand and which I rather vaguely hoped to visit. What could be more attractive after glancing – no more – at some of the racial problems of a huge half-continent than to go to a tiny and certainly beautiful and romantic island and see America's 'race relations' in tropical minuscule.[56]

First I have to settle with my conscience that this is a legitimate enterprise for me under the terms of my Fellowship. But then I really have no terms. At least there is no harm in playing with this beautiful idea and making tentative inquiries.[57]

The news is that America is having trouble with the natives who, both in her own Tutuila and New Zealand's Upolu and Savii had formed an anti-Government movement known as the Mau.[58] But even in Washington it was difficult to learn much more. It appears that the

Naval Governor[59] of Pago Pago is one of the most complete despots in the world. It also appears that, in 1900, the Americans had omitted the rather necessary precaution of formally annexing the islands.[60] After all the candid kindness shown to my other investigations, the negative response which the Naval Department made to me about their island was puzzling. This is certainly a silent service. In the end the Naval Department told me that they would give me a letter, but it would not be of much use. The decision lay with the Naval Governor. It so happened that a change of governors was imminent – I gathered they changed every two years – and that he would be sailing shortly from San Francisco. *If* I could get on to the same ship and *if* I could win his confidence he *might* allow me to make the visit.

So in San Francisco I have been making inquiries. I have found out about the Governor's ship and have managed to book a passage on her.[61] Through Mr March, my kind acquaintance at Berkeley – where it seems that every problem under the sun is subject for a PhD thesis – I have found someone[62] who tells me that the leader of the Mau had come to the States to give evidence before a Committee of Congress, and that when he tried to get back on to his island he had been arrested and deported with his white wife. He is thought to be living in or near San Francisco; his retreat is said to be some fifteen miles the other side of Berkeley. Mr March was game to try to find this man. So we motored at high speed through the lovely residential quarter of Berkeley, where every householder has followed his own sweet architectural whim, from Spanish to Aztec, Elizabethan to Georgian, and California has kindly smothered them all alike in a flamboyance of shrubs and creepers. And so on to the so-called slums, really clean little wooden houses, each with its garden and garage. We found the house and went in.

The room was crowded with relations, of all shades of colour, in what I supposed was true Samoan fashion. The two principals detached themselves. The woman was a plain, straw-coloured, keen-looking American, the man the first Samoan I had seen, very striking, with his copper colour, broad pleasant face, melting dark eyes, and upstanding black hair. She did all the talking, and was as sharp as a ferret, pouncing on the points. She grew more and more impassioned; he only nodded and smiled gently. She waved a copy of the Governor's printed orders in my face, but I was not able to get hold of it nor borrow a copy. She said the island was the most complete autocracy in the world; the Governor was supreme and utterly uncontrolled. Nor had this position ever been legalized by Congress. Was such a state of affairs American? Was it tolerable in the twentieth century? There was no appeal from him even in matters of life and death. There was a murder case, and the Governor, the judge and another man tried it. The third man disagreed with the verdict and the victim's counsel appealed to the President and the Supreme Court of the USA. 'I'm afraid you're out of luck,' was all the Governor said, 'for I am going to hang him this afternoon.'

There could be no justice, she said, and no progress under the naval government – no proper education. Everything was static. So it went on, the husband nodding, the relations of all colours open-mouthed. Then he described his arrest and deportation and claimed to be the accredited representative of the Samoan people to Congress.

We hurried away. I feel that I have got to get to the bottom of the Samoan problem. I am now resolved to go there and to keep my mind open until I do get there. I can only hope that my paymasters of the Rhodes Trust will consider this enterprise a legitimate item in the study of race relations. It is, of course, a very small island. But then America has not got a very big empire. And issues of political principle are not commensurate with square mileage.

In the evening the Vice-Consul took me to the Chinese quarter for dinner. I had just time to dash back to my hotel and plunge into a fluffy frock before he came. We walked up a hill like the side of a house to find ourselves in a kind of exported China: Chinese names on shops and Chinese notice-boards, Chinese style street lamps, Chinamen stretched out full-length in the windows of barbers' shops. Here was the GHQ of the Kuomintang, not long ago a revolutionary club, now its flag is the flag of the Chinese Government and hangs everywhere.[63] Here is the Chinese telephone exchange, built pagoda-fashion, where the Chinese girls are said to remember everyone of the two thousand subscribers in the quarter. We went into a restaurant where, as an anticlimax, they served us with a perfectly respectable European dinner.

Then we strolled into the streets. In the provision shops ducks and hens filled the windows and were settling down quietly for the night. The newspaper boys were shouting news of imminent war between China and Japan but there was no ripple on the surface of the thousands of placid, inscrutable faces. My host gave in to my desire to visit the Chinese theatre. A huge crowd was trying to get in, but a sort of hired bully with a heavy stick took charge of us, forced a way in and intimidated my companion into letting him get our tickets. As we came noisily into the theatre the huge audience turned as one man and stared at us and I saw we were the only white people there. I knew nothing of the Chinese and this massed gaze communicated nothing. I did not even feel embarrassed and could read neither curiosity, resentment nor interest in those hundreds of eyes. But the sense of non-communication was strangely unpleasant. We took our seats. All the Chinese were eating nuts and spitting out the shells: the sound of many hundred mouths crunching and spitting was like that of a dripping waterfall. . . . [The original manuscript gives a long description of the play.]

Then to my hotel to try to get some sleep before starting tomorrow for my Pacific voyage.

2

The Pacific Islands

I write on my first night on board. It has not been easy to extricate myself from San Francisco. After we left the Chinese theatre my academic friend[1] took me back to my hotel and stayed talking until after 1 p.m. He had been so kind acting as my adviser, courier and transporter that I could not drop hints to expedite his departure. The hotel manager did his best, opening the door a dozen times to throw an exasperated look at us. There were so many things to do in the morning that I reached the dock one and a half hours late. But the ship[2] was still there.

It can be a desolate business embarking alone on a ship and leaving one strange place for another. I felt rather grim as I stood well out on the wing of the chattering crowd hanging over the taffrail. Alongside me and below on the dock was a crowd of well-dressed, vociferous Americans. Everyone but myself seemed to have friends afloat or ashore – though I should mention that the unseen long-suffering Mr March sent a great bunch of flowers to the ship. Suddenly, cutting through the American voices, I heard the unique low drawl of a cultivated, perhaps over-cultivated, English gentleman, with its occasional cutting edge and abrupt clippings. Why, I wondered, does that tone convey such measureless assurance? The Americans were assured enough, in their high-spirited, high-pitched way, but they were on their own ship in their own port. There was another English male voice, which seemed to belong to a younger, more self-conscious man. I leaned out and examined the row along the taffrail. Yes, there they were, in well-cut English flannels, correct, restrained, with club ties.[3] One of the men looked ordinary enough but the second one was strikingly handsome, tall and slim, with a long well-shaped head, brown hair brushed well back with a slight ripple and a feathering of red-gold; well-set grey-blue eyes, a fine nose and a rather scornful mouth. About thirty, I judged. I wondered whether in this crowded

69

ship I should meet this man and whether his character could match his appearance.

The band struck up a sprightly tune; the sun blazed down upon us; the stewards dashed up and down the gangway carrying great boxes and armfuls of flowers; thousands of streamers appeared, thrown between passengers and their friends below until the boat was attached to the dock by a tangled web of colours.

Where, I wondered, is this – to me – all-important Governor-designate of Pago Pago?[4] I scrutinized more closely the row of faces along the taffrail. Do American sailors carry the same facial hallmarks as British sailors? I selected as my choice a shortish, grizzled, rather dried-up looking man with cautious eyes. For that was surely the local Congress man paying him a loud and breezy farewell and wishing him success. I was glad to see that my selection for governor did not seem to like this loud well-wishing. I was glad he was not the breezy type but I feared that he looked rather too forbidding, and the woman I picked as his wife looked equally so.

The band now struck up a sentimental tune. The streamers increased until they made a multicoloured mat between ship and shore. Then came that always dramatic moment when a strip of dirty water shows up between ship and dock: the streamers snapped; the faces and the voices on the quay diminished; our ship gave an ugly bellow as if in pain and we moved into the great bowl of the harbour, with the chunky little ferries scattering at our approach. We passed the island which looks straight out seawards from the harbour and which is crowned with a huge flat prison.[5] One has to pass through San Francisco's Golden Gate to appreciate how narrowly it opens upon the sea, and then turn back and see the line of coast with the almost invisible break in its continuity. Little wonder that the first explorers sailed by without seeing that behind that low patch of coast lay a vast natural harbour, big enough to take all the fleets of the modern world.

As we drew out to sea the cold became piercing and I put on the fur coat I had dragged rather shame-facedly across a broiling America. The sea was rough, the decks impossible, the portholes closed. Without being sick I am a rather unhappy sailor for the first two days of a rough voyage. So I fled to my cabin to wrap myself for some hours in darkness and as much sleep as I could achieve.

I crept out for dinner. I found myself placed at a table headed by the handsome Englishman whom, for no very explicable reason, I have since named to myself as Petronius. His English companion, two colossal Australians and an American woman were around us. I kept quiet, partly because I felt rather shaky and partly because I had decided that it would be wise to keep silent about my mission, both general and particular to this voyage, until I had studied my human environment with its possible dangers. Fortunately Petronius talked – and looked – as if only he and his companion understood the English language.

We are now all settling down to our seven days between America and Honolulu. I have made contact with Petronius. It appears that he and the other Englishman are in the Colonial Service *en route* for their posts in the Pacific. We paired off and I found him clever, conceited, arrogant and fascinating. I tried hard not to give myself away but alas! his training – he is in the legal service – and ruthless self-confidence have defeated me and he has dragged my story out of me, including my plot to land at Pago Pago and my intention to stalk the Naval Governor. I have sworn him to secrecy but I doubt whether I can trust him.

I have made my first contact with the Governor, who is treated as the Great Man on board this ship. He was so reticent and vague that this first interview accomplished nothing. Then Petronius plotted to bring us together in a bridge four with the Governor and his lady. I was dubious, as I am an impulsive player, and I understood that the Governor and his lady were advanced practitioners. We played, I very badly, and the atmosphere was sticky. Petronius' easy banter, warning the Governor against me as a dangerous agitator, and his claim that I was not to be allowed to land in Fiji, completely misfired. Worse, I had with me the novel[6] I wrote about Somaliland and Petronius lent this to the Governor. As it is all about colonial politics and the conflict between the civil and military authorities, this may prove fatal. But as Hawaii grows nearer, the Governor, and still more his wife, are beginning to surrender a little to Petronius' charms. But Petronius' constant sparring with me does not really help my cause. Last night I played my last card and showed the Governor the letter I had from the Naval Department. But these letters must have a code which is secret from the bearer, as the effect appeared to be nil.

Hawaii

Every day *The Polynesian*, the ship's paper, has been lashing itself into an ecstasy about the paradise which we are approaching and the commercial advertisements have been almost hysterical about the hotels and restaurants, the flowers and trees, and the air perpetually filled with the sobbing, throbbing ukuleles. There was even one suggestive advertisement which promised that if you were the sort of person who, having been worked up to expect a place of simple beauty, reacted against the Americanization, there was a special number you could ring and ask for an experience of unsophisticated native life. That, too, it seemed, had been artificially preserved – at a price.

Petronius and I decided not to go with the boat's official sightseeing party but to make our own way. I got up at 6 a.m. in order to see the mountain mass of the island rising out of the Pacific with what looked like a tiny emerald rim along the water's edge. On the quay were crowds of people of several colours and there was much garlanding as we disembarked. Petronius bought two garlands for me, of cream and coral frangipani. We hired an impressive-looking car and we had not the heart to bargain with its fat and cheerful Hawaiian driver. . . .

[There follows a description of the island's natural beauty.]

Our driver was marvellous. I am sure he had the essential spirit of Hawaii, the pre-American Hawaii. He had a creamy voice and his throat was filled with almost continuous low laughter. He was intelligent and witty. He would have been cynical if he had not been so amicable. He laughed at everything – at us, at the Americans, the Chinese, the Japanese, at his people's loss of their land and independence, at the spoliation of their islands and the decline of their race – most of all at religion and the missionaries who had, in his view, betrayed them to the Americans. He had never been out of his island: he was a pure-blooded native and yet he was our equal in wit and intelligence, and surely our superior in his philosophy and realism. He was quicker than most foreigners, not only at following our English, even our colloquialisms, but at sensing unspoken meanings. I wish I could remember his own *bon mots*. Unfortunately I can recall only his charm and philosophy. By the end we were as wax in his hands and yet, as we learned later, he charged us less than the proper fare.

We went to the aquarium. . . . [An account of the many kinds of fish follows.]

We lunched at a hotel hanging over the sea and then went to call on the British Consul.[7] He motored us around and instructed me upon Hawaii as an educational centre, an intellectual melting-pot of the races and the locus of the Institute of Pacific Relations[8] which we visited. He expounded all this to us as we sat in his lovely house and garden.

Then down to the sea for a bathe. My readers must be getting clogged with my superlatives but then Hawaii *does* have the most famous bathing beach in the world. You can take your choice – if you have the skill – of riding the great waves standing or lying on a board or shooting them in an outrigger canoe. You can also see the human form in what is probably the widest range of shape and colour in the world – from black through the dark brown of Hawaiians and Filipinos, through the copper of Samoans, the yellow of Chinese and Japanese, with all the half-caste modifications, and down – or up? – to the Caucasians in the full range through scorched pink to our own white, which, by contrast, looks so very much more unattractive in its pig-coloured nakedness than any other body colour. All these variously pigmented forms were there, swimming or lying on the white sand in dazzling coloured wraps and costumes, on a beach framed with palms and flowers, backed by the rose-coloured walls of the Royal Hawaiian Hotel. I learned with awe that its tariff is six guineas a day! But, as we left the water, there seemed no way of avoiding dinner in this palace.

To get back to the ship we took a tram. We heard American voices in the seat behind us. 'Just look at this place after Suva. It makes you think.' 'Oh well,' came the responding voice, 'you know what the British are. They take everything and give nothing. It's all those damned officials lounging about like God Almighty that blight the place.'

Yes, it does makes you think. I have come away from America almost crushed by my impression of her power, riches, vitality. But I did imagine I could at least expect to feel superior about Britain's imperial activities, even after allowing for the exiguous size of America's empire. I have now seen my first American 'colony'.[10] The ruling power has turned upon Hawaii, a week's voyage away from wealth of California, the full blast of her energy. She has developed the islands to their limits. Native labour being inadequate in numbers or in will, America has imported many thousands from China, Japan, the Philippines and elsewhere. Now the labels on sliced Hawaiian pineapple glow at you from nearly every grocer's shop in England. Then there is sugar, tourists, big hotels, American luxury and hygiene, American efficiency in education, town planning, all that sustains this golden prosperity I have just seen. The mingled races look well-dressed, clean, co-operative, cheerful. There is also an intellectual life. At what cost? Only that of pushing the former owners of the islands into the background, the happy-go-lucky Hawaiians, who are being painlessly extinguished with every modern convenience by these waves of immigrant power and luxury. And if our driver is a fair sample, they are quite prepared to smile at their own painless extinction.

American Samoa

The Governor has been much fêted in Hawaii, smothered in garlands, dined, but not wined, since prohibition reaches across the ocean. But he has now become a worried man. Until now he has confessed, with disarming simplicity, his very large degree of ignorance about the island and so of the problems which will face him. But Samoan affairs have some links with Hawaii. The so-called rebels, the Mau, are demanding a civil government. We hear that a commission of Congress will be coming out next summer to look into the situation.[11] The navy, it seems, is trying to prevent the Mau from developing into the degree of rebellion it has reached in New Zealand's Samoa, and so far, it seems, with success.

Tonight, the night before we are due to reach the island, after bridge and when his wife had gone to bed, the Governor, Petronius and I sat on and talked until 1 p.m. I had with me an article from the *American Mercury* defending the naval government and this led us on to one of those talks in which you feel you are cutting through the loose earth to the rock. We began by discussing administrative organization. I had, rather rashly, lent the Governor my novel, *Major Dane's Garden*, and this raised questions in his mind, as it is about a British territory, Somaliland. Petronius and I explained the division of functions, military, political or administrative, and judicial, in the British Colonial Service. As far as the Governor's hazy information went, it seems as if in Pago there is a distressing confusion of these functions.

From structure we drifted on to policy. We went on to ask, 'Ought these Polynesian people to be preserved?' It is clear that they cannot stand what we call development (or progress?) or only when it is slowed down to a pace that to us is a standstill. Apparently strong and beautiful, they wither away before Western pressures.[12] Long isolated in their islands, with the coconut palm to give shelter, meat, drink, thatch – almost all they need – with fish easily caught on the reef before their doors, with *taro* in return for scratching the earth and breadfruit dropping from the trees, they have had no incentive to contrive and struggle, still less to reason. Nowhere in the world is life easier; that is why they sing and dance and put hibiscus behind their ears. But now we have caught them in the net of the world economic system, and their beautiful leisure is menaced by the hunger of the Western markets for coconut oil and by the bee-like perseverance of the imported Chinese labour through whom that hunger can be satisfied. Well, as some Australians on the ship said, and as the Americans have practised at Hawaii, 'Let them go! You need not do anything violent – just cease to shelter them, open the door to the other races, and, still singing, they will disappear.'

Accepting that this argument is economically sound, should we not act upon it? The Governor thoughtfully, but very strongly, gave his 'no', and gave it on purely moral grounds, so purely moral that he was too embarrassed to give reasons. I naturally voted with him but analysed a little and rather less on moral grounds. Are we omniscient enough to judge any race, especially when we are plaintiff, judge and executioner in one? Have not these hasty decisions always been regretted? And have we not always to reckon with the demoralization, however slight and subtle, of these who commit these racial murders? As for Petronius, he represented another shade. He accepted the British sentimental policy because it was that of a gentleman, adding that gentlemen are generally wrong. He pointed out that in the Pacific the decision was purely sentimental because we had very little to lose economically, whereas in Africa the humane policy was in the long run the best policy – no, I rather think that sounds like my idea.

But, granting we should try to save them, *can* we save them? The Governor was really moved here, envisaging his job in a new light. But, in so far as their best chance of true survival depends upon the maintenance of their tribal life and customs, is that not already broken through? I instanced from an anthropologist I am reading[13] how in Tutuila the school hours have already smashed up the elaborate divisions of labour, on which village economy depends, by abstracting a definite age group of workers. Already the work provided by the white man on the wharf, in the police, etc., has menaced the communal system by individual wages and undermined the chief's position by encouraging individuality and removing young men from his authority. And there is religion. Though here the native has shown a certain resistance, or rather a power of assimilating Christianity to his own religious ideas. It is true that under the new God a great many more things are *tapu*[14] but then, under Him, if you do break the *tapu*, it is so easy to avoid the consequences. You just say you are sorry and get forgiven.

We decided in the end to save the Polynesian, partly on moral grounds and partly because we must still regard the charge of economic worthlessness not proven. And so to bed, and a weary write-up of this diary.

To bed. But not to sleep, at least for me. For I had now realized how terribly embarrassing it would be for the Governor to land as a stranger in the island, bringing in tow an odd foreign female he had picked up on the ship, a self-confessed investigator of a reported rebellion. The governor-to-be would be the guest of the governor *in situ*. And this was a naval, not a civil government. I saw the new Governor did not know even as much as I did about the difficulties of finding accommodation. Last night I therefore gave a vague reassuring answer to his kind but not very pressing offers of help, and went, belatedly, to bed.

I was too excited to sleep more than an hour and soon after 4 a.m. I put on my dressing-gown and went up on the bridge. No one stopped me. Above me were all the stars of the tropics, enough to make the black sea insignificant. It was so calm that the light in the mast moved quite unswervingly among the stars.

It was only the slowing down of the boat that told me land must be approaching. I made out a jagged portion of the blackness that neither shone with stars nor reflected them. An uninteresting grey and green dawn came and showed me that we were approaching two islands, a small one to the east and a big one to the west. The westerly one rolled up quickly into black mountains. The colours changed, the sea from black to indigo and from indigo to grey, the land from black to grey and then, with the light, the sea slowly turned blue and the land green. Green is never more beautiful than after a long track of ocean, but I do not think there can be any green so rich and deep as that of a South Sea island.

While it was still dark a figure in white came and stood beside me. I could just see the dim form. I assumed it was a ship's officer, and, being in *déshabillé*, though still almost invisible, I replied rather reservedly to his quiet 'Good morning' and went on gazing at these dark masses, trying to imagine what life and what beauty they contained. Suddenly that life expressed itself. Dots of fire sprang up at the water's edge, and out of these grew little flaming wheels. The unseen natives were sending a message of welcome – or was it of defiance? – to their new Governor, as the ship glided past their villages.

Suddenly I realized that the light had caught me. Turning to my companion I saw that it *was* the Governor, erect and very impressive in his white uniform with blue and gold epaulettes, braided cap and medals. We must have stood an hour together. It was clear he was in serious mood. Gazing at his islands, as they revealed themselves through the solemn stages of the dawn, we spoke in whispers, both in the same mood. I envied him his job – and his sex.

I had to run from the light. Petronius, in a very gorgeous but restrained silk dressing gown, emerged below, and one or two naval officers with their wives, anxious to see the first of their new eighteen months' home. The spell was broken.

When I got back, dressed, I had the experience that Robert Louis [Stevenson] counts the most wonderful in life – the first view of a South Sea island.[15] The land rose almost sheer out of the water, very evidently the summits of a range of submerged mountains. These peaks were clothed to the top with trees, and the velvet effect this always gives was richer than anything I had ever seen. A tiny ledge rimmed the island, a strip of golden-white sand with a natural avenue of coconut palms running along the ledge. The coral reef caught the full force of the sea which broke on it in enormous waves, holding it off the shore. Beyond this was a calm lagoon and, peeping here and there between the palms, were the soft brown huts, the *fale*[16] of the natives, mushroom shaped and without walls.

It is, of course, the palm that gives character to these islands; without it they might be impressive but not so unlike other islands; the palms, with their exotic and romantic suggestions and their feathery beauty. Their loveliness is therefore often dependent upon how far the setting shows off this beauty. Growing in a thick mass on a straight bit of coast the palm is lost, the view almost commonplace, but let the coast reach out slender arms around a bay or throw out an atoll or two, then the palm has its chance. I wonder if the world holds anything more glorious than these Pacific shores, with the deep cobalt sea throwing white breakers on the coral, the green lagoon, the black, volcanic rocks and white sand, and the crags behind, cloaked with

feathery green trees. The sky was full of white clouds which cast
moving shadows on the lower hills, while there were mists wandering
about the higher peaks, shot through with sunshine and rainbows.

Suddenly the boat turned and we saw before us the entrance to the
land-locked harbour that makes a crooked arm into the heart of the
island. The harbour looks what it is, the crater of an enormous volcano,
which means that the rocky walls, covered in trees, rise almost sheer
out of the water on all sides.

Turning the elbow of the harbour, we see sophistication, America in
paradise. Two colossal wireless standards rear up beside the mountain;
a small wharf with sheds; and dotted among the trees the officers'
quarters. These are scenically tactful, with soft green roofs, while
Government House, perched right on the summit of a spur of a rock
which thrusts into the middle of the water, and buried in trees and
flowers, is in a position in which no human being is quite good enough
to live.

As we heave slowly up against the wharf, we see that the band of the
native marines, the *fita-fitas*[17], are drawn up and playing on their silver
instruments. They are fine, dull copper men, with broad faces, not
unlike the European cast, but with a suggestion of Asia and the
Mongolian. They wear a scarlet head-dress like a hollow fez, spotless
white vests, scarlet sashes, and navy blue skirts with scarlet stripes at
the hem: a very handsome uniform. A big car sweeps on to the wharf
and, amid salutes, the present governor comes aboard to greet [his
successor] and take him away. As I watched this performance I felt
how right I had been not to embarrass the new Governor.

Passengers and crew, now lining the taffrails, gazed at the island and
the little wharf. I was the next performer on this empty stage as I
resolutely disembarked under hundreds of curious eyes. My baggage
was dumped beside me. Leaving it there, I followed a road through the
overhanging verdure and found an office, apparently that of a – or *the* –
shipping agent. He was a German with a Samoan wife. At my first
obvious question he shouted gutturally at me, 'Do you think I have
nothing else to do but look after people who come here where there is
no accommodation?'[18] I retreated and wandered dismally on. I found
the store of a trader. I had been told about this man. He was a partner
of Nelson, the notorious half-caste trader, a leader of the Mau, who
had been deported from Western Samoa by the New Zealand
Government for his political activities.[19] I found my man in the middle
of a crowd which showed wide gradations of colour. I was not

altogether sorry to be roughly denied accommodation in his unattractive looking household. I found my way to what seemed to be the rather modest administrative building. Here I was asked to show my passport. It appeared that this place was also the office of the judge, the only civilian official on the island. I explained my difficult position to a clerk. He went to an inner room from which I heard an angry shout.

'Well, what the hell can I do about it? D'you think I'm going to have her to sleep with me?' (Laughter)

Then he came out, a great, coarse, handsome creature. As he was my last hope, I swallowed my antipathy, and did my best to get his help. He did some telephoning, with no result.

Would I stay with a native? There was one who was building a European house. He sent for him, looking him very hard in the eye and said, 'You understand me. You are to take this lady down to your house and let her stay with you.'

The man was clearly angry and terrified. He dared not answer. He just wriggled. So off I went. I had no sooner started than in broken English he began to put me off. He did not take visitors, the house was not good enough for whites, etc. As it was terribly hot I decided to stop and go back. He implored me to come on. I saw that he was afraid that if I turned back the judge would know he had put me off so I had to walk about a mile in the blazing heat down to his house which he was building European fashion but which was swarming with children and relations. Once there, and having said I would not stay, he broke out with all his resentment. Clasping his youngest child, called Overland (after the car), he said, 'Why do I build my house *foapalengi* (European fashion)? Because I have money. Because I want pleasure. I build for myself and my people.'

This passionate stance was clearly not one that could be moved by a bribe even if I had wanted to join his extended family. So I dragged myself back with the man jogging alongside and imploring me to say that he had shown me his house and that I did not like it. His fear was obviously so great that I felt that I had to do what he asked. This, of course, effectively cuts me off from any further help from the unhelpful authorities.

What to do next? I was now very tired. I went back to the quay. The ship was still there. My luggage was still sitting on the quay, I sat upon it. The two or three hundred pairs of eyes still gazed down at me from the overhanging tiers of the ship. They had not much else to look at. The gong rang for lunch. I was in an agony of indecision. I was hungry.

I longed to creep back to my lunch, to my cabin, to Petronius and my other acquaintances who were calling to me from the ship.

Then I realized that I still had time to round off my diary-letter and get it off on the steamer. So here I am sitting on my luggage writing this letter home. I am still being horribly tempted to get back to the ship and sail away from Samoa in all the security and comfort which the liner can offer. Or shall I sit optimistically upon my baggage, hoping there will not be too much 'liquid sunshine' – or moonlight – and wait until the American navy is forced to emerge from its elegant reservation and do something about me?

The steamer makes a warning hoot. I can post this but I fear it may be some weeks before you hear what happens to me. But you need not worry. Something is sure to turn up and, even if I have to go and beg food and shelter from the natives, they are not cannibals!

Days have passed since the *Sierra* sailed away from the quay. And as it turned out the natives *have* taken me in and I am writing this in a native hut, while my hosts sit around gravely watching me.

But I must go back to where I left off.

As my ship, looking very large and incongruous, edged herself out of this lovely little harbour the unexpected happened. This was in the person of a tall, dark handsome young woman. When she spoke I knew she was English. She at once offered to help. It seems that she is an artist and is staying with one of the American officers and his wife while she does some paintings.[20] I told her my story. She thought my only course was to try and live with the natives. She told me that one of the men working on the cargo deposited by my ship was a chief, Ava by name. We went over to him, a fine looking, slightly grizzled man, dressed only in a loincloth. He spoke no English but another man spoke a few words and my new friend seemed to think that Ava would receive me in his village. The plan seemed a little surprising to me with some knowledge of Africa, surprising but attractive and exciting.

My new friend said that she was sure her naval hosts, the Governor's aide-de-camp and wife, would give me some lunch. I certainly needed some. So we went to the naval quarters, pleasant, green-roofed bungalows alongside the water. I was greeted kindly – how much kindness can mean at such moments! They fed me lunch and persuaded me, without any difficulty, to spend the night with them.

In the afternoon we went out and bathed. We dived off the

Governor's private pier and swam out to a barge. It was a glorious bathe. The water was soft, clear and warm; it lay as in a deep basin with the mountains almost encircling it, and with the palms leaning over their reflections at the water's edge. Marvellous fish, yellow and electric blue, darted along the edge of the coral. We were swimming out in mid-harbour when, to my astonishment, I found that a big grey warship had rounded the narrow entrance into the harbour and was bearing down upon us. This, I soon learned, was the *Emden*,[21] the new *Emden*, built to replace the German raider which had been so fatal to our shipping in the war. She was on a goodwill – or reconciling – cruise and was paying a visit to the American navy after a rather mixed reception in New Zealand. The crew were standing in long white rows upon the deck staring at us as we swam rather frantically out of their way. The band was playing 'Deutschland über alles'. There was an Iron Cross and an imperial crown upon her bows. It was all very exciting. We got on to the barge and watched. The *Emden* fired a salute of seventeen guns which in that bowl of mountains made a terrible concussion. Then the Governor's ADC made a preliminary call. He was certainly a quick-change artist. One moment he was lolling near us on the bank in shirt-sleeves, sweating and looking incapable of his job. The next, by the addition of his coat, cap, sword and gold cord, he looked a marvel of official dignity and acted it too. He went off briskly in a launch, counting, he told us, on a drink. Unfortunately the Germans, out of consideration for the laws of their hosts, kept the key on their beer. Then the Governor, my ultimate quarry, a big, handsome bulldog of a man, made his call, with the *fita-fita* to drum him down the pier. He too, to his fury (for, as I learned later, he loathes prohibition), drew blank. Then the German commander, Arnauld von Perrier, who, I was told, sank more allied shipping than any other U-boat commander in the war, made his call. We swam in for this and sat drying under a palm, near the landing-stage. He looked a man: quite young, stringy, alert as a cat, a fighter in every look and movement. He marched close past us without more than a glance our way, a pretty good effort, for my English companion is rather a beauty and especially good in her bathing-dress. He had hardly gone when I began to sting and throb and found I had been stung all over by a poisonous creature that drifts in the water. In spite of this, I swam again in the evening, when I encountered the judge again in the water. Then someone suddenly said, 'Meet Governor Graham', and I turned to see that big, rugged face close to mine. We shook hands, at which, in my embarrassment, I promptly sank, so I never heard his kind words, if any.

There was a reception and dance at Government House that night for which I unpacked my blue dress. There were fifteen or twenty German officers there, a fine looking crowd, in white uniforms and gold epaulettes. The commander was covered with medals, including the Iron Cross. . . . I did not like the idea of shaking hands with the German commander and resolved to avoid it. It was impossible without a scene. The Governor brought him up to me and at once he held out his hand, seized mine and gripped it hard. I had a long talk with him. I have not met a man who gave such an impression of being packed with virility, of power under perfect restraint, and yet ready to leap out the moment the occasion presented, like his own torpedoes. Bad, good, inhuman? Adjectives did not seem to apply. He was just force, to be employed by his country as she thought fit. I talked to the other officers, too – they all talked English; they danced beautifully. Much as I liked the Americans, I had a strong, unexpected and unwelcome feeling of being far more at home with the Germans. There were so many things that they, in their long history, had proved as we have: their scale of social, if not moral, values was nearer ours; they were, until yesterday, like us, an aristocracy. There were things we both understood, I felt, and hated to feel, almost as though we understood even the war better than the Americans, even though they were enemies and the other allies.

Two of the *fita-fita* were now called in to dance, a couple of ukuleles providing the orchestra. The Samoan dance is peculiar. The dancer shifts his heels the whole time, with the accompanying necessary movement of the knees, and upon this jerking base he carries out elaborate movements with his arms and hands. It is at this level that he displays the beauty and significance of the dance in so far as there is any of either. He reproduces in a rippling, conventionalized form all the day's work, making *kava*,[22] washing clothes and building a house. Sometimes the movements are traditional and almost unrecognizable. Sometimes the dancer improvises boldly. It is all done to the monotonous rhythm of the ukulele, of nasal song and clapping hands.

Suddenly to my surprise, the Governor's wife leaped up and joined the two natives, then my English friend, then another woman. Slowly the tempo speeded up, the clapping became louder, until, in a frenzy of rapid movement, the five dancers, all acting independently, rounded off the dance, the ladies retrieved the shoes they had kicked off, and the audience duly applauded.

The next morning I set out in a rowing-boat to which was attached a little outboard motor. It belonged to a Samoan teacher who had been recruited to provide transport and who brought two friends. In this small craft it seemed to take a long time even to get out of the harbour. But at last we reached the open sea and turned sharply westwards parallel with the coast. We clicked our feeble way amongst the huge Pacific rollers. . . . Then suddenly we found ourselves in the blessed calm of the lagoon with the thwarted waves piling up on the reef behind us. Beyond the lagoon I saw the soft-coloured houses nestling against the trees and the bases of the mountainous cliffs.

The Samoans soon came out of their houses. They gazed at me with astonishment. I gazed at them, curiously, anxiously. They were a beautiful colour – a kind of rosy bronze, surely the best of all colours for the human form. For the first time I saw the famous *lava-lava* – the short brightly coloured skirt which they wore below the naked torso. Bodies were tall and broad, hair dark, the eyes turned upon me were curious – surprised – but gentle. My only recollection of Polynesians was drawn from Gauguin's paintings. Here they were, come to life and against his own rich green background they seemed almost too beautiful to be real. They appeared to speak no American but their whole attitude spoke of interest and welcome. Where, I wondered, is this rebellion?

I knew only one word, 'Ava'. They shook their heads and pointed further. And so, carrying my small suitcase, I walked on between the lagoons and the mountain cliff, past the beautiful mouse-coloured houses. 'Ava?' I said but was always sent further on.

At last Ava, grizzled, courteous, but quite astonished that I had assumed he was to be my host. There had obviously been some misunderstanding at the docks. His family – in anthropological terms a very extended one, I thought – gradually collected round me. But communication seemed almost impossible. (Why, I thought desperately, had the Americans stationed here for nearly thirty years, never taught these people their language?) But Ava's wife made little cooing noises of hospitality and welcome. And at last a very beautiful boy of fifteen or sixteen was pushed forward. I gathered he had been to school. And tied up in a corner of his *lava-lava* was a little dictionary and phrase book. Slowly, inadequately, we spelled out our communications. No, I was not expected. But I was welcomed. More and more people came round. There was an air of hospitality, almost of *fiesta*.

Now began a game of guesswork. I knew nothing of their customs
and to every suggestion I put forward the only answer made by the
young interpreter, with the difficult help of his dictionary, was 'As you
please'. Finally, in desperation, and thinking that the elders might be
glad to be rid of me for a time, I suggested a walk and set off along the
track between the lagoon and the forested wall of mountain. My
interpreter and three big boys followed me, looking very handsome
with their well-built copper bodies and brilliant green and crimson
lava-lavas. A crowd of tiny boys, mostly naked, hovered about us like
flies, and like flies were brushed off every now and then by the older
ones. . . . We walked along the shore with *fales* every few hundred
yards until we reached a breadth of firm sand. Feeling rather desperate
with this Pied Piper kind of procession I called a halt and with the help
of gestures and the dictionary, organized some Olympic Games. First
we had putting the weight with lumps of coal. Then I taught them
ducks and drakes with large flat shells. They were quick to learn and
soon beat me at my own game. . . .

Meanwhile the sun was beginning to sink and the sky to turn pink.
Exhausted, we sprawled on the sand and wrote our names upon it.
They decided that they liked my first name best and murmured it
luxuriantly as a Frenchman might – 'Ma-jé-rie'. My dictionary boy
wrote his name on the sand. 'Kalamete'. We wandered back. I longed
to detach myself from my attendants in order to indulge myself silently
in the beauty and strangeness of the place. But I was not allowed to
linger outside Ava's place. They fetched me in. . . .

I was now called to come and join them for prayers. What a joy to
find they were fellow-Christians! A very fat, half-naked chief intoned
the prayers in Samoan. I heard my own name several times. The others
joined in. A lamp flickered on the floor. Even the dog, the cat and the
babies kept still. I think the prayers lasted a good twenty minutes. I
could only try to look as devout as the natives.

Prayers over. Would I have my meal? But was it time to eat?
'Whenever you please!' Very well, now! I was served alone and with
much ceremony. First, freshly split coconut milk to drink; then chicken;
then baked breadfruit; then fish, wrapped in leaves and baked in ashes;
then *taro* root.[23] One of the men waited upon me. The food was spread
on bark-cloth, the hammered-out bark which they paint in black
and brown designs. They all sat in silence waiting. Both hunger and
manners caused me to eat well.

'Now is *kava*,' whispered Kalamete.

I saw the famous ritual drinking of the South Seas for the first time. The *taupo*,[24] a virgin chosen for her beauty and skill by the high chief to be a kind of princess and mistress of the ceremonies on important occasions, made the *kava*. . . . Besides being maker of *kava*, she goes round when the chiefs visit other villages and leads the dancing. Her marriage is an important occasion. The honour of the chief and the village is bound up with her chastity, and after the wedding there is a public defloration, with terrible disgrace if she proves not to be a virgin, surely a difficult achievement in Samoan life. The law now prohibits this public test.

The *taupo*, a grave looking and beautiful girl, squatted before us. The *kava* bowl, a round, shallow basin supported on numerous legs, the whole cut out of a block of a special redwood tree, was put in front of her and a liquid poured in. She then took what looked like a large handful of straw-coloured raffia and whirled it round in the basin. With graceful, traditional movements she wiped round the edge of the bowl, then suddenly flung the skein back and out through the posts. It was caught by the half-seen figure of a boy who whirled it round and round in the air and then threw it back. This is to strain out the sediment of the crushed *kava* root. The girl repeated these ritual movements five or six times. Then she dipped a polished half-coconut shell in the fluid. The talking chief, whose special business it was, called out my name 'Ma-jé-rie' with – I imagined – appropriate compliments and the girl brought me the drink. I had been coached in this. I poured out a few drops on the ground to whatever local gods still existed, raised the shell, and drank. It was horrible, rather bitter, with a dull tang at the back of it. I believe the taste grows on you; I was told that the present governor can't have enough of it. I could hardly swallow it. I hoped that it was no longer the custom for the girls to chew the *kava* root into the proper state. One by one the chiefs and *matais*[25] tasted the *kava*, then the bowl was removed.

There was dancing in the evening. Dim figures appeared between the posts, laughing and murmuring, until there must have been about fifty people in and around the *fale*. First some young girls danced, then a tiny boy of five or six, uninvited, joined in, and made his babyish attempt to follow his elders, mostly getting in their way. He was not reproved. Here, in the dance, the Samoans seem to find self-expression, elsewhere disciplined by the communal system.

Dance succeeded dance, to the accompaniment of a semi-visible orchestra of ukuleles, half in, half out of the *fale*, songs and clapping sometimes reinforcing the rhythmic strumming. The big boys would disappear and come back, copper limbs glistening with coconut oil. They had put on collars, cuffs and anklets of banana leaves, torn into streamers. Garlands of flowers round their necks tossed as they moved and filled the *fale* with scent. Then the *taupo* danced, a grave, beautiful and subtle dance. Then, at my request, two old chiefs performed. Over and over again, with gestures, they urged me to dance. At last, feeling that my refusal might give offence, I rose, though I knew I could not perform in their way. I took off my shoes and stockings. The chiefs hung three heavy, scented garlands round my neck: the women bound my waist and ankles with flowers and dressed me in a skirt of raffia palm. I began with something like a solo waltz. But as the music of the ukuleles was too fast for this and was growing faster I was forced to whirl around in almost apache style. First one then another of the young men joined me, trying to dance in response to me. The audience clapped, shouted and roared, and at last rolled on the floor giggling. Fortunately I realized that this did not mean that they were laughing *at* me but rather *with* me in delight and surprise. So I carried on. But at last I danced off the mat on to the sharp coral and this brought my dance to a somewhat painful end. There was no end for them. They went on and on. . . .

The morning of the inauguration of the new governor everyone was very excited. Ava and the other chief men went off before dawn as they had to take their places at the show. The young men, who lived in a separate *fale*, asked me to join them for breakfast. We sat in a circle waiting for the food to be brought in. At last it came – an immense devilled octopus! Each of us was expected to take one tentacle and pull all together. I saw that mine would inevitably bring an eye with it. I had to decline, whatever the offence.

They said that I must have a Samoan name given to me before I went and that I must give my inseparable admirer, Kalamete, an English name. I christened him Christopher and told him as vividly as I could the story of the name. He then named me Tolufalo. I asked what that meant, waiting rather complacently for some complimentary interpretation. After some discussion plus research in the dictionary it came.

'Swallower of blood.'

This was a great shock. Seeing I was not pleased, Kalamete tried to explain at great length that it was a famous and good Samoan name. He tried hard to convey its meaning, and I gathered, or guessed, that when the blood rushed up in anger or resentment and you swallowed it back and kept your temper, you showed a restraint highly respected among these amiable people. I could only hope that this choice of name for me did not mean that I had appeared throughout to be showing great restraint under provocation.

Alas! It is time to go. The boat is launched. . . . It took us over an hour rowing along that lovely coast and harbour to get into Pago Pago. . . . Seeing we should be late, and as the naval personnel with fashionable wives were already walking down the path to the *malai*,[26] and as I was filthy, dishevelled and hatless, I asked them to drop me at the Governor's pier. I decided to tidy up at the house where I had spent the first night and had left my luggage. Kalamete, all gallantry, sprang ashore nimbly to help me to land. Alas! the step was slimy with weed; he fell and grazed arm and knee badly, and blood stained the spotless *lava-lava* he had put on in honour of the great occasion. Here was, I saw at once, a first-class tragedy. In utter dejection, he left the boat and dragged along with me. The naval people looked wonderingly at us. We must have looked a sorry couple. Poor Kalamete was almost in tears. He could not go to the ceremony at all. No! no! What would the Governor think? What would other people think? It was a distressing end to our happy time. I begged him to go to the ceremony and tried to minimize the damage. In vain! His standards were too high. As a last resort I told him I had a new *lava-lava* for him, not actually in cloth, but all ready and waiting in the store for him to change into. It would be my parting present. I forced a dollar into his closed protesting hand and ran into the house. It was empty. I bathed and changed hurriedly and ran out to join the crowd.

Everyone had gone to the *malai*, the patch of flat land beside the harbour. It was brilliant green from the constant rain. It is backed by all the shipshape naval buildings that make up the station. It was indeed an impressive assemblage that I found. The two naval governors and their wives were on a dais surrounded by the other officers in their white, blue and gold uniforms. The wives, in their pastel shade dresses, blue, mauve and lemon, looked like a bed of flowers. On one side of the dais were all the chiefs, aristocratic in bearing and dress. On the left were the officers of the *Emden*. In the middle, on brilliant grass, in their navy and scarlet uniforms, were the *fita-fita*, going through various evolutions to the music of their band. Beyond them, against the background of the harbour, the Samoan crowd, mostly male, squatted on the grass in their crimson, blue, orange and green *lava-lavas*. The whole joyously coloured scene was backed by the steep rain-green mountain.

I crept up as unobtrusively as the last arrival could. The commander of the *Emden*, which still lay in the harbour, made me a place next to himself.

The whole ceremony was simple and impressive. After the *fita-fita* had performed, the three leading chiefs made speeches of farewell to the retiring Governor and of welcome to the new one upon his inauguration – how Kalamete loved mouthing that word! The speeches, when interpreted into Samoan, took three times as long as in American. The retiring Governor read out his orders of appointment and revocation. He then made a short speech which had every mark of sincerity, even of his being moved. Seventeen guns were fired with alarmingly impressive effect in that enclosed valley. Then, in complete silence, his flag was hauled down. The new Governor's flag went up and his salute was fired. The new Governor then rose, so did the judge, my *bête noire*. He administered the oath of office. The new Governor made a conventional speech which made me decide that he is unlikely to equal his predecessor in projecting himself. Then *his* flag went up, his salute was fired. Followed a prayer. Then came the *kava* ceremony. . . .

Before I left Pago I had reason to laugh at the fears which had caused me such anxiety before my ship arrived. The retiring Governor showed himself friendly and helpful. He sent me round with the *Emden* officers to see the school, the effects of which had so completely failed to reach Kalamete. . . . The naval doctor explained his work to me at great length. Tuberculosis is the great destroyer, probably due to wearing clothes in this wet climate. After this comes filaria, which can lead to elephantiasis from a growth of worms. I saw some terrible cases of men and women with legs like huge bolsters. I saw, too, a lot of ugly blindness, largely caused by their own drastic treatment of scraping an infected eye with coral. It was terrible to see these beautiful people blighted in these two ways. The doctor's road is hard: he uses compulsion only for communicable diseases: he dare not make a wide use of compulsion as he might lose the people's hard-won confidence. Even now he has to endure their bringing cases too late for him to help or, conversely, just when he hopes for a cure in hospital, the relatives suddenly take the patient away to certain death at home. He has tried to train Samoan girls over a three-year course, but as soon as he sends them out to the villages they are promptly lost through marriage, or thwarted by the old 'wise women' or by male disapproval. The doctor told me that the only time he really lost his temper was when he found one of his nurses prescribing for a chief – upon her knees!

The retiring Governor took my education in hand. He had none of the fears and hesitations of his successor and this not only because he was about to leave but because he was a man of different temperament, bluff and open. He sat me down alone in his own office at the administration building and put out all his reports to the Navy Department and left me to read them. He presented me with a collection of these reports and even showed me his latest confidential dispatch to the Naval Department.

The readers of this diary will not want all the administrative details which went into my notebooks.[27] It will be enough to say that such unrest as there was in this lovely dependency seemed of a very mild character and largely stimulated by a few exiles in the United States and carried along the Pacific route. Such discontent may well grow more serious with time. But I doubt whether a visitation of political investigators from Washington will bring the millennium.[28] In the absence of any trained staff like our Colonial Service these naval men are probably the nearest thing for the job.[29] Anyhow, greatly daring, I am going to send an article on the Samoan troubles to *The Times*. But that will be after I have been to compare the situation in New Zealand's Samoa.[30]

It was a wrench to leave Pago, the nearest place to Paradise on earth that I shall ever see. And I knew I should never see it again.

I had a bit of a crisis getting away from the island. I think I have mentioned the dirty little coaster of eighty tons in which I was to sail to Upolu, the chief New Zealand island of the Samoan group.[31] It was impossible to find out what time it would sail (there was a faint atmosphere of Conrad about the *Lady Roberts*). I went back later but neither the Captain nor the mate, when roused with difficulty from sleep, would divulge the secret. I had to thank a stranger, watching my efforts, for the information that the horrid little boat would certainly not set out until the liner to Hawaii had come and gone.

While I was peacefully having supper with Benedicta's kind naval hosts – and I needed all I could get because the Americans seemed to live on salad and ice-cream – my host leapt to his feet. His nautical ears had identified the feeble siren of the *Lady Roberts*. I tumbled all I could find into my suitcase and we ran for it.

The *Lady Roberts* was still there when we reached the jetty. The rush and the crowd on the horrid little ship rather spoilt my host's gesture in draping me with *leis* of red, white and blue flowers. I forced my way on to the stinking little tub. There was hardly room to put one's feet down on the deck, such was the crowd of passengers, and the air was rancid with the smell of oil, sweat and of those who seemed to be prematurely seasick. Crowds of copper-coloured bodies pressed against a steel wire barricade saying goodbye to friends. One climbed outside the edge of the barrier and leaned perilously over the water, hanging on by one hand and one toe. Through the noise I heard a familiar voice.

'Ma-jé-rie, write me letter. I write too. God bless you, Ma-jé-rie, always.'

'Goodbye, Kalamete. God bless you.' We pushed away with harsh screams from the siren.

I looked round the ship – very small, very dirty, very crowded. An enormous figure advanced upon me in the quarter-light, dark and half naked. He seized my hand. I shrank back from the first impression of brutal strength.

'My name Centenary,' he yelled against the noise of the ship and the sea. 'Call me Cente. I go to Apia to train for pastor. I look after you.' The light flickered upon him and I saw a mild, good face.

But at that moment we passed out of the harbour and into a storm. There was a crashing and jostling, groans and cries. I fought my way into the tiny saloon. It was crammed full with all kinds and colours, from a silvery-golden Swede and a white Roman Catholic monk to a half-caste Samoan woman with a cluster of varicoloured babies. I tried the deck. It was drenched with spray and running with oily bilge. Even the Captain admitted it was a bad storm. I struggled below. There were no bunks, only shelves with pillows fouled from a dozen voyages and tattered strips of American cloth. I managed to insert myself into a space with my head between the boots of a man, who, being very drunk, kept them fairly still.

I did not sleep. I lay thinking of the Samoans of Tutuila. I knew I should never see them again. They had opened for me a new perspective of beauty. Beauty of their land, of their bodies, of their apparent happiness, of their manners, their dignity and ordered courtesy, their warm, gentle kindness to myself, an unknown and unexpected apparition. Could people, I asked myself, be more different from the other exotic people among whom I had lived, the slender, sinuous, fierce Somalis trekking about their brown semi-desert country in search of scarce water and grazing? Samoa was green with its liquid sunshine: its fish, coconuts, breadfruit, *taro* and a dozen other natural riches offered free or for the minimum of effort. Of course I had only seen the surface of their lives and that only for a brief time, but what I had seen was true even if there were other less lovely truths I could not know. I asked myself with anguish whether the Western world must utterly violate the still surviving beauty and innocence of these islands. The American navy could hardly hope to continue to keep the door shut upon the world and its tourism. Indeed, I know now that they have not done so.[32]

That night, as we fought through the Pacific rollers across the seventy miles which divide Tutuila from Upolu I felt that just as we are destroying species of birds and animals so we, the West and the Westernized world, kill with our love – our exploitation of the exotic – beautiful, precious, ancient and fragile ways of human life. Perhaps the Samoans would survive not only physically but culturally. They have accepted our best gift, of which we have been trustees, the Christian faith,[23] and have built it into their culture. Perhaps, as increasingly they take charge of their own destinies, they will preserve some, at least, of that beauty of their own character and of their own islands, of which I have just had my brief and unforgettable experience.[34]

Western Samoa

During my wretched sleepless night on the abominable *Lady Roberts* I had time not only to think about the American Samoa I had left but to try to adjust my mind to the other and larger group of islands to which I was sailing, those which New Zealand has held under League of Nations mandate since they were taken away from Germany during the war. . . .[35]

Samoa has long fascinated me. For the lectures I gave at Oxford on the mandates system I had to read the voluminous records of the Permanent Mandates Commission, with Lord Lugard[36] and other international experts on colonial affairs spending long days cross-examining the New Zealand representative.[37] And all this for two little islands with less than 40,000 inhabitants, while large territories like Tanganyika, Iraq, Syria and, above all, Palestine, were demanding their attention. I followed up my work on the documentation by visits to Geneva to study records and meet officials at the headquarters of the Mandates organization. So . . . I feel I must insert a page or two about the background in order to make my doings intelligible. This seems the more important as I shall try to get to New Zealand to see the political background of the Samoan problem with, of course, a simultaneous glance there at the Maoris.

Like other Pacific islands Samoa early attracted the attention of intrusive Europeans, adventurers of all kinds, whalers and other exploiters – and the missionaries![38] These arrived in 1830 and by 1860 almost the whole population had been converted. Germany, Britain and America put consuls on Upolu, the most important island. When, in 1885, the Samoans indulged in civil war between their two important rival dynasties, the three nations sent gunboats to overawe them. This only gave the Samoans the first of many opportunities to make European intruders look silly. It happens that the capital, Apia, does not have a continuous reef to shelter it from the Pacific breakers and in certain weather conditions these can sweep into the bay. This now happened and six of the warships, those of Germany and America, were driven on to the reef or the beach with heavy loss of life. Only the British, by stoking up with everything combustible in the ship,[39] rode out the gale. The point of this story is that the Samoans, instead of watching with glee the destruction of the interlopers, flung themselves into the raging sea to rescue all they could. . . .[40]

In 1899 the three powers got tired of struggling with each other and with the incomprehensible Samoans and made a deal which left Tutuila to the Americans, and Western Samoa to the Germans, while Britain – of course – obtained compensation elsewhere. If the Germans did not attempt to crush the Samoans (and, as I have said, there were less than 40,000 of them when I was there) by the methods they used in East and South-West Africa to coerce defiant natives,[41] it was partly because there was something irrepressible about the Samoans, and partly, I suppose, because of the large number of watching missionaries. Moreover, the German governor, Dr Wilhelm Solf,[42] was a man of great intelligence and moderation.

Soon after the outbreak of war in 1914 New Zealand occupied the islands and in December 1920 was confirmed in her position by the grant of that new international device, a mandate under the League of Nations. But, alas! this was not the beginning of a golden age under the humane New Zealanders, determined though they were to make a success of their new international trust, but the beginning of troubles leading two years before my arrival to the development of a rebellious movement known as the Mau. Between the well-intentioned New Zealanders, the Christian and aristocratic Samoans, and the puzzled and sometimes almost exasperated Mandates Commissioners, how was the underlying explanation of the trouble to be found? This is what I had come to discover. . . .[43]

We sailed into the harbour of Apia. This is the capital of New Zealand's mandate of Western Samoa on the main island, Upolu. I must confess that after my night on the dirty little *Lady Roberts*, which I was told had been condemned three years ago, I was not in a very impressionable frame of mind. But the kind giant, Centenary, led me on deck and showed me the dangerously shallow scoop that is the harbour of Apia, and pointed out the sharp ridge against the sky where Stevenson is buried and the grand wooded mountains rising beyond.

The official doctor, on instructions from the Governor, took me ashore in a launch and here the billeting officer was waiting to take me to what must be the only hotel. It was still early morning. I was tired after that awful voyage and, after Pago, Apia made a very poor impression. The dirty, neglected beach, the semicircle of shabby buildings, above all the tattered, half-derelict hotel, all gave an impression of decay and inertia. The hotel, once a fine block of offices for the main German planters' firm, had mostly been turned into flats for government officials; the remainder is run by a shrivelled little Chinaman and his fat Samoan girl at 15/–6 a day.[44] After the defilement of the ship I tore off all my clothes, bathed and lay down and went fast asleep, thus failing to make my call upon the Governor as instructed by the doctor. His Excellency sent me a note remarking this omission and giving me another chance on Monday.[45] I was well punished. This was Saturday. I felt very ignorant, neglected and forlorn. However, I assumed that in this small place, and sponsored by the Governor, the officials about the building would make contact as a matter of course. Not they! In the public rooms and in the garden they passed me by, almost deliberately, so it seemed, looking the other way. Was I being sent to Coventry as one spying upon their local rebellion? I dragged myself out for a walk along the slovenly 'Beach', as the waterfront is called. Copra warehouses; tangled looking stores run by half-castes; some old-timers in shabby topees; a rather gimcrack Roman cathedral and, dominating the harbour, the rusted, broken-backed carcase of the long ago wrecked German warship *Adler*.[46] The Samoans in the street were quite different in manner from those of Pago, looking at me in a half-insolent manner. Many deplorable dogs and ponies.[47] At dinner, as at lunch, there were a few white officials but from none did I get so much as a glance. . . . Of course I should have taken the initiative. But I fear I am not brazen enough for this job I have taken on. And I was tired. I hope I shall get stronger and tougher as I go on with my travels.[48]

My morale was not improved by a little incident this evening in the hotel. When the *Lady Roberts*'s siren had summoned me at Pago Pago I had hurriedly stuffed some clothes into a suitcase. My best dress, in which I meant to call on the Governor on Monday, was badly crushed. The Chinese hotelier assured me with words and gestures that he could and would press it for me. An hour or so later he brought it back to me very carefully folded. But as I shook it out a huge burned hole was revealed. The dress – my best – was ruined. It was a very serious blow, as my wardrobe is very restricted, and though I think I am reasonably good-tempered, on this occasion my nerves were frayed and I really exploded. As I spoke, though I am sure he could not understand much of what I was saying, he slowly crumpled up in a way that I should have thought impossible for the human body, so that in the end he lay completely collapsed upon the floor at my feet. This broke my anger. I felt bitterly ashamed as I realized that our confrontation was really based on race. I could not have spoken like this to a white man or woman, and no one of my race would have collapsed under the stroke of my tongue. I did what little I could to repair the moral damage which had probably hurt me more than the Chinaman.[49]

Sunday today. The morning dragged on. The hotel was full of somnolence. So was the waterfront. I felt that I could not sit around waiting for someone to speak to me. So I set off on a long walk straight inland. After half a mile or so on a road of a kind, and on which at first I met nobody, I found that some trees had been felled blocking the road. I clambered over them. This obstacle appeared several times. I went on. One or two Samoans passed. They stared at me as if surprised but ignored my greeting. This seemed to me very odd for this courteous people. I went on further. I noticed that one or two of the men were wearing a navy-blue *lava-lava* with some white bands round the bottom, rather like our hockey skirts at Oxford. At last I came upon a large, round, open-sided hut rather like a bandstand. Inside a circle of men were sitting, all with the navy-blue banded skirts. I waved and shouted a greeting. They all turned round and stared at me but made no reply.[50] So, feeling snubbed as well as puzzled, I turned round and walked disconsolately back, stepping over all the logs again and drawing unfavourable comparisons between these Samoans and those of Tutuila.

On my return I found that several cards had been left for me and decided that human nature was not so bad after all and that I must toughen up if I were to make a go of this circumnavigation.

This morning I called upon the Governor at his office. I was anxious to see this man who had been sent to retrieve his country's reputation in Samoa.[51] He greeted me demurely and spoke in a small repressed voice, very slowly and weighing every word. He has been here more than a year now but I understand that he is still an enigma. Neither European nor Samoan, I am told, knows what goes on in his head. What a contrast with what I begin to hear about his predecessor, the open, rash ex-sergeant-major, General Richardson,[52] whose hopeful plans and failures were familiar to me from the minutes of the Mandates Commission.

I returned to my hotel for lunch and made notes on the interview. Then, this afternoon, the Governor called on me to take me up to Stevenson's house, Vailima, now Government House, for tea.[53] He arrived in a dilapidated little car with the imperial crown at the back and the flag in front. He sat in the car as if he did not mind, so why should I be imperially snobbish enough to mind for him? We picked up his little son en route and also a vital, cheerful young man whom I will call Jim[54] and who, I later learned, was casting New Zealand behind him and setting out to make his fortune in America.

Vailima stands on a hill, a buttress of the magnificent mountains which rise in the middle of the island. It is a low, friendly, wooden house looking over a lawn and through a half circle of splendid trees, through which, from three miles away, shines the sea. Jim and the boy were sent away to play and the Governor and I sat down to talk. He put the points of his fingers together and talked for an hour, softly and with much precision. Not much of what he said stayed with me. I find that unless the talk is rich in facts and ideas it goes straight through my head.[55] I hear so much that my powers of reception and retention are wearing down. But I know the general impression he gave me. It was of great detachment, a coolness that was too cold, of almost too much patience. But perhaps this is a snap judgement on too brief an encounter. Certainly, I thought again, the most extreme contrast to his bustling predecessor. He said he thought that things were improving but he gave no evidence of it as he revealed how bad they were – the proportions of the Mau, their insults to himself, the complete uncertainty of the future. Yet he spoke as though these things did not really matter but were just mildly interesting. Perhaps it is his form of self-defence. Samoa, after all, as he told me more than once, is a very small place. Perhaps so, I thought, but it has made a sizeable international row and put New Zealand in the dock in the international and colonial spheres.[56] Incidentally, he told me that in my outing yesterday I had actually walked into the middle of the area held by the Mau and that my so-called bandstand must have been their headquarters. My conclusion was that this must be a pretty mild kind of rebellion and that, as no lives had yet been lost, there could be hopes for a peaceful solution. Yet in the civil wars in which the three consuls had been concerned in Stevenson's time the competing chiefs had helped themselves to their enemies' heads.

So the Governor sent me away thoroughly puzzled. As I went out I found Jim in the Governor's car. It took us back to Apia. There we decided to drop politics and enjoy ourselves. He raised a car and we collected our bathing gear and went out along the coast as far as a car could go. We then plunged into the jungle and swamp until we came to a creek. It was almost sunset: palms against fire on one side of the bay, palms against early stars set in pale green on the other. We hoped the reef was of the effective kind which kept out the sharks and swam out. It is not often that moments are what one dreams they might be but this bathe was one of them. The water was warm and silky with cool currents flowing through it. The palms leaning over us made two sounds in the slight breeze, one of silky caress in the upper plumes and a dry whispering in the brown fronds that hung down the trunk.

We dressed and struggled to find our way back through the now black jungle. There was one more delight in store for us. We reached a creek spanned by a bridge made of a single log perilously perched on two posts. We had crossed it with difficulty in the brief twilight: in the dark it seemed impossible. From the other side of the stream came five points of blazing light. A Samoan girl came to the bridge holding high a torch of flaming palm-leaves. The red and gold light played upon her copper arms and breast and thick black hair and showed how erectly she trod the narrow bridge. The lights behind, carried by her companions, lit up mangrove, banana and palm, making a luxury of green, all doubled in the still water. When they had crossed over they stood, holding their torches for us. . . .

Before the night was out we saw a less pleasant side of native life. Some Samoan boys beckoned to us and led us behind the town to a *fale* in the bush. We stepped through a crowd of Samoans playing on guitars and ukuleles and saw a mixture of whites and natives dancing in the hut. But the spirit was very different from that of Ava's house. Two fat, very unattractive-looking women were running the show and dancing like jellies. A handsome, dissipated-looking woman was lying prone on the floor very much in *déshabillé*. Every now and then the fat women would conduct one of the whites to a hut full of drinks. There is strict prohibition in Samoa. They were furious because I would not drink or dance and infected Jim with my attitude. One of the fat women sidled up to me and said that I was too good for them.[57] I said good-night and went out through the ring of spectators. Jim followed but he had to pay – heavily.

I have now been in Samoa for a week and hard at it every day. On the whole I have been disappointed with the beauty of Upolu Island. The morning after that splendid bathe the Governor took me for an expedition along what seems to be the only proper road – or perhaps the only road left open by the Mau? – for some thirty miles. We wound along the coast passing villages which Samoans always build close to the sea wherever there is a protecting reef, sometimes passing European-owned plantations, with palms planted in rows and cattle underneath to keep down the undergrowth. But there was no vista; many of the villages were untidy, and here and there a corrugated-iron roof effectually shattered the Arcadian atmosphere. There were churches everywhere, of no particular architecture, built by the natives out of coral rubble, whitewashed and weather stained.

I suppose never in history has a heathen race embraced Christianity with quite such a fervour as the Polynesian. You can see the Samoans trooping in to the churches two or three times a day on Sunday, all in spotless clothes and carrying huge prayer books. As for building a church, nothing is easier. These people, who live apparently in such primitive simplicity, can easily raise, in two or three villages (and the village is not a very large unit), £3,000 or £4,000 to build a church and do the actual work of the building themselves. Merchants and officials comment rather bitterly upon this: 'If the Samoans can do this for a

church, why not for profit, so that we could count on regular
production?' For the Samoan raises the money simply by collecting
the fallen coconuts and cutting them into copra instead of simply
letting so many of them lie. I was shown churches that had cost in cash,
not counting the labour, as much as £7,000. And that is not all. The
Methodist and London Missionary Society missions, as far as I could
make out, with their village schools, boarding schools and training
schools, are well supported and the Samoans even contribute men and
money for the conversion of the heathen – the Papuans, for instance.

On our trip the Governor and the Director of Education were
inspecting schools. The first one was in a church; rows of boys and girls,
going up in ages from about six to about eighteen, squatted on mats on
the floor, the local pastor and the teachers hovering about them. A long
programme for our benefit was written on the board in the beautiful
missionary-Samoan handwriting. Mental arithmetic, English nursery
rhymes, singing, etc., one of many such programmes that I still have to
inspect both here and, I anticipate, in Africa.[58] Then, at the prompting
of the education official, the Governor made a prim little speech. I was
told to make a speech too – not so prim, I hope, though it is very
difficult to know what to say on such occasions. Afterwards the
children vanished and, from the door of the church, we witnessed
rather a beautiful ceremony, the ritual offering of food by a whole
village. The donors were very effectively grouped, advancing slowly
step by step, singing, the villagers bringing the food, hens, *taro* and
nuts down to the very little ones offering eggs. The Governor,
seemingly not yet broken in to this kind of thing, awkwardly refused all
but one squawking hen which was put into the car, there to continue its
lamentations all the long way home. He explained that this was one of
the few loyal villages in that part of the island. Certainly, elsewhere we
were wholly ignored or received contemptuous glances. No representative of HIM [His Imperial Majesty] could have travelled his domain
with a poorer accord or in meaner estate in that ancient, shabby
gubernatorial car.

In the afternoon the Director of Education invited me to meet the
whole government educational staff and I had to sit in the middle of a
circle and make conversation addressed to all of them. I could not but
feel as I talked to them how unfitted they were as a group to undertake
the supremely delicate task of educating a primitive and temperamental
people. But perhaps we ask too much. Can we, of the white ruling
nations, hope to staff all the outpost schools in the subject world with

people of vision and intelligence, especially when a good deal of their work must be very elementary? Yet the future of these peoples demands no less. But before I depreciate these teachers I should ask whether I would devote myself to such work. It needs a missionary's faith to commit one's whole life to such service in exile.

If you are not interested in education and conversion you had better skip the next page or two, for in much of the colonial world education is mainly in the hands of the missionaries. It is due to them that the people of so many of the Pacific Islands were 90 per cent literate in their own language long before the same could be said of many European countries. When settled government came to Samoa in 1900, the Germans recognized the *fait accompli* and Dr Solf, according to his own notes, which the Governor showed me, appreciated the work of the missionaries, though he criticized the LMS[59] for what he called the main fault of the English, a lack of *bonhomie* and a Sabbatarian puritanism.

The LMS are the great people here. Of the 38,000 Samoans they claim 28,000 as their adherents. They have a self-governing and self-supporting system, with a highly developed financial side to it, so that the whole organization with its schools, pastors, training college, printing press, boats, plus the cost of the missionaries themselves, is self-supporting. Government officials even tell you that a large but unknown tribute leaves the islands for the benefit of the headquarters in Britain. This last fact the head of the mission, when I asked him point blank, denied, though not very emphatically. He said that the Samoans did contribute to foreign missions and even sent their own Samoan missionaries to New Guinea, but as to whether they were on the wrong side of the balance sheet in the end it would be almost impossible to say. It was, he said, all a matter of bookkeeping. He was a sharp little ferret of a man, but not an unpleasing ferret, and he frankly confessed himself more of an organizer than an ecclesiastic.

It is easy to see, what I never could understand when I read the books, why these islands attracted so many missionaries. Easy conversion, boundless amiability and hospitality on the part of the natives; on that of nature a corresponding hospitality, an equable climate free from noxious animals, insects and disease. And how beautifully easy to run a mission! The natives give the land and build the huts or houses; the pupils can keep themselves entirely, as they do in all schools here today, by spending one day a week in the *taro* patch, cleaning the bananas and picking up the breadfruit. With a little coconut plantation attached they can, with the minimum of work, actually make revenue for the school, as they do even for the Government school in Savaii. I am not intentionally cynical; the fact strikes you as soon as you visit the mission stations. But what about the martyrs' death at the cannibal feast? I can only think that cannibalism makes such a good story, or, I fear, a good joke, that its statistics have been somewhat exaggerated! In Samoa (I am almost sure) no missionary was killed, far less eaten; in the slightly more truculent Fiji, I believe, a large memorial school speaks for the one famous tragedy.

The mission schools are simple. Throughout nearly all the island there is in every village a Samoan pastor, both schoolmaster and parson (if RC, he is called a catechist), and sometimes two of different sects. He lives in the village and teaches the rudiments, the three Rs, with a good deal of Bible study. Picked boys are sent to a boarding-school, where, probably, English is taught as a subject, and, with the help of English, New Zealand or Australian textbooks, a very little geography and a little more arithmetic are added. When teachers speak of agriculture they mean the weekly planting day: when they speak of handicrafts they mean they teach the boys to make what the mission needs, boats, desks, houses; and with the Roman Catholics, elaborate carving for the church. The best boys from these schools go on to the training schools, Methodist, Roman Catholic or London Missionary Society, there to learn for two to four years to become pastors, studying, almost entirely, the Bible. The LMS have a huge place and run a printing press. I visited also the Methodist centre, run from Australia. The RCs, with the usual Catholic tolerance for the frailties of humanity, make marriage a condition for a catechist's post; he has his wife with him during his training so that there is a little village of Samoan *fales*, complete with children, within the station. The Methodists go so far as to have a special girls' school to educate wives for their pastors and they pair them off, apparently arbitrarily, as the pastors go out.

Along comes the hearty New Zealand Government with an energetic, rather boisterous Director of Education and a group of young, imported men and women from New Zealand. They have set up in the islands a number of grade II schools where a government teacher takes the children on from the village schools and gives them, as far as I could judge, a rather useless education. The mental arithmetic was useful, perhaps, but much time was given to singing, which they do anyhow; English, which is not really necessary, and which they express in conversations learned by heart and in nursery rhymes. As a compliment to me in one school I was treated to an excruciating recitation of Stevenson's 'Under the wide and starry sky'.

The Government provide as a next stage – Sir George Richardson's pet scheme – two boarding-schools, one in Savaii, one in Upolu. . . . In each of these about sixty boys, living in native *fales*, electing their own prefects, make a few more slow and difficult steps towards the quite unnecessary New Zealand proficiency examination, the leaving standard for the sixth form in the New Zealand Government schools. Although only the best boys actually take and pass this examination, yet, of course, the education of all is dominated by it, and it means a great deal of time spent in the difficult acquisition of English and a good deal of unintelligent cram. The so-called agriculture cannot amount to very much, since the New Zealand schoolmasters who lead their boys to the plantations have had no special training and probably know much less about handling *taro*, coconuts and bananas than their boys. The last stage is the boys' school at Apia, where the final New Zealand examinations are actually taken. Here the teaching of English reaches its climax, New Zealand textbooks are in use, the New Zealand school journal provides the reading, and a certain amount of patriotic talk about the King and the Dominion is offered to the boys.

These boys, Europeanized up to a point, and with an education divorced from religion (some of them are boys expelled from the mission schools) are now on the market. Their one object is to be clerks in the Government. As one letter I saw had it, 'I have been to school and learnt English. A job, please, only a little job, in government.' Failing this, many of them hang about town, become taxi-drivers (there are few roads but many taxis in Apia). They present the usual problem of the half-educated primitive, too good for his village and no good out of it, that we seem to be producing all over Africa. Heaven knows what the solution is![60] The Government knows that its schools are filled just because they offer English; only so do they compete with the missions. The Roman Catholics, hard pressed by the others, offer it too. The Methodists and the LMS are strong enough to refuse.

The real problem of education in Samoa and in similar islands is that there is really little you can teach these people. They have, and they know, nearly all that they need; the missionaries bring the Christian religion and so add a new interest and depth to village life, plus the hobby of church-building. All this seems to have little or no disruptive results. What else can you teach them? They build one of the best houses in the world, they need little furniture, they make their own boats, and they know how to get just what they require from nature with the minimum of effort. How can you offer such people an agricultural training, or any handicrafts, and why should you bother them with English, except the very few who should be absorbed into government and commercial work? No one can give a good answer to that and I felt that the Education Department should at least be thinking out an answer: in other words, have a policy, not a vague idea of activity and progress and a lot of generalities about making good Samoans. Though personal relations between government and missions seemed civil, the missions, from their old-established ground, watch the rather hectic activities of the Government with such measure of contempt and condemnation as their vocation allows them.

I may add here that the missions keep severely neutral in the political conflict. That is to say they do nothing to help the Government and I suspect that any benevolence in their neutrality finds its way to the native side. An LMS missionary who had lectured in New Zealand, and who was held to have condemned the Mau in certain matters, had to resign shortly afterwards. Meanwhile, the New Zealand Government, conscious of these large, old, far-reaching institutions, whose staffs watch their troubles with coldly critical eyes, complains that there is no New Zealand mission in the place – missionaries are English, Australian, American (Mormons) and Roman Catholic (which means French, German, American, etc.), anything but New Zealand. (What *is* the adjective for this country?)

Rummaging among the papers at the Native Office I found some wonderful evidence of the daring shown by these people and their thirst for religion and education. Three young girls in the Tokelau Islands, some four hundred miles north of Samoa, determined to go to school in Samoa. They persuaded a boy-friend to help them and in a little, leaky open boat, with thirty coconuts, they launched away in the dark. Then follows the bald narration, written down by an interpreter, of their eight days of privation and peril – three days and nights of rain, the feverish baling, then becalmed, the rudder torn away in a storm, finally drifting on to the coast exhausted, with only one coconut left in the boat. And that is not the only such story.

Before leaving the missions I must insert that on a later visit to – if I remember rightly – an LMS establishment, when we all went in to look at the large and excellent church, the numerous pupils all filed into the seats and I was asked to speak to them – from the pulpit! What was expected of me? A sermon or a bit of secular uplift? But one could not be unresponsive to all those beautiful, trusting, reverential, uplifted faces. So I did what I could but cannot confess, even in this diary, what that was!

This digression about education all arose from my expedition with the Governor. We went to another school where we had a further dose of mental arithmetic and nursery rhymes and speeches. I was again presented with a huge bouquet and had to make a speech. Ignorant though I was of the country, I had a feeling that the Governor was doing everything just wrong.[61] A great feast had been prepared for us but he hurried away without much apology, and all his utterances and actions were marked by the same shy brusqueness. Coming home, in discussion, he said he wondered if the Polynesian people were worth preserving – words that, coming from the Governor, had a chilling effect on me. I had the sense that he did not like them, and I think that without a genuine, human liking for his people, a man cannot govern them successfully. I get the impression that General Richardson, whatever his faults, had that. I can already see that it is going to be difficult to criticize governors who are, in a sense, my hosts and upon whose goodwill I am dependent.

Indeed, I had hardly been a few days in the island when I began to question whether the New Zealand staff as a whole were fit to handle the Samoans. It is not easy to speak of this even in a private diary, for these people not only entertained me but also exposed themselves (and each other) with the utmost frankness. Also, one must guard against the temptation of thinking that the English public-school type has an exclusive monopoly of the art of governing.[62] These men are very different – men with little general culture, little powers of generalization, many with the outlook of a clerical grade, and with no inkling of their own ignorance about native administration. They are of two types: men who are seconded for short terms, eighteen months to two years, and who have no time to learn their work, or else the more incompetent who stay because they have nowhere else to go. It is hard to decide which of these alternatives is worse.[63] But what else can be expected from a small country dealing with small islands? The Samoans, like most tribal people, are an aristocratic society and they recognize and admire aristocratic qualities: courtesy, courage, self-confidence, dignity, firmness. They get little of these from New Zealand's Samoan Service; they may get good intentions, heartiness, diligence, honesty perhaps. I realized as never before what a very expert business native

government is, and what correct proportions of strength and sympathy
are needed, and at the right times. The New Zealanders have tried
hard to understand. But when firmness was needed they wavered, and
alternately bullied and indulged the Samoans. They do not appear to
have seen their charges in the round. At first, charmed by the
amiability of the Samoan, they expected too much of him. Then, when
the inevitable differences in their culture and character appeared, they
reacted against him and depreciated him. From that one turns to read
Dr Solf's memoranda left in the archives, with their brilliant insight
into native and European alike, their judgement and balance. I began
to think that New Zealand cannot yet produce the men to run Samoa:
she cannot produce the patience and vision in her government. Samoa
is a small island, but big enough to test New Zealand and find her
wanting. It is absurd that national pride and the chance of distribution
should divide the Samoan islands between two powers. Would it not
have been better for the expert, England, to have added this small
concern to her big business of colonial government?[64] I had better
defer answering that question until I have seen more of British
administration than that of Somaliland.

The amazing indiscretion of these officials!! They not only gave,
they pressed upon me, sticks of dynamite with which I could have
blown them all up. What they thought of their colleagues, of their
chief, of the Governor, of the government at home – *this* scandal, *that*
incompetence. All with the slightest knowledge of my position and
character. I had to keep an alarm bell ringing in my head at every
meeting lest I should betray knowledge of what I should not know. I
was actually told that one of the highest officals joined regularly in a
drinking and gambling place in the middle of Apia with Mau
policemen posted round the hut as a protection! There was hardly one
of the officials I met who made any attempt to hide the plight of the
government, though very few seemed able to diagnose the causes. But
many of them finished by saying, with a shrug, 'The only thing is to
hand it over to the Colonial Office.' Not a healthy condition for the
service to be in?

I cannot here tell the whole story of the Samoan [Mau] 'rebellion',
which alone would explain the political situation as I found it.[65] There
are gaps which I must try to fill when I reach New Zealand. It is the
story of a difficult people, monarchical and aristocratic, who, by reason

of many changes of government and a long history of international complications, have come to have an inflated sense of their own importance, a people who have never been conquered, which as a past fact is an ever-present psychological factor with most native races; a people with too much time for politics and a complicated loose system of chieftainship that fosters intrigue and jealousy. Little New Zealand, with her inevitable limitations, takes over the islands and sets to work with the best intentions. After a series of 'incidents', many of them farcical, they are now in a position of deadlock. Three-quarters of the people belong to the Mau, maintain a policy of passive resistance, refuse to pay taxes or keep the law and actively resist arrest by the inadequate police forces who, the Samoans know, dare not use their revolvers. Meanwhile, in defiance of the law, the Mau parade the streets of Apia in their uniforms of a blue *lava-lava* with white stripes. They even call at the Native Office wearing it! The police tell me that their position is impossible as they have strict orders never to let a situation lead to bloodshed.

One night a man I had asked to dinner at the hotel was talking to me afterwards and I was saying that the Mau seemed pretty tame. He was denying this and getting rather worked up about it and at last jumped up and asked if I would dare to test the Mau. In great excitement we got a car – it was about ten o'clock – and drove inland from Apia towards the Mau stronghold into which I had strayed on my first day here. At a junction of the road ahead we saw many torches and, coming closer, a crowd of men on both sides of the road. Some were standing beside logs, ready to roll them on to the road, and others were drawn up with great copra-choppers or big stones in their hands. We had to draw up and they flashed a bull's-eye[66] into our faces and into the car and then let us proceed. We had to go slowly until we passed a second picket, a few hundred yards further on, which was ready if the first picket failed. If they had suspected us, or if we had been police, they would have held us up. As it was, it made one pretty hot to submit to it and, as we drew away, my companion insisted upon putting himself between me and the group armed with stones in case any should be thrown. And it did not make one feel better when a girl cried out tauntingly (translated by him as), 'The white people dare not drive through because they are afraid of the stones.'

The local half-caste leader, O.F. Nelson,[67] a wealthy trader dominant in the copra export trade, has now been deported, but he directs the 'rebellion' from afar in Auckland, after trailing round

Europe and knocking in vain at the doors of the Mandates Commission and the Privy Council. (Samoans do not, it seems, despise half-castes especially if, like Nelson, their Samoan blood is of aristocratic quality.) The Mau collect taxes and send the proceeds to Nelson. They also adjudge the land away from loyal natives to themselves, and there will be the devil's mess in land titles when, if ever, the whole affair is settled up, as the government is not strong enough to defend its own native supporters.

There are a thousand Chinese in Samoa. They are brought in as indentured labour though, owing to the provisions of their own government and the protests of the New Zealand Labour Party, most of the evils of indenture, as far as the labourers are concerned, are removed. But is the system good for the island? The Chinese are brought in one ship once in three years, and are supposed to be repatriated, but government and planters do their best, mainly for reasons of economy, to prolong it to four. They are said to be a low class of Chinaman, very young, and they are under no legal obligation to work or stay with the same master. In fact, they shift about a good deal and, as there is a shortage of labour, the bad planter gets small chance. They are not allowed to bring their wives and they may not marry Samoans. The result is obvious. Useless to say they may not enter Samoan houses and much more useless to say Samoan women may not enter their camps. The Samoan women are amiable and free; the Chinaman makes a good temporary mate. He works hard and pays her well in clothes and jewellery. So the cross Chinese-Samoan children are always on the increase. When the Chinese sail (and they do their best to hide and miss the boat, so good are the conditions in Samoa) the temporary wives, accompanied by as many babies as the men have spent years in the country, gather to say a sad farewell, with the Chinese promising to tell their friends coming out in the next batch all about them. And though the Samoan men hate the Chinese, yet the little half-breeds are always taken into the village and become part of the family. They are said by the teacher to be the sharpest part.[68]

While I was there, there was trouble. Two rival gangs of Chinese quarrelled. One demanded the dismissal of a foreman of the other party. This was refused. Whereupon two or three hundred of them went on strike and marched into Apia from a plantation run by one Hughes, near Apia. For three days I saw them sitting on the steps of the clock tower (given by Nelson), chattering excitedly or lounging up and down the beach with deliberately insolent manner. On the fourth day they went to the Chinese Commissioner's office and rushed it. He had only two police with him. They fired at close range into the crowd, which broke and fled, only to find Samoans, including prominent members of the Mau, waiting outside and giving each a bang on the head as he passed out. Some were very seriously shot and taken to hospital. The Chinese vanished from the waterfront. Whereupon Mr Hughes rushed his terror-stricken wife into Apia, fearing their return, maddened, to his lonely plantation. He brought her into the hotel with her baby, both in a state of nerves, and one of the officials' wives and I soothed her. Then this wife and *her* baby got infected with the panic, and what with the rumours coming in, and hysterical women and screaming babies, and what with Mr Hughes, very strong and silent, saying goodbye and going off in a storm, alone, to the plantation, it was all very dramatic. However Mr Hughes survived; the strike collapsed; the planters congratulated the government and a few days later I saw fourteen scared and bandaged Chinamen huddled in the dock for trial.

No one likes the Chinese but they seem to be a necessary evil. They are the natural enemy of the Polynesian, having learned in a hard school those qualities by which they could oust the easy-going islanders out of their fertile lands were it not for the defensive hand of white government.

The plantations are quite interesting, though I gather they are not run, nor do they pay, as once in German days. One or two former German owners are now working at a small salary on their own former plantations as managers, rather a pathetic sight.[69] The main product is copra, with cacao, and some rubber, which does not do very well. I visited several plantations and was shown all the processes and presented with cacao pods and squares of raw rubber, which I had to get rid of afterwards. Some of the planters have Samoan wives with the usual tribe of relations and half-caste children filling their houses. The plantations are beautiful with their lines of palms or cacao trees brilliant with pink and orange pods; tall para-rubber trees, delicately incised, and, here and there, the huge masses of the wild rubber tree, each tree a small forest in itself.

The great enemy of Samoa is a beetle. The huge rhinoceros beetle was introduced either from Ceylon or Java early in the century and is slowly spreading. He breeds in rotten wood and eats the young shoots of the palm, just as they appear. Thus nibbled, when they grow out, the branches form a striking shape of clear-cut, large angular incisions in the fronds of the palm. As a result the ravages are easily recognized by night or by day. But not so easily checked. Only by keeping the plantation clean, cutting away the surrounding bush and destroying all rotten wood, can the enemy be kept at bay. The Government has passed elaborate regulations. One whole day a week was to be given to cleaning and collecting beetles and larvae. These were all to be counted and credited to each individual, with records kept by headmen. All this, difficult enough in normal times, has broken down entirely now and so the beetle steadily and visibly advances: the fans of the palms are serrated and then die, until only a bare, flexible mast remains. As the palm is all in all to the Samoan, giving him poles for building his house, fronds for his curtains and roof, fibre for binding the fronds, milk to drink, and cups to drink from, beside food and money, the loss of the palm could be the loss of all.

But the Samoan will not realize his danger. To spite the government he spites himself. It is the same in health. Now that the Samoan refuses to pay taxes the Government refuses to give him free medical attention, although New Zealand rightly prided herself on a splendid health service. The Samoan does not seem to care. When things are very bad he may go to the doctor, but he has given up all sanitary and precautionary measures, so that the Government is in the dark. Of births, deaths and communicable diseases it knows nothing and lives in fear of some epidemic starting and running uncontrolled through the island. While I was there a mysterious pneumonia was rife which they refused to call influenza, remembering the dreadful disaster of 1918, when a quarter or more of the population was wiped out. So yaws, hookworm and elephantiasis are creeping back after the vigorous and successful efforts that the New Zealand Government made to combat them before the trouble.

Well, I could write indefinitely about the affairs of Samoa, but I must summarize. I had a busy time working in a room given up to me at the Government buildings.[70] Here I spent most mornings, having many conversations with officials and others, motoring or riding out to see plantations or villages, schools or missions, going out to dinner, and sometimes getting a game of bridge – no stakes! I dined at Government House, which was always rather chilly, where the Governor might spend the whole evening talking business in an undertone to the Secretary. Yet he was not only kind but tolerant to put up with an inquisitive and critical young woman of whom he knew little. I had secret meetings with the Assistant Secretary for Native Affairs, who insisted on bringing me confidential documents from the office for me to read at the hotel. I interviewed an old, besotted beachcomber who is Nelson's *chargé d'affaires*, once a British gentleman, now a wreck in a shabby, broken-down house, with a native wife, and a pedigree by the front door, showing his descent from the Plantagenets.[71] And I got very run down as I could not eat the food at the hotel, because it was so dirty, so I had to live on bananas and got very little exercise.

Activities reached a climax just before I had to go. Many people came to see me off in a high sea on the *Lady Roberts*, as small and as foul as ever. I was en route for beloved Pago to catch a boat there to Fiji. This time I carried the wherewithal to cover her dirty bunks and pillows; and a large tin for eventualities.

I shall not forget that evening. It was as bad as the voyage to Apia. We sailed at four. This time I had a monk and a nun, a couple of natives, the Chief Engineer, and an indomitable dried-up little American woman whose lonely perseverance in uncomfortable travel remained a mystery to me. She had been at the hotel and was the biggest bore I ever met, not so much from what she said as the way she said it, all on one note and never stopping all the time. There were very few natives aboard as typhoid had broken out at Pago and the doctor at Apia refused to allow anyone to go who would be returning. He warned me solemnly against going. Meanwhile the other doctor, his opposite number in Pago, insisted on calling the Western Samoan pneumonia influenza, a dreaded word after the terrible recent epidemic, and refused to allow *his* people to go to Apia. (The doctors carry on a sort of feud.)[72] We bumped into a strong wind and sea head-on the very moment we ran out of the channel through the reef and, instead of watching the Samoan wooded mountains disappear in cloud and sun, I huddled into my filthy bunk. It was infinitely worse than the last voyage. I never realized before what little boats can survive. At times we were simply lost in valleys of water that cut off the sky: sometimes we went right *through* waves, and, at the worst, there were times when the sea seemed to hit the rearing ship a blow, as with some solid projectile or as a boxer catches his opponent on the jaw. At these times the ship seemed to stand suspended, shivering in mid-air, before the next plunge. Even the Captain, who stuck to the wheel all night, said it was a *very* bad crossing, and he has sailed the South Seas for fifty years. I felt sick, which was not so bad as the awful results after I took a drug bequeathed me by Petronius, which gave me hot and cold fits and prevented me being sick – but I draw a veil. The run should be ten hours, and it took fourteen. And I only did it for the love of Pago and to fit in my visit to Fiji.

At last we turned into that thrilling, beautiful harbour. We tied up at 7 a.m. I staggered out and rang up the Governor. He and his wife were both in bed but they responded warmly. Very different from the first was my second landing in Pago! The Governor's great car was sent down to the dock and I was swung up the concrete drive to the wonderful eyrie where Government House hangs over the bay in a wreath of palm and hibiscus. Only when the Governor's wife had appeared to a delicious breakfast served by smart Chinamen did she confess that she was suspected of typhoid and the next minute the doctor arrived to take a swab.

The Governor was naturally in a very worried state, but very nice to me. He drove me down to the ship – the Matson liner had swung in past our windows without our noticing – and bullied the Captain and that horrid local German agent into taking me on and also giving me a cabin to myself. Then he took me off to interview the Secretary for Native Affairs, whom I had not talked to before, also the Director of Education. I had a great time and all the naval officers were most kind and welcoming, in spite of their anxiety about some of the children down with typhoid. The English artist was there, and the ADC and his wife and a crowd came to see me off. The swagger *fita-fita* played and sang. There was the usual throwing of paper streamers, and as we glided away out of that glorious mountain bowl I could see the people waving handkerchiefs and branches of palm, and the Governor and his wife waving to me high up in Government House terrace, until we ran out of the harbour mouth and turned away west along the island. It was horrible to think I could get no news for a long time of the typhoid and of the Governor's wife. I had a feeling for Pago that I had not for Apia, and it was not only because of the beauty of the place but because of the kindness of all the people there, not forgetting Ava and Pele and my 'brother' Kalamete, whom, alas, I did not see this second time. I stayed glued to the rail to watch every yard of the passing island, while all the strange people aboard went to their meal. It was most wretched to think I should never see that loved and lovely place again.

Fiji

It was Wednesday when I boarded the ship, the SS *Sonoma*, and we landed at Fiji on Saturday, but then we missed out Friday altogether, which was just as well as I was sick again and utterly alone in what, in my state of mind and body, seemed a very unprepossessing crowd of Australians en route for Sydney. On Saturday morning, August 25, in drenching rain, through which capes and bays and many ranges of mountains appeared and disappeared, we crossed the reef and sailed into the wide harbour of Suva.

I must cut Fiji short as I am getting far behind my current date in this diary. Nor do I feel that I had time to grasp Fiji.[73]

The island, or rather its capital, Suva, received me with the utmost indifference.[74] Petronius had urged me to come but I expected little from him, himself a newcomer, who could hardly be expected to sponsor a strange, inquiring woman picked up on the boat. Anyhow he had not been warned to expect me on the SS *Sonoma*.

The contrast between Fiji and Hawaii! I remembered what I had overheard those damned Americans say in Honolulu.[75]

Suva is a most desolate port in which to land, with an untidy dock, derelict land around it and, when the town is reached, just a shabby, largely Indian town. I did not know where to go. The Fijians quarrelled over my luggage; the Indians quarrelled over my taxi; but at least the doctor let me off quarantine for typhoid. I went to a dirty hotel, squashed in the middle of the town, with all the noise and hot smells of the narrow street coming in through my window. I had to take a deep breath before setting out through heat and rain to attack Suva. As a stronghold manned by the British Colonial Service, I knew I had a job ahead of me, as I had no introductions here and was yet determined not to be dependent upon Petronius.

I walked through the town, cheering up as the rain stopped and I suddenly saw the glorious bay of Suva. I found a ramification of mustard-coloured wooden buildings which, I was told, were the government offices. I walked into one big one and asked for whoever was boss. I was told that the new governor had not yet arrived.[76] The Acting Governor was away on tour. The Acting-Acting Governor was away for the day. Acting-Acting-Acting Governor, however, Mr Johnson,[77] would see me. I went in and explained myself. A smooth, poker-faced man, very suspicious, with the authentic English public-school and service manner. He had been at Oxford, too, and still had

his undergraduate attitude to the woman student. This was the first
British colonial government I had tackled since Somaliland. I
presented my credentials, all I had being a copy of the letter the
Colonial Office had sent round to the other governors – I had not
planned to visit Fiji – and which they had typed abominably on a bit of
thin, unstamped paper. I cannot imagine a more dubious kind of
document.[78] However, this man was kind in his cold way and sent for
some juniors[79] and made them bustle around to make me room in one
of the offices, where I had a big desk and all available papers. I started
skimming over the yearly reports to the Colonial Office and, not
surprisingly, found them far more meagre than the reports of the
mandated territory to the League of Nations.

With Saturday afternoon coming on the office now shut, so I
wandered out and found football matches in progress – two Fijian
teams kicking with their bare feet against a seemingly half-caste team.

So far quite the most striking thing I could see in Fiji was the Fijian.
He is a tall, and a very savage-looking person, a great contrast to the
pale, beautiful Samoan, and much darker in tint. But, most
characteristic, his hair, henna-tinted, stands, or rather perhaps is
trained to stand straight up, with the effect of a busby. It is impossible
to believe, looking at him, that, like the Samoans, he is, as a rule today,
a gentle, religious creature. Even his voice sounds ferocious, a deep,
guttural voice, his expression, gestures, stride, all suggest truculence.

In the evening Petronius called, and on the next day, Sunday
morning, took me for a walk. He poured out a story of mutual
jealousies of a small, English official society, infected with intrigue and
gossip. Every man seems to have told him outright his very low
opinion of most of the others: indiscretion seems to have become
licence here. Indeed, Fiji seems very much of a Cinderella among the
colonies; it is the furthest away from the metropolis and feels herself
forgotten. Men store up their leave too long; the climate is bad for
morale, and politics are dominated by a 'Big Four' of traders who have
the economic fate of the place very largely in their hands and who sit on
the Legislative Council.[80] Meanwhile the imported Indian (said to be
'of the lowest type') steadily gains on the Fijian, nearly 70,000 to the
Fijian's 85,000 in the last census, and the Chinaman is just beginning
to encroach on the Indian.

We walked past Government House. The town may be for the most
part an Indian quarter and the Government Offices a tangle of wooden
sheds, but Government House is superb, cresting a hill in a large,

beautifully wooded park that goes right down to the sea.[81] On the seafront all the fashionable world was motoring up and down and greeting Petronius, who has clearly made a great hit with his charm and good looks, and favouring me with a long measuring stare. He told me that the Acting-Acting-Acting Governor would be furious if on Monday I presented myself to his superior, who would be back, and the superior would be equally furious if I did not. Better offend the lesser man, he thought.

Which I did on Monday. It was all very funny. No. 3 called in No. 4 – the man I had seen on Saturday, and snapped orders at him as if he had been the office boy, telling him to look after me, and see I had all I wanted, with the natural result that I got little more as No. 4 was like ice from that moment. I did my duty by bravely calling at Government House where I found Mrs Acting-Governor. She sent me, by her secretary, a letter to say that she was almost completely and indefinitely engaged, but that if I would call at 10.45 on Wednesday morning she would be able to see me for a short time. Petronius having poisoned my mind against her, I refused.[82]

Petronius asked me to a party at the 'Batch' where were six others, youngish men in the Colonial Service, all sharing the house.[83] Petronius, being apparently socially superior to the rest, talked them all down, held the floor, criticized their bridge and completely dominated the scene. I found the evening a great strain and came to the conclusion that though the best Englishmen are the best in the world, the average Englishman only gets at the public schools an immense, unwarranted assurance, loses any reverence he may have been born with, and has no idea how to treat women. Why do the Americans know this, whatever their other faults or limitations? It is impossible for a woman in my position not to speculate a good deal about it and I cannot help thinking that the qualities that make it possible for American men – of most sorts and kinds – to treat a woman like myself as they did, are very important ones: a healthy self-confidence, sympathy, the open mind, a proper perspective about sex. The lack of all these is rather serious. Added to this difficulty was the sense of feuds between the men, very thinly veiled with banter, and it will be seen that my attempt, as the only woman, to be bright, social and interrogative, could not be much of a success. I was glad to bury myself in bridge, even at a shilling a hundred, and gladder still to go back to the ghastly hotel, the first time since leaving home that I ever went back at night unescorted. All this reads as rather an elaborate excuse for an unsuccessful evening and perhaps I was as much to blame as they. I should therefore add that the evening went tolerably well on the surface. This travelling makes one over-observant and over-ready with comparisons. Also I am short of time and those I contact are not. I am here to learn, but if they are bored or indifferent about their work they are not anxious to teach.

I struck oil before long in the Director of Education, a New Zealander.[84] He helped me enormously and took me out for a whole day's motoring trip to see the schools, and, incidentally, the island. We drove out through the back of Suva, through the Indian shops, with here and there a Chinese interloper, out through the miserable Indian hovels and plots of ground, scattered about without any order or, apparently, any minimum standards of hygiene; then uphill until we could look back upon the huge inlet to Suva, with the white line of the reef and the scattered islands, and magnificent wooded mountains. Distance conveyed to me the enchantment I had so far missed. It was long before we reached our first native (Fijian) village. I was disappointed. The Fijian house is quite unlike the Samoan. It is exactly like a very faded haystack in the distance, but nearer one can see that the thatched walls are covered with dry leaves to keep the rain out. A chief's house, or meeting house, is marked by a very steep roof. But as they are so slow in building and as the roofs tend to be leaky, they are now encouraged to build or patch with corrugated iron, with its shattering effect upon the harmony of the scene. And inside, though cunningly made and decorated, the hut seems dark and stuffy after the airy, adaptable Samoan pavilions, and the effect is increased as one's feet sink deep into the rush-cushioned floor. Yet they are a fine-looking people, and obviously the less mild climate dictates their form of house. They offered me enormous prawns packed in cleverly woven little baskets of palm.

After that we went through some glorious bush, growing up and down precipitous slopes so that each strange shrub and tree showed its shape. Heaven knows what they were: together they made a most exotic, lush, tropical scene. Most striking were the lovely tree-ferns, which I saw for the first time, with their black, scale-patterned trunks and delicate canopy of fern-fronds. I was delighted to hear that I should meet them again in New Zealand. The wild banana, too, was a romantic looking creature, with its huge glossy leaves, and there was the ivory pandanus from whose spiky blades the pine mats are woven, while vegetable parasites of all kinds dripped, or mossed, or trailed or hunched themselves about its growth.

We reached our first objective, one of five Government boarding-schools for boys. It was placed in a fertile valley, but, alas, in Fiji they do not use enlarged native houses for schools as in Samoa, and the buildings are wood with tin roofs and very ugly. Not a soul was there. It was a place of the dead. Then the Director guessed that it was plantation day and we went out into the fields. No wonder we had not seen these brown, almost naked bodies, half sunk in mud of the same colour, [which] with others were buried in the huge arrow-headed plants of the *taro*. The schoolmaster, with not much more on than the boys, emerged and set up a crying which, relayed by them, brought them all running and tumbling, covered with sweat and mud, to the road. They were of all sizes and looked such a jolly lot, with their earthy implements in their hands. I was pointed out the highest chief of all and very much respected. He was a little atom, with a cherubic expression and only a muddy rag round his middle. Then they sang to me in their deep, harsh voices, and with great energy, Fijian and Maori songs which had a swinging rhythm.

We went on until we reached the big Rewa River, beside which lay the huge crushing mills of the Colonial Sugar Refining Company, the firm which dominates Fiji.[85] The plains were squared with bright green sugar-cane plantations and spotted with the miserable shacks in which the Indian workers live. Here we visited several Indian schools. The Indian children seem very feminine and fragile after the sturdy, barbaric-looking Fijians; they look subtle too, and the boys, by our biased standards, effeminate. Their education has been almost completely neglected. Now they come to the mission schools, for lack of others, with texts and Bible pictures all over the walls and prayers every day, and remain convinced and unalterable little Moslems and Hindus. Wherever possible the parents take them away and send them to a school of their own creed.

Here, as always, the great business of the day is learning English, and all the specimen lessons were reading and reciting. In one school I asked the upper form a lot of questions about India to see how much the children of the indentured coolies knew of their own country. They were very vague, though the world Gandhi raised a response.[86] Not one wanted to go back to India. Asked what they wanted to be, they nearly all said schoolmasters, though a few said carpenters and mechanics. I asked this question of all upper forms, and only about 1 per cent professed a desire to be farmers. The Director remarked, almost sadly, upon the charm and frankness of the Indian children, as compared with what they would be later. There seems to have been great prejudice against the Indians as ex-coolies. It almost seems as if, having brought them here, the government has resented their presence and has feared to educate them. Yet many of the boys look intelligent and responsive. Seeing the Indian after the Samoan and Fijian, I realized how racially close the Indian is to us. Many of those boys, but for their colour, were the exact counterpart of English boys. . . .

The relations between the two peoples are of complete detachment. They neither mix nor quarrel: there is practically no intermarriage, and though sometimes one sees little Fijian and Indian children playing together in the road, it is very seldom that one sees the adults walking about together. Each I am told, despises the other. The Indian regards the Fijian as a savage; the Fijian despises the Indian for his poor physique and his alien status.

Going on to more Fijian schools I found some of the boys squatting in little platoons all over a derelict church. It is impossible not to warm to the jolly little children, visibly struggling into the first light of knowledge. They are more cheerful than the Indians. As with Samoans and Somalis, their loincloths are spotless, as are their shirts (if they wear any).

We then went on to the big Wesleyan centre. This is a huge estate, with an orphanage, a girls' and a boys' school, and a training college for teachers.[87] The interest of this last is that the experiment is being tried here of mixing Indians and Fijians. I went into a class-room where they were having agriculture and saw a dozen of the small, slender, velvet-eyed Indians sitting among the big sprawling aborigines. The teacher told me that there was not much difference in them in standards. They were studying from a book produced – as seems usually the case here – in the Philippines by the Americans. I tried to talk to them a little, but they were too shy to answer.

In the drawing class was one of the most beautiful human beings I ever saw, a young, slender Fijian, with the heavily marked features common to them, the lips full and yet not too full, the high cheekbones, aquiline nose, but all more refined than in the usual type, with enormous dreamy eyes and a great crest of red-black hair. He was dressed in a spotless white *lava-lava* and shirt open at the neck. I walked round to get his profile – he was equally beautiful that way. I went up to speak to him, but he only bent his head with the look and gesture that accompanies a blush (though no blush was visible) and went on with his work.

Afterwards I went to tea with the local missionaries. Here I found was an American expert from Honolulu and Manila reporting on the education of the Fijian for the missions. He was very voluble and rather superior. He expatiated on what America had done for the Philippines and Hawaii, and he brought out fine phrases as if the very coining of them was a final argument in itself. He was shocked to find the Colonial Office had done so little for the native. I did my best. I tried to point out that our methods differed as well as our objects; that we tried to understand the native and, having done so, to develop him on his own lines, struggling where necessary, to slow down rather than speed too fast. I even hinted that we should not be proud of Hawaii but ashamed of their destruction of the native and his society.

The American point of view must be different. His great achievement is a material one; he works at it, wonders at it, almost worships it. It is the essential bond between the different elements in his country. Tradition, nationalism, the nationalism of a thousand years or so – the customs and culture of a people hammered out through centuries and moulded upon their land and its products – how can they even evaluate that? Putting aside the accusation of selfish exploitation, the most generous policy for them seems to be to give of their best, and their best is organization, increased production, a higher standard of living. I think that we, perhaps, undervalue that as they overvalue it. Certainly I think it should have been applied to the Indian, already uprooted, and in need of adjustment to a new setting without the risks that attach to quick-change methods for the Fijian. I admit that the town of Suva, mainly an Indian town, and the Indian quarters dotted about the countryside, are a disgrace to the Colonial Office. But, it might be asked, can you organize and improve the Indian, and conserve the primitive simplicity of the Fijian at the same time? The one will all the more surely oust the other race. To that charge, what indeed is the answer? It is very dangerous to interfere with the natural distribution of races, to put Indians in Fiji or Jews (after two thousand years) in Palestine, or Chinese in Samoa.[88] Yet communications and economic development will increasingly ignore racial frontiers.

The officials, however, do not seem at all worried about the future. When I tried to paint frightening pictures of the Indians gaining year by year upon the Fijians, the clever, adaptable, individual Indian against the easy-going and communal Fijian, the answer was: 'But the Colonial Office will see to that. We shall protect the Fijian. That is our policy.'[89] *Can* the Colonial Office, half the way round the world from England, put up the huge artificial barrier that is needed against the Indian, against frontal attack of masses and the insidious undermining of economic and social forces? Add to that the Indian is a born politician, with all the weight of his vast, self-conscious country behind him, bitter with the inferiority complex, poisoned by the memory of indenture. The Fijian, by contrast, it seems, is tractable and placid, perfectly willing, perhaps, to consume away with the same grace and fatalism as the Hawaiian. While I was there the town was full of the campaign of the first Indian elections to the Legislative Council and once the thin end of democratic representation gets in, the whole wedge called 'democracy' will follow, however slowly.

Scares, however, are easy to work up on paper. There are two possible mitigations in the future. One is that the Fijian will make up and assert himself. Already the contact with the Indian is making him a little more self-conscious than he otherwise would be. The other is that the Indians' grip on the land may not remain complete and firm. Already the second generation of plantation labourers is turning to the towns and the white-collar jobs (here the Chinese are better men, though small in numbers now). If the Fijian can stick to his land, and learn to develop it, perhaps he will be safe.

Meanwhile, everyone loves the Fijian and dislikes the Indian. This had driven a white doctor[90] here into such opposition that he has taken up the cause of the Indian, edits a paper for them, shares his house with them, and sings their wrongs continuously. A rather amusing incident about that. The Acting-Acting Governor told me that the one man who could tell me about the Indians was this doctor and arranged for me to go and see him that afternoon. I lunched with some people, and in hurrying away I said to my hostess I was going to him. They seemed surprised. I said, 'The Acting-Governor tells me that he is the one man in Fiji who can tell me about the Indians.' 'Really,' she said coldly, 'I should have thought that as my father is the Indian Commissioner. . . .'[91]

Well, I backed out of that and rushed off to the doctor, a hideous man, who told me that he felt no revulsion from the Indians, regarded them as our equals, liked living with them, and hotly denied that their morals were worse than ours. The Indians told him that there were only about three moral white women in Fiji. They had seen them dancing and they believed that dancing of that kind was incompatible with morality.

It is maintained that the Indians here improve with transplanting. The women are in a great minority and so automatically their status rises. They are never veiled, they have considerable freedom, and there is even some intermarriage between Moslem and Hindu. Their standards of health and hygiene improve – that gives me some idea of what India must be!

Meanwhile the planters cry out for more labour, the government hesitates to recruit more 'coolies' from India, while the Indian Government will have nothing approaching indenture. The big American firm at Hawaii has bought a huge tract of land in Fiji to start up a pineapple plantation and tinning factories, and that will ginger things up and raise the labour problem acutely. So the future of Fiji and of Indian and native is still open to question, one I cannot try to answer.[92]

3

New Zealand

I boarded the very workaday steamer,[1] a dirty little tub which does the round between New Zealand and the islands, taking from them copra and bananas and bringing to them merchandise of all sorts with tourists, missionaries, members of parliament, commissions and committees. She had brought a cargo of hogs on her last round. These had been packed under the dining-room and after disembarking at Apia they had left their memory behind them. She was now carrying back bananas, which were bunching out of the hold and festooning the bridge. She was also carrying, much to my delight, two Mau chiefs, going to consult their exiled leader Nelson in Auckland. One was a famous rebel and a mighty man physically.[2] The little Highland Captain carries them all, rebels and rulers, and is acquiring quite a philosophic view of the Samoan question, but as he transports both Government mails and Nelson's stores he dare have no politics. However, after we got well acquainted, he invited me to his cabin and opened out there.

We had a very rough trip. (Oh, this Pacific Ocean!) When I arose, after a day in bed, I found that the sterner sex were sitting in alternate seats at nearly all the tables, the women being down below. I found myself opposite a dry little American professor from Minneapolis,[3] an alert but rigid man, and, by the time I got aboard, thoroughly at odds with all the New Zealanders round him. They had jumped at the chance of accusing America, in his person, of soulless dollar-chasing, of claiming to win the war, and of playing Shylock over war debts. I was able to soothe him by paying some compliments to his country, and soon found myself put with him, with my back against his wall.

I settled down to taste the New Zealand flavour aboard the ship, and at once conceded their claim of being 'so English or, rather, Scottish'. I liked them. Most of those I met were not so aggressively nationalist (with the special nationalism of a new country) as Americans and

Australians, partly, perhaps, because their isolation allows them to be more complacent. Yet they do suffer from a measure of inferiority complex; they shrink from criticism and are quick to suspect patronage. They try to disarm you by saying their country is minute and off the map, but they will not admit the more serious difficulties under which they labour. At the end, when the coast came into sight, several men to whom I had never spoken came up and begged me to remember, 'ere I judged their country, that she was not yet a hundred years old. They are intensely proud of their scenery; I find that no people speak with such a possessive pride about physical features as colonists, some of whom may not have reached their new country until they were twenty. An American on the *Homeric*[4] held forth about the Grand Canyon and the ancient giant redwood trees until he almost convinced us that they were of American manufacture – he a German immigrant of the first generation! . . .

The New Zealanders are not blatant like that, but even with them one wonders whether they have yet earned the right to talk about '*our* mountains' and '*our* lakes' in just that tone of voice – even '*our* Maoris'. As to the two first, perhaps they have; as a people of farmers, they have worked hard and effectively upon the land. And, come to think, how does one come to possess mountains and lakes? Is it only by living with them for a thousand years and breeding poets to honour them?

I naturally had my eye upon the Samoan chiefs. One Faumuina was, I knew, of royal blood; the other, one of the most prominent Mau leaders. As the Samoans are a highly aristocratic and ceremonious people I went about it carefully. I consulted the Captain. He told me he was much relieved that they had decided not to come into the dining saloon as he had thus been saved all possibility of embarrassment, which made me wonder whether the equality of the Maori was quite so complete in practice as on paper. He went and interviewed the chiefs. There seem to have been difficulties. I learned afterwards what they were. Would I promise him (a) not to let them know that I had been in Samoa, (b) not to contradict what he said in his introduction? I refused the first and told him he was to tell no lies in the second.

The two chiefs had a special, big cabin on deck. They were both wearing the uniform of the Mau, blue white-banded *lava-lava* and purple badge, and were bare-legged. For their rations they had a palm basket full of bananas, *taro* and breadfruit. The Captain made a speech. He said that I was not just anybody but was of great importance in my own country; that I habitually played tennis with the

Prince of Wales and was a great friend of the Duchess of York. He then discreetly vanished.

The chiefs asked me in and I squatted on a berth. I confessed at once that I had been in Samoa but impressed upon them that I was English and had no connection with the New Zealand Government. At the same time I warned them that I thought they were largely in the wrong.[5] For a long time I could get nothing out of them. Faumuina was a giant of a man, his courteous and benign Samoan expression soured by bitterness and defiance, and he proved very hard to coax. But in the end he gave way and, with his colleague, agreed to meet and talk to me. In broken English they spoke of their wrongs; of their determination never to give in even if they had to die. Faumuina especially spoke of his devotion to Nelson and of the injustice of this man's banishment. If anyone gets killed it will be Faumuina, and I could not help thinking as I talked to him that it should not have been impossible to handle dignified and moderate men like him and to avoid getting into a position in which the only way out may be to shoot him.[6]

Meanwhile the poor rebels, never having been out of this island before, were shivering with cold, and as, like all Polynesians, they are helplessly vulnerable to chest complaints, I spent a long time urging them to put on some warm underclothing and to keep themselves wrapped up, and painted as luridly as I could the penalties of ignoring my advice. Next day it was warmer. Faumuina at last came out on deck and I played croquet-golf as his partner and, playing for the first time, he then beat all the men at deck quoits. I never saw such accuracy. The other passengers were surprised but seemed fascinated rather than offended.

(If my writing is worse than ever, I am in a very rough sea; it is 8 o'clock in the morning and the old S S *Maunganui* keeps standing on her prow and waving her stern in the air.)[7]

Auckland

We sighted land early in the morning and ran south past a string of islands and along the horn of New Zealand, past Kawai Island, where Sir George Grey, the famous colonial governor who became New Zealand's Prime Minister,[8] had his reputedly disreputable home, and past the dark, volcanic island of Rangitoto. The Maoris, I am told, say it is sulky because it was uprooted out of the mountains – where there is a lake exactly the same size – and it is always wanting to get back. And certainly it is most extraordinary how, on the most brilliant sunny days, the slopes of the island mountain are sullen with shadows.

I had made great friends with the Captain – not, I hope, wholly for self-interest – and he now took me up on to the bridge with him as he steered us into the big rambling harbour and showed me the points on the large-scale charts by which he guided the ship. When I came down I found the usual excitement on gliding into port, the same acute self-consciousness among all who had a part share in it, that I had found upon going into New York and San Francisco, with a good deal of talk about the 'finest harbour'. The Australians were quite serene, certain that Sydney would knock out all the others. Some New Zealander said 'Wait until you see Wellington!' My own feeling generally is 'What a litter man has made upon a beautiful natural site', and I try to imagine what it must have looked like when the first European ship sounded its way carefully in. No one can pretend that the thousands of little red and white cubes scattered about shores and cliffs, plus the accumulation in one part of bigger and dirtier cubes and rather more smoke, has any claim to beauty or even grandeur. Yet it is really their own work that the locals are asking you to admire, not the contour of the harbour basin or the line of the hills. No, the best harbour, by my standards, is Pago Pago, left almost as God made it.

I had not expected anyone to meet me in Auckland and was surprised when the Captain told me that two good-looking young men were waiting for me in my cabin. I went there and found two reporters from the rival newspapers, the *Sun* and the *Herald*, sitting on my bunk. One was turned out into the passage while the other did his work. I gathered from their methods that a little American influence had trickled along the steamship routes into Auckland. However, I let them do their job. When you are a short time in a place, and want to get hold of people quickly, it is rather a convenience when they know something about you.

The second man insisted upon my staying at the best hotel in Auckland and motored me there himself. Coming down the gangway I had seen in the crowd an enormous dark face on an enormous fat body, with eyes staring up at the ship, and, with almost comical effect, a bowler hat on top.[9] My reporter told me what I had already guessed, that it was the exiled Mr Nelson meeting the two chiefs. Asked if he would interview them, the reporter said it was no good. They would have the strictest injunctions from Nelson not to open their mouths to anybody, above all not to speak to anyone on the ship. I determined, if ever I brought myself to see Nelson, not to give Faumuina away. I was interested in the way the reporter implored me to give my opinion upon Samoa, tried all ways to trick me into dropping an opinion. Seeing that they would make something even of my negatives I dictated a sentence to the effect that I refused to make any statement until I had studied the problem at the New Zealand end.

I had three days in Auckland, which was the wettest and most expensive city I had struck, though a nice, clean, cheerful, spread-out place. Seen from Mount Eden it looks enormous, a city of at least a million inhabitants instead of the quarter million it accommodates, but that is because it is a city of small bungalows each in a small garden. These bungalows, made of wood, painted cream, and with red tin roofs, I saw everywhere I went, more or less turned out to pattern; and speaking of the very general, but very moderate, level of comfort in the Dominion. From an architectural point of view most of the building is commonplace, almost ugly. Decoration on the bungalows is of a standardized curly metal variety: most of the large new buildings in the cities are the American steel-and-concrete type, and the majority of churches I saw are wooden reproductions of the mid-nineteenth-century English chapel. It must be said that earthquakes discourage stone and that the southern cities are said to be better, but my three weeks' dash gave me the impression of a country very innocent of art, always with the exception of what is left of Maori art.

I imagine New Zealand will long remain very much what she is, conservative, 'English', moderately prosperous, with the virtues and limitations of a small, isolated, largely farming community. They certainly are extraordinarily kind, though, being English or Scottish, it is slower work to make contact than in America.

My main object in Auckland was to meet the two protagonists in the Samoan drama, the much debated ex-Governor, General Sir George Richardson, and his erstwhile friend and later enemy, the deported half-caste leader and trader, Nelson.

Richardson was easy. I rang him as soon as I arrived in my hotel, reminded him of our meeting in Geneva,[10] and went out to see him next day. I found him in a smallish bungalow, with his wife and daughter, a maidservant, and a good new Austin 12 (most New Zealanders, like Americans, go for a car before they go for a maid). I imagined that in all his troubles he would have learned more reticence than he showed in Geneva – but not a bit of it! He overflowed Samoa from the moment I entered. He never paused even to ask me what I meant to do with the information. He simply laid everything bare, his hopes, his regrets, his hatreds, his bitterness. I had a most fascinating three hours, and in the course of them I learned a great deal about the Samoan trouble, for I realized how much it arose from the personality of this man, his virtues as well as his faults. He is charming and persuasive, full of vitality which he cannot hold in, ambitious, vain, overbearing, and, fundamentally, a promoted British NCO. Watching him I can imagine how he flung himself into his work, studied the language, loved the Samoans, stimulated them, speechified, paraded, reformed, and generally keyed everything up. I can see how difficult it was to oppose or criticize him. I found myself that he made it almost impossible for me to dissent, how a remark I made about external political influence was at once worked into a general opinion that *that* was the sole trouble, and that he congratulated me on my insight. His wife, a very handsome, silver-haired woman, with the kindly, patient expression of one who is married to a boy, tried to hold him up now and then but soon gave it up and went out. The only remark she made when I mentioned Faumuina was, bitterly, 'Yes, and to think how often I have invited that man and his wife to Government House to teach them tennis.' There was only one answer to make to him. 'Yes, you are splendid, keen, clever, vigorous; you did everything you could for Samoa. The only fault is that you had no knowledge of native administration, of Samoan traditions and character, nor had those who had appointed you.'[11]

Now, how to approach Nelson? Banished from Samoa by General Richardson, he tries to run his island business from an office in Auckland and travels, corresponds and intrigues on behalf of what he sees as his people's interests. I felt some disinclination to have any dealings with him at all after the part I thought he had played. In the end I wrote him a letter to say that I thought it only fair to tell him that I took a very adverse view of much that I had heard of him, could not forget the impression he had made upon the Mandates Commission (who said he was a self-seeking adventurer) but that if, after knowing this, he still cared to meet me and put his side of the case, I would listen with as open a mind as I could under the circumstances (I should never make a good journalist).

In the afternoon I called to see a Samoan woman, widow of a German who died in internment during the war. She knows Nelson well and she was horrified to hear what I had written to him. Of course he would have nothing to do with me now! How could I expect it? Not even by her influence would she now be able to bring about a meeting. However, in the morning came a letter from Nelson which surprised and disarmed me. He could not understand my taking my point of view but, in spite of it, if I would call at his office, he would do his best to put his case.

So I went down and found him in a small office, with a staff of two or three whites. His own private office was so small that there was hardly room for his immense, seated bulk, a table and myself. Henry VIII was nothing to Mr Nelson. His immense jowl makes his face almost a triangle, with increasing rolls of dull brown skin and fat eddying out of his collar. This gives, perhaps, a false impression of his having small pig's eyes, so lost are they in his cushioning face.

He talked for an hour with hardly a word from me. He told me how everywhere he had been maligned and misunderstood; of how his business had been ruined; how unfairly the papers had treated him; how he had never had a chance to put his case properly before the Royal Commission.[12] He spoke bitterly of Richardson, who had deported him without trial or even inquiry.

'It is all right for him. What is Samoa to him compared with what it is to me? It is my own country, my only country. All my interests are there. I had everything in the world to lose. But my honour was at stake. I could not lose that. I ask nothing but British justice, and some day I shall get it – when it may be too late. Though the mills of God grind slowly. . . .' He spoke with apparently deep emotion. 'What are the Government going to do now? They have deported me, sent over military police to Samoa and they can do nothing, nothing. They are absolutely helpless. The Samoans will never give in, never.' I asked how it would end. 'In bloodshed? If there is, the Government will be responsible. The Samoans will give no cause to shed blood.'[13]

He is a strange mixture of sharpness and simplicity. I am told that experienced men who examined him at the Joint Committee of Parliament say they never met such an alert and clever witness. He was all over them. And yet he went to England thinking that the Privy Council would hear him, though his case was not an appeal, and all the time the lawyers were bleeding him of his fortune, in New Zealand, London and Geneva. A schoolboy could have told him that the Privy Council would not hear his case. Yet in Samoa I was shown letters, intercepted, from him to the chiefs, written from a Mayfair hotel, and still hoping to pull it off (incidentally dunning various chiefs for old loans of £5 or so). As for Geneva, he still did not understand why the

Mandates Commission had refused to see him, and it was left to me to explain the procedure of that body and how in 1926 Chamberlain and Briand had turned down their request to be able to hear petitioners.[14] But, and this was very interesting to me, denied a public hearing he went round to try to see them in private. Lord Lugard, very correctly, refused, but three of them did see him, the Swiss and Dutch and another, the French, I think.

In the end I could not help feeling very sorry for him. His faults are the faults of his half-blood or, rather, of the position in which it puts him. He must fight now, for all is at stake for him. I am sure he thinks himself in the right and undoubtedly he has reasons for complaint. Richardson first encouraged him too much and then, finding he was, in his view, not all white in his conduct, recoiled from him and regarded him as the evil one. He is not *quite* honest. He professed to have nothing to do with a body called the Samoa Defence League,[15] which has been founded in Auckland to propagate Samoa's wrongs. (such is the entanglement of Samoa in New Zealand politics). When I asked if he could let me have any of their literature, he said vaguely he really knew nothing about it. They had an office of their own. Then he called in his clerk, rather a stupid-looking man, and said, 'By the way, you know the Samoa Defence League. Would it be possible to lay hands on any of their stuff for this lady, do you think?'

'It's all in your cupboard, sir,' said the man blankly, and flung open the small cupboard beside Nelson, which proved to be full of little else.

All the same, I shook hands with Nelson as I went away, which is more than I could bring myself to do coming in. I could not but feel sorrow about the situation, and for both men. For there is Richardson, with his ambition broken, his reputation shadowed, and with a sense that this is a world in which energy, honesty and altruism cannot flourish. On the other side there is Nelson, tied for ever to Samoa by his mother's blood, and drawn by his father's into ambitious paths, beyond his skill and character to walk.[16] Great friends at first, now their only hold upon their own self-respect is to accuse and revile each other. Meanwhile, the beautiful island and the beautiful race are being spoiled. Samoans are dying for it none the less because there has been no violence so far, but because of the breakdown of the excellent health service.

Nelson sent to my hotel a great armful of literature, pamphlets, etc., for which, in spite of determined efforts on my part, he would not let me pay.[17]

I must leave Samoa for a while, until I get to Wellington, and concentrate now upon the Maoris.

I had studied the Samoans and had made my – to me – fascinating diversions into their islands more for pleasure than intellectual duty, though I had the excuse that they offered an example of the working of the mandates system. But the Maoris – the cousins, more than once removed, of the Samoans – were of the real stuff in the history not only of race relations (and as such they had figured in my lectures at Oxford on British Native Policy) but of imperial history. I knew that I could do little more on my present visit than get a glimpse of the Maori today as he is after nearly a century of domination by white emigrants. It is an astonishing story, this contact with an isolated people, with such contrasts in their character: fierce cannibals yet responsive at once to Christian teaching; highly artistic – much more so than the Samoans; struggling physically, politically and spiritually in the sudden grasp of an utterly alien race and culture.[18] I could not expect to learn much but I could hope for glimpses that would light up my studies.

The first thing I did was to climb up to a dark and dirty office of 'Arotia', the Maori Association, a society in Auckland for protecting the interests of the Maoris, who mostly live in the districts just north and south of Auckland.[19] Here I found a half-caste, Graham, and a full Maori, Ranga Tiki, in charge, and several others hanging about and waiting for help and advice.

The Maori seemed to me much darker in colour than the Samoan, his brown is blacker and has less of that lovely copper tint that seems to me the perfect colour for the human body. His features, too, are heavier, and harsher, more distinct; there is less of the mellowness and placidity of the Samoan race, less of the expression of lazy merriment. All this is due partly to the Melanesian strain, I imagine, and partly to the harder climate, partly, perhaps, to contact with the whites. One feels them much closer to us physically than with the negroes.

The clients at the office were nearly all men taking cases to the land courts, those courts where efforts are made to disentangle the inextricable muddle of tribal claims and individual ownership, of promises, compansations and confiscations, most of which lead back at once to the famous Treaty of Waitangi and the war of 1856–65 which finally crushed the Maoris.[20]

There was a dear old grizzled Maori who was being sued by his white neighbour for trespass and was trying to show that there was no other way to his land. He was terrified of the court and was being painfully coached in its procedure. All this was in Maori, but they translated for me. He said his English was so bad that he could not stand up to cross-examination without an interpreter. In the end, much to my relief, he induced Mr Graham to promise to come to court with him.

The next business was even more interesting. A very well-dressed Maori, with a handsome, intelligent face, came in. He was a member of the Native Land Commission and also one of a Commission of Three appointed by the Government to inquire into the employment of Maori women by Chinamen. The Maori Association had been the chief mover in getting this Commission and it is one more aspect of the whole many-sided problem of the contact of races in the Pacific.

There are, I think, about five thousand Chinamen in New Zealand, and, as in Fiji, America and Canada, they are store-keepers and market gardeners. Right through New Zealand the greengrocer's shop, with its fruit arranged in complex and attractive patterns, belongs to Ho Ling or Chow Lung. On the outskirts of the towns are market gardens, cultivated with a patience and intensity with which no European competes. When he wants extra labour – it being difficult to get Chinese women into the country – he cannot get white men, nor Maori men, but he can get Maori women. This is the more convenient as they will act as wives or mistresses. The Maori, like the Samoan, has a fear of the Chinaman which is very well founded, for, as a race, the Polynesian is the natural prey of the Chinaman, and would perish before him, without need of violence, but for the shield set up before him by the white man. When I was asking Ranga Tiki about it he answered with impressive gravity, 'The Maori fears the Chinaman.'

With his small numbers, it is for the Maori more than a matter of honour that his women should not fall into the clutches of the Chinaman.

The next day the Maoris arranged for me to visit two old-established C of E Maori schools, one for boys and one for girls. A Maori woman called for me, rather a plain, pinched little woman, and we walked out to the schools. She told me that she had married a white man and that their daughter could not speak Maori. She spoke of the rapid Europeanization of her people, of the gulf between the generations as a result. She still went back to visit what was left of her tribe, but she did not think her daughter would. Her great desire was that the daughter should have the best possible European education.

All the girls, about eighty, were paraded into one room for my benefit. They stood in perfect silence, going up exactly in heights, every one in navy tunic and blouse, black shoes and stockings and yellow tie. They gave, in the mass, an impression of very dark skin, great black eyes, thick, though not unpleasingly thick, lips, more purple than red in tint, and abundant, shining black hair, breaking out of plaits, springing away from confining ribbons. The contrast between their rich, barbaric appearance, and their ordered silence and ugly dark dress, was almost painful. It was so clear that they should have been naked to the waist, with bright-patterned petticoats, singing and running free. Equally great was the contrast between them and the rather prim-looking schoolmistresses facing them.

The head discussed them at the top of her voice as if they had not been present so that I longed to get rid of her and talk to them alone. Among the Maoris were other islanders, one from the Ellis Islands, one from the Cook Islands, one, I believe, from the far, wild Tokelaus.[21] These were pulled out for inspection, the drab blouse and tunic almost succeeding in standardizing them, except that their hair sprang even more vitally out of control, and their big, dark eyes looked more bewildered.

I had to remind myself that they were not prisoners, that they had come of their own accord, some from so far across the Pacific, to get that dimly conceived, powerful treasure, education, the key to the mysterious white world, the sign of superiority over their fellows.

They sang songs – some in English, some Maori. When they sing their own language, in husky, toneful voices, and with great expression both of voice and of face, one imagines one is getting something of the real expression of the race, what they cannot give you in talk and are forgetting to give in the arts. I felt this with Samoans and Fijians (less with the Indians) and to me its effect is almost overpowering in its beauty and pathos. One might feel it with a crowd of children at home because their youth is passing, but here not only youth is passing, but the race, that corporate personality, a precious, ancient, individual thing, which, once lost, can never be re-created. The numbers of the Maori may be increasing but, it seems, the true Maori is not.[22] What lives is a changed, increasingly mixed race, which has largely lost its lands, and its pride and its art. And these children will go out into all the difficulties of a time of change, trying to adapt their natures to the new and forget the old, imitation Europeans. Yet the Maoris are supposed to be better off, better treated, than almost any coloured race. And here I thought of the Amerindians. The Maoris have at least been allowed to keep a little more of their pride. That may be true. And yet one cannot help thinking that Western wisdom and altruism might have made the contact very much less painful and more constructive, might still do much more than is done to understand and to help a race it has made prisoner on its own islands.

The boys' school was rather jolly. A square, strong Maori master [and] an English headmaster, with the tone of the public school in his voice and love of his boys in his eyes. The atmosphere free and friendly. They, too, sang to me in parts, a jolly song with a kind of bark in it, which made the little boys wriggle with delight in the singing of it. They looked very vigorous and healthy, as do all these vulnerable Polynesians, and so attractive and clean that one is not surprised that they can win white women. (No unbreakable colour-bar here.) Some looked very pale in colour. The headmaster's own boys were at school among them. We went out into the grounds where the head boy, a high chief, led a *haka*, the Maori gesture-song, a great performance, though one difficult to describe, a virile affair. As in Fiji and Samoa, questions about discipline produced no answer at all. There is no problem and the native needs none of the discipline which white youth demands. My Maori guide confirmed my impression that the tone of the boys' school was better than that of the girls, who were too much suppressed.

My half-caste friend, Graham, and the Maori on the Chinese Commission took me up to the Auckland Museum. This is the War Memorial; a huge Greek-style building, of Portland stone, which caps a hill and looks far out to sea. It is not open yet, but my guides had access and it was rather fun to see a museum in the making, with all the experts labelling, grouping and mounting. It is – inevitably? – mainly devoted to Maori art, and in the big hall is a full size Maori meeting-house with carved ancestors on all the beams, their mother-of-pearl eyes winking wickedly in the half-darkness. Right along the centre of the big hall – how long I cannot remember – runs a war-canoe big enough to hold at least a hundred warriors, with finely carved prow and stern-piece. It brought home the realization of Pacific islanders' migrations. I imagine the Maori stands high as a designer, his green-stone implements and wooden boxes – even his ordinary tools – have beautiful and intricate patterns. The Samoan cannot touch him, in fact the Samoan exhibit was one of the poorest of the lot, while the head-hunting Solomon islanders ran the Maori close. One of the most horrible things I saw was a man-catcher from New Guinea, a very long stick ending in a big loop, within which was a sharp spike. You ran behind your man, threw your loop over his head, and pushed forward so that the spike pierced the back of his neck. I understand it is still extensively used. One gets a little sick at looking at the elaboration of instruments to slice and stab and trap and torture. It makes one inclined to agree with Hobbes that the life of the natural man is nasty, brutish and short. (But what of unnatural man?) The Samoans seem always to have been a comparatively gentle people.

I noticed that in restoring a Maori house, they had some Maoris designing the work, but a white carver executing it.

Urewera

On the fourth day I started for Rotorua. By instruction of the Maoris in Auckland, I got off the car at a small country town – it is difficult to call a New Zealand main street, all wood and tin, a village – and found my way along the banks of a green river until I found the gate into a Maori *pa*.[23] It is not difficult to recognize a Maori gate or a Maori house, with its carved posts and figure on top. Only on this *pa* was written 'Absolutely no admittance except on business. No camera allowed inside the place.' This was awkward, as though I had business, I had also a camera.[24] So I surreptitiously photographed the gate, walked away, hung my camera inside my jumper – where it made a suspicious lump – and again addressed myself to the *pa*.

I should explain that the *pa* is owned by Princess Te Puea, sister or cousin of the Maori King. She has collected all the strays of her tribe, especially orphans, organized the *pa*, built houses and, lately, a huge meeting-house on the old-style, now the biggest and best in New Zealand. To raise funds she trained a troupe of men and women dancers and took them all round the country: they were a great success and made thousands of pounds. She then induced the government to let her Maoris off going to school and she made her own school, her own church, providing from her own fields. I was shown photographs of the opening of the meeting-house a year or so ago, when five thousand Maoris of all tribes collected and camped on the spot, with the then Prime Minister, Mr Coates, looking very tall and soldierly – the man whom I am hoping to meet – standing beside the Princess, with her broad, shrewd, aristocratic face.

I was expected, had been expected for hours, and a very intelligent young woman, one of the troupe, who spoke English perfectly, took me all round and entertained me to tea in Te Puea's house, which was the most amazing medley of lodging-house stuff, aspidistras, shell frames, antimacassars, the primmest kind of lower-middle-class respectability, plus Maori mats, weapons, kiwi feather rugs, etc. It typified very glaringly the meeting of the cultures. Te Puea is struggling gallantly to save what she can of the past, to rally Maoris to her meeting-house, her Maori regatta on the river and her dances. The danger will be that her *pa*, only fifty miles from Auckland, will fail to infuse reality into the old and remain as a sort of museum piece for tourists. There is money to be made that way. The New Zealander is sentimental about the (old) Maori. He will subscribe to a new *whare*, he will pay to see *poi* dances and hear *hakas*.[25] Still more will the growing numbers of tourists. From an antiquarian point of view a commercialized survival of that kind might be better than nothing, but it has little relation to the life and pride of the race and could even degrade it.

I sat out in the road for an hour, hailed another car and drove on to Hamilton. Here, in a large country town, I had two hours to wait and amused myself by remarking how many British goods there were in the windows, and by going into the War Memorial Park, built on a precipice over the river, where some kind of rare tree had been planted for each local man killed in the war and named with his name; a beautiful place, I thought, and a beautiful idea. I watched the people flocking out of the town after work, a happy, healthy-looking crowd. No poverty apparent, no luxury, and as English-looking a crowd as you could find out of England.

It was almost dark before we left Hamilton and set off the eighty-mile run to Rotorua. I grudged not seeing the country and was glad to get there, stiff and tired, about 10.30. I got a very cold reception at the hotel. In the lounge a tight semicircle stared at me but refused to break, so I abandoned all hope of warming myself at the big logs. The proprietress said it was too late to get any food: by labour laws all meals in hotels must be finished by 7.30 (or is it 8?) unless they can put on a special shift for a late supper.[26] I could not even get my hot-water bottle filled, so went to bed disconsolate, not much comforted by remembering that it was my birthday.[27]

What worried me most was that I could find out nothing about my plans for tomorrow. These concerned my desire to get into the one place where I understood there was still a remnant of Maoris living in something like their old way, the heart of the old King Country, where the Maoris had made their last stand. I had heard rather vaguely at Auckland that the most promising and the wildest part of the North Island was the Urewera country (a Maori name, too shocking to be translated),[28] that it was very inaccessible, about eighty miles from Rotorua by a very bad road, and there was no communication with it at all except for that provided about once a week when a half-caste bush policeman drove his car into Rotorua. In the morning I got up early and walked about making inquiries. At last I struck the half-caste himself, a dark, hulking fellow, by name MacPherson. He was in a garage, desperately tying disreputable luggage all round his car with ropes and string. The car, too, seemed to sag, dispirited with systematic overloading, and almost disintegrated by banging along bad roads. MacPherson, being three-quarters Maori, was much too amiable to refuse me. His car was supposed to hold five, but as the teachers and missionaries were at this time going back to their work in the bush, he had already agreed to take nine. I was the tenth, plus my luggage. I imagined for a moment the agony that lay before me, the cramp, the bumping, the cold. Where could I stay the night? Well there was a police post at Te Whaiti, where they would perhaps give me a bed, and about twenty-five miles further on there was another policeman – another MacPherson – who, also, *might* take me in. So I sat down and hoped for the best.

The teachers and missionaries arrived, all heavily laden with packages, mainly wooden boxes of groceries to sweeten their fare in the wilds. They were Presbyterians, grizzled, sturdy, plain, badly dressed women, returning to their work in the last true remote Maoriland after a short holiday. They were all on Christian name terms and when it was realized that the car could not possibly hold them all their glances made me feel the Jonah. I was a mystery, too. Who was I? Where did I think I was going? Where staying? Our dark driver was questioned in whispers but he knew nothing. When it seemed that three of them would have to stay out and wait another week, I volunteered to abandon my seat and confessed myself a mere inquisitive traveller. MacPherson smiled weakly, anxious to please everybody and yet not lose my £3 fare. The women, extending some of their Christian charity to me, decided to attempt what seemed impossible and all pack in. The luggage was hung round the mudguards, packed round the bonnet, laced to the footboards. A plank was rigged on boxes just in front of the back seat. Three sat on this, with one lying on their knees, two crushed in beside the driver, three of us squeezed into the back, with one sitting on our knees in turn. But unless you have ever been with eleven plus luggage in a five-seater no description will suggest the anguish of our position. A crowd had collected, and, among amused and amazed bystanders, we crawled away.

For twenty miles we wound among low hills from which rose Rainbow Mountain, the sand of whose slopes is scarlet, green, purple, gold, blue, each in neighbouring patches. (It was so amazing that I broke my rule of not loading myself up with souvenirs by buying, after my return to Rotorua, a glass cylinder containing examples of the sand.) . . .

We stopped at the main forestry station where there was a crowd of Maoris working. One holding a motor-bike, and standing with shirt open, and cap back to front, disappeared shamefacedly to do up his shirt and turn his cap behind the hedge. He was an ex-pupil of one of the teachers. The missionary standards of decorum must be high.

It was now one o'clock and the others produced lunch baskets and had a picnic while waiting for the car to go on. I went and hid among the pines, pretending to eat mine, and wrestled with the pangs of hunger. Aboard again, I had to nurse on my cramped knees the heavy Maori servant-girl going out to work in one of the mission-houses. I had to embrace her tightly the whole time for fear she should lurch right out of the car. . . .

I must enthuse for a moment about the scenery of New Zealand. Neither in England, nor in what I have seen of Europe and America, is there anything to equal it. One feature is the variety; there seems to be everything in the north island – grassy downs, bracken moors, pine forests, native bush, low wooded hills, snowy mountains, rivers, waterfalls, tarns, lakes, crags. There is another feature, I think, though I could get no one to explain it. All colours in New Zealand have a value much greater than ours, partly owing, I suppose, to the clear atmosphere. Blue mountains in New Zealand are really blue: I could not help staring at them, measuring the startling depth of colour and trying to store it in my memory. But it is the same with all colours, the green of leaves, the green or blue of water. It is as though in England we see everything with scales upon our eyes. If I try to picture New Zealand it will be with rushing green water in the foreground, and leaning over the water, trailing their vivid spring-green hair in tresses ten and fifteen feet long, the weeping willows: for a touch of strangeness there will be the sturdy palms, black trunked, with sudden spiky manes that the New Zealanders ungratefully call cabbage trees. And always, in the distance, range upon range of mountains, each a different shade of blue. All this under a sky full of beautiful clouds that race along, drawing shadows after them on the ground, and yet never obscure the sun, except when sudden rain falls to wash the colours still clearer.

Except the forestry station, we had not passed farm or house since we set out. But now the car had to proceed some miles over fields to drop the wife of the state rabbiter as near her home as possible. The teachers spilled thankfully out of the car to rest, while I went on with Mrs Rabbiter to see all I could. She told me she hardly ever got away from their place: that she had come out from England only a few years ago (as a domestic servant under the Government scheme,[29] the teachers told me) and here she was for life, utterly cut off from the world. They had a huge mixed pack of dogs. Her husband went out every week hunting wild horses on the mountain slopes in order to feed the dogs. (Do even the dogs in New Zealand turn up their noses at rabbit?) She sketched in for me a hard life; herself a hardening, discontented, disappointed woman. We dropped her by the edge of that lovely river, under a row of Lombardy poplars that caught the sunlight in their leafless branches and turned it silver. We left her to her dogs and rabbits, with all her parcels strewed among the reeds beside her, shrilling abuse at MacPherson for taking her no further. There is a scheme in this country, financed by wealthy farmers in gratitude to the Royal Navy which kept the seas open for their cargoes during the war, to import and train English public-school boys. One of these was apprenticed to the rabbiters; he came up and the woman turned on him as if he were a dog himself and yelled at him to bring a pack-horse. I could only hope the poor boy found consolation in the scenery.

On the way back we passed two wretched looking huts. A long row of ponies was tied to the wire, and near the huts crouched a number of Maoris, muffled in ragged, unsuitable European clothes. It was a *tangi*;[30] they were wailing over the dead, an intelligent and popular girl, who had died in Auckland hospital where she was a servant. They had brought her body to this outlandish spot and now her relations had come from all over the north island, sixty odd of them to keen round her coffin, extol her virtues, and indulge in the death feast. For this they had thrown up their jobs, run away from school or abandoned their farms. Civilization's clutch upon them is insecure, it slips at a *tangi*, as many schoolmistresses and employers afterwards told me in sorrow or indignation.

We crammed into the car again and went on through the heart of the valley. In a tiny, new, yellow wooden hut we found a Maori girl operating the telegraph, her shaggy pony tied up outside the door. She was very handsome, with her hair bunching out like clusters of grapes on each side of her face, and merry black eyes set under a wide forehead. We met several of these girls on their shaggy ponies, with harness mostly string. They probably, most of them, had a dash of white blood in them; they were not so atrociously dressed as their elders; their only blemish was their fat, rather ugly legs. The teachers told me that even after several years at boarding-school, like the one I saw at Auckland, they return to the *pa* and almost revert to becoming pure bush-Maori. Their relations all say, 'Good, now you have been at school, you can cook for us, sew, wash for us.' And the girl becomes a general drudge, and gradually abandons her school standards of cleanliness and efficiency. Not quite, however; and for the sake of that 'not quite' the teachers still have faith to go on.

I should explain here that the Urewera country, popularly called Maoriland, has been almost entirely left to itself by the Government. It was, as I have said, the scene of the last Maori war.[31] For a long time the Maoris were very sullen, and just before the war attacked the surveyors and road makers who pushed through the road to Te Whaiti and Kuatahine.. There was also quite a serious shooting affray a few years ago[32] when a police patrol was sent in to arrest the local prophet, Rewa. The Presbyterian Mission turned its attention to the district about twenty years ago, and sent in women, entitled 'Sister', and then teachers to run village schools. They lived in little shacks, not much better than those of their charges, and endured hard and lonely lives. A few years ago the Government took over the schools and built schoolhouses and quarters for the teachers, but in all cases could only get Presbyterian missionaries to fill the posts, as no one else would go to such remote places and harsh conditions. So, all through the district, the only whites are the missionaries. One of our party was the teacher for Te Whaiti and [she] lived with a certain Sister Dorothy. There was much excited talk, as this missionary gave the returning teachers all the local Maori news.

It was pitch dark when we set out again. We drove at once into mountainous country clothed with the famous native bush of which New Zealanders are so proud even while they destroy it. It is utterly unlike any other kind of forest I have seen. . . . It is all doomed, except where it is artificially preserved. . . . There is less sense of tragedy about its disappearance than with that of the forests of North America, for the Maori (all but a remnant) has been weaned from the bush, and delicate, weakened, and much changed, the race is learning to live upon the fare of civilization.

Rising out of the valley, we twisted through a pass in the mountains and at twilight, in a cleft between steep wooden hills, found Te Whaiti, a small Maori village. My heart sank when I saw the filthy little wooden shack where MacPherson lived. It was surrounded by hovels from which peered dark, full-blooded Maoris, wearing ragged overcoats and old mufflers, half-hiding their faces. Here and there, neglected and rather incongruous among huts of tin and planks, stood a carved Maori house, with its huge gables, or a store, stilted on carved posts. In the twilight, the prospect of being confined in this valley with these disreputable-looking aborigines was not alluring. I got down and began to drag at my luggage.

Out of the shack, which was the only building in the valley apart from the Maori hovels and which was post office, police station and store, came a pretty but bad-tempered looking Maori girl, also, I think, bearing the name of that indefatigable Scottish patriarch. She took a parcel from our car (which, incidentally, is the Royal Mail) and vanished quickly inside the house. The driver, urged by me, went in very timidly to persuade his cousin (?) and came out crestfallen, chased by her, her face convulsed with rage. Hardly able to look me in the face, he said it was quite impossible for me to stay there. Where then could I stay? I could not go back. He was now going on through twenty miles of bush to the next and last place on the track, Ruatahuna, but I could not stay with him there because – well, there seemed to be reasons. It was now rapidly getting dark, and the women in the car were impatient. There was nothing to do but to throw myself on their mercy. I felt very much of a fool, especially as I did not know when and how I could get back from this inaccessible place. I had never realized that there were such wild parts of New Zealand.

When I announced my plight they whispered together and finally two sisters, who lived in a mission school house beyond Ruatahuna, said they would take me in. They were plain women, in all senses of the term, and they made no elaborate attempt to disguise the fact that they were accepting a disagreeable necessity. So, humbled, tired and hungry, I crept back into the car.

Our road was now very rough, cut in the precipitous side of the valley, and the lamps picked out of the blackness every variety of strange shrub and fern, and limbs of tree bearded with pea-green moss. We went very slowly, bumping down every now and then into gullies cut by the mountain torrents. Once we had to get out and push. We were all very cold and miserable. But our adventures were not quite at an end. I smelt a strange smell and saw a faint glow on the sky. It was not difficult to guess the reason. What was puzzling was that though the smell of burning grew stronger every moment, we could not see the fire. Then, suddenly, rounding a corner, we saw the beautiful and terrible sight of a forest fire at night. [There follows a description of a forest fire.] The driver was in a great state and I felt very cold inside. The other women did not seem much perturbed. Spending the night there or going back were equally unpleasant alternatives, and as human beings generally prefer the risk of death to the certainty of discomfort we naturally elected to go on. We could not go fast owing to the dangerous corners of the road, and I never enjoyed any fifteen minutes less than those. . . .

We emerged from the bush about 10 p.m. and passed a camp of surveyors who are examining the possibilities of bringing electricity across this country. We stopped at the police post. Near it was a Maori *pa* where the Maoris and their horses were circled round a big fire, and the men called out deep-toned, cheerful greetings to the sisters in Maori and one leaped on the footboard, and chattered all the five miles on from the Ruatahuna post to the mission station. All the women in our party were fluent in Maori and I learnt that most of the Maoris here could not speak a word of English.

We got into the school house about eleven o'clock. We found the house locked up and had to set to work to light fires and make beds. I naturally did my best to make myself both useful and agreeable, but my two rather grim hostesses were a type I had never met before, and they regarded me with a certain amount of disapproval and suspicion. One reason was that I had to use them as interpreters to barter with the Maoris for a horse for me the next day. I had forgotten tomorrow was Sunday, and even if I had remembered. . . .

After a night on a very uncomfortable camp bed, unable, for cold, to sleep much, I woke to a glorious morning and to realize the wonderful position of the house. It was on a clearing cut out of the bush on the side of a hill, and with a view for miles up a steep wooded valley, all untouched native bush, with a sky-blue river rushing through a deep gorge.

The only signs of life were two Maori *pas* on the other side of the valley.

Realizing that I had hurt the feelings of my hostesses I had a brilliant inspiration by which I could improve relations and combine the best of both worlds. The pastor for the district (whom I will call Mr White) had started on his round to some of the *pas* to take services. I elected to go with him. He had already started, but I obtained a horse and caught him up at one of the *pas* after riding about five miles through the bush.

Alas for my romantic hopes! A Maori *pa* is a most sordid-looking affair. In the ones I saw there was a rough stockade enclosing about an acre of land. In this there is generally one real Maori building, the meeting-house, which may be very old. It represents the best New Zealand and still retains aboriginal art and architecture, with its elaborately carved posts, its woven walls and the handsome red, white and black designs on the rafters. There may also be a carved storehouse. Scattered, quite without plan, are the living huts, ugly, small, square sheds made of tattered timber, with tin roofs generally in the last stages of rust and disrepair. The Maoris, the horses, the dogs, all combine to give you an air of poverty and wretchedness. The old women, especially, fat, out-at-elbows, with coarse, black manes straggling over their eyes, old caps and greasy mufflers, sometimes gnawing a pipe, remind one of the dark gypsies one sees in the south of France.

In the first *pa* we found the pastor, very correct in black suit and boots, very young, pink of face, Scottish of course, shy but dogged, his eyes full of zeal. He greeted us rather shamefacedly. He feared there would not be much of a congregation. They had all gone away somewhere. I learned that this is a peculiarity of the Maori: you never know where he is. *Tangis* account for many of his disappearances; for the men, seasonal work, shearing, or occasional work on the railways and forests. Their old life, with its sequence of duties and proper interruptions for recreation and religion, has not trained them for the regular work on one job that our system demands of them. They offer an exasperating refusal.

We tied our horses to a fence, off-saddled because it was raining, and crouched on the edge of the porch of a Maori house. The congregation consisted of a filthy old hag smoking a pipe in one corner, her dark tattooed face hardly emerging from a shawl; an equally dirty old man, out at knees and elbows, holding a child whose cast-off European clothing hung about it in a way to expose most of a body stained with dirt and sores; and myself. Throughout the service the child, upon whom I, all unwilling, exercised a powerful attraction, struggled to reach me and to clean and wipe itself upon me, with some success as its guardian seemed half asleep.[33]

Shivering in the wind and rain, my companion and I quavered out three long hymns out of a Maori hymn book, of which, of course, I could not understand a word. Then came a long, impromptu prayer, also in Maori, and then, when I could have screamed with cramp and cold, our pastor began his sermon. All I knew about Presbyterian sermons was the opinion of James I.[34] Pitilessly the pastor went on, earnest, fluent, in the staccato, harsh Maori language, with its short words seemingly all ending in vowels. The rain drifted in waves, obscuring the valley, the horses drooped lower and lower in dejection, the child tickled my back and slobbered over my jersey, the old man and woman were all but snoring, but still the parson went on, his face rapt, his voice running up and down all the scales of feeling that a sermon can contain. It was sublime.

After this we rode on to the next *pa*. The young pastor had no small talk, and guessing that after delivering himself of a sermon like that he could hardly yet have come down to earth, I respected his capacity for sublimation. At the next *pa* there was some sign of life; there was some rather inefficient ploughing in progress and a group of young men sidled quickly out of sight behind some sheds. At the meeting-house the pastor rang the bell, but though we waited long our congregation in the end consisted of an idiot girl, convulsed once in five minutes with epilepsy, and a large duck, which settled down beside her. Believing that the pastor meant to preach to them, and fearing a serious chill if I had to crouch under that again, I made my excuses and rode off, the other woman with me. But I could have beaten those young men.

When turned out in the morning, my companion and I had been told that we could return for a meal at six o'clock.[35] It was now half-past one. We counted our provisions; they consisted of a twopenny bar of chocolate and two apples. We were ravening. We rode until two and then consumed our portions. My companion was English, from some provincial university, Reading, I think, and she was teaching in one of the Diocesan Schools, through which, I think, New Zealand tries to maintain that 'Englishness' of which it is proud. This woman could say nothing good of them; her school, it seemed, existed to foster snobbery. And the men! She was the least attractive women possible but she hinted darkly in such a way as to suggest that the New Zealand men were such that she had a precarious struggle to defend her modesty, if not her chastity, from them.

She was not the ideal companion for a day riding in that glorious bush so I tried to detach myself into two parts, and give up one to appreciation of the solitudes around us. The sun came out and dried our clothes. It also threw reflections of the trembling, bespangled tree-ferns upon the river, and picked out the shafts of the white pines. Our track was so narrow as to be almost impassable even for one pony and it led up and and down the deep valley in paths so steep that we slithered down the one and had to haul our ponies up the other. I do not know why the sense of being in virgin country is so enchanting; I wonder if New Zealanders and Americans feel it as we outsiders do. The struggle against the wilderness is still so new to them; the bush is an enemy to be attacked with axe and fire, and its solitude one of the hardest conditions of a hard life. As for the Americans, I shall never forget the disgust, almost the shame, with which they pointed out the unproductive bluffs of Nebraska and the deserts of Nevada. But I could not help regretting, with the Maoris, that the road is to go on from Ruatahuna to Lake Waikaremoana, and so link on to Gisborne and Napier.

To my horror, upon our return there was neither food nor shelter for our tired horses. They were simply turned out in the cold evening into a small, fenced enclosure, in which the grass had been already gnawed to the roots by the ponies of the Maori children, who ride miles to school. This, although both had to go on to carry mission teachers twenty miles through the bush to Maungapohatu. All I could do was to tear armfuls of grass from the so-called garden, which soothed my conscience rather more than it filled their stomachs.

After tea, the sisters Clemence said they supposed I should like to go over to the mission house for the evening service. Perforce I said that their supposition was correct and we set off with a lantern. We had already seen Sister Annie, a gigantic, ugly woman, who looked as if she had been cut out of wood with an axe, coming back from her rounds, with an almost obliterated pony staggering under her. Sister Annie was the first white woman to come into the Urewera country twenty years ago and the children had then run away from her strange face. There, in a living-room as much a mixture of Maori and lodging-house as Princess Te Puea's, we found Sister Annie, the pastor, two teachers and the servant who were going on tomorrow to Maungapohatu, and also some Maori men. We were told that out of consideration for us the Maori service which they always held would be followed by an English service.

The Maori service consisted of four hymns, a prayer long as only, I think, a Scot can make it, and a sermon. Our hymn-books were Sankey and Moody translated into Maori, and I was quite startled by the way in which all the whites present, though they had quite normal speaking voices, screamed out the hymns in a nasal whine, without any attempt to keep in tune. I had read of this without believing it. Perhaps this was an old tradition, exported and preserved in this isolation. The cavaliers used to sneer at the canting Presbyters, psalming through their noses. The custom must have the dignity of a tradition, one appalling even to me, utterly unmusical as I am. Followed, for my benefit, the English version of the service, the same number of hymns and prayers, and then the pastor read us a sermon once delivered by one of the elders of the Church at a conference of pastors. A sermon, delivered to such an audience, was longer than ordinary, and not very closely applicable – at least to me, by now feeling very sinful.

But it was impossible not to admire more and more the pastor, young, good-looking, full of force, who had chosen to exile himself here, and work upon such unpromising material. Presently a child cried, and a dark, pretty little girl was brought in, the offspring of the pastor's predecessor by a Maori wife. He took the child on his knee and his rather dour face lighted up, yet I wondered whether he would not have inflicted any correction upon it in the name of religion.

Now the two leading Maoris of the district announced their intention of making speeches. Sister Annie interpreted. They represented strikingly the two different types of Maoris I had noticed, one with broad, rounded faces, as if moulded in rubber, the other long, sharp cut. One of these men, with long dark moustache, was more like an Italian than a Polynesian. He had only one arm. He made a courtly speech, telling us how they loved this house as the house of God, of the beautiful Maori name they had given it, how they welcomed back the teachers, deeply appreciating the education they were giving to the children. The next man was a bit of a humourist. He spoke in a deep, jolly voice, and though half blind and wearing an eye-shade, having just had an operation in Auckland, his face twinkled with good humour. The pastor translated his final words. 'I cannot think,' he said, 'why you strangers should come to this desolate country. Did you not know that its name meant something too bad to be translated? Why do you come so far to see a waste land and a handful of savages who are so uncivilized that they cannot even speak English? But since you have come, we welcome you.'

I replied, saying that in England there were those who were

interested in the native people throughout the Empire, who wanted to meet them and hear news of them. That their country was not desolate to me, but beautiful, etc. etc.

I learned afterwards that of those two country Maori gentlemen, one had lost his arm through the explosion of a stick of gelignite which he had stolen from a mine, and that the other, having been sent to Auckland by the mission, the doctor found that he must lose the sight of one eye because the treatment of magic had turned it septic.

They told me much of the prophet Rewa who lives at Maungapohatu, which is also the headquarters of the pastor. Rewa has founded a new religion of which he is the prophet and from which he draws tribute. Many stories were told me of his rascality and shrewdness and of powers almost hypnotic. It is said that he can walk upon the water, but the missionaries say that he drew his disciples down to the beach and there harangued them until they were in an ecstasy. Faith, he urged, was the great thing, they must believe that he could walk the water, it was their belief that mattered. Did they believe? Oh, yes, yes. Well, then, there was no need for him to walk, it would be wrong to do so: faith without sight, did not the Bible say, was the great virtue.

Asked why he had assumed divine powers he explained that his followers had made it necessary. When he was leading them to the land where they should dwell and they came to Ruatahuna, they had to go on to Maungapohatu through the bush by night. They were terrified and dared not go on. Only by assuring them that he could keep at bay all evil spirits could he induce them to proceed. At Maungapohatu he has built a great temple and a huge *pa*, and there, all but cut off from the world, challenged only by the pastor and the school, from which he bars his followers, Rewa maintains a last fool's paradise for his race.[36]

This is only one of several Maori sects. At Te Puea's place when I asked what sect their Church was, they said, our own Maori sect, a *hau-hau* Church. I believe this is connected with the last Maori war, the Hau-Hau, when, in a reversion to a sort of biblicized savagery, the Maori went into war barking like dogs, *hau-hau*. (Incidentally a better interpretation of a bark than our bow-wow?)

I have put down this about Rewa because it seems to me interesting. The Maori eagerly absorbed Christianity and quickly become literate. The white man's god had greater power and more *mana*[37] than his. But now, surrounded and subjected, in a last reaction against assimilation, he tries to make the white God his god, re-creates him, dressed in a curious mixture of Old Testament and Maori tradition. Chilled out of

1 Margery Perham in the twenties.

2 Margery as a tutor at St Hugh's College, Oxford, in the late twenties.

3 Margery Perham as a young lecturer at Sheffield University in the early twenties.

4 'Crossing the line' on board SS *Sierra*, August 1929. The figure in the lawyer's wig and gown is probably 'Petronius'.

5 'My own police guard' is how Margery Perham endorsed this snapshot taken in Fiji in August 1929.

6 Margery's self-appointed guide in Pago Pago, Christopher Kalamete, in August 1929.

7 Margery Perham as an Oxford don in the 1950s, taken when she had published the
first volume of her life of Lord Lugard.

the white man's churches, crushed by the white man's civilization, he creeps into a corner, shuts his ears, and asks to be bewitched into believing that the Maori still possesses some magic. Only so can the rapid growth of these semi-religious impostures be explained. There have been similar developments in Africa and for all of them the Old Testament is a rich mine. But I found it impossible to learn much about these movements. Nothing much has been written on them and the missionaries, who do know, speak their own language in telling of them, for to them they are wiles of the devil.[38]

Early the next day, in drenching rain, the Maungapohatu party set out on horseback, with pack-horses to carry their gear, and I was called for in a battered old Ford, already swilling with water, and driven by still another Maori MacPherson. My hostesses and I, now on the best of terms, parted with regret. We splashed through fords and puddles. Our MacPherson, a splendid-looking young fellow, at least three-quarters Maori, spoke of the Maoris with the detachment of a scientist. Yes, these people were very poor, but then they would not work. When they were not asleep, drunk, or at a *tangi*, they might or might not scratch the ground. He himself stopped and chatted with every Maori we met, so that I had to remind him that I was getting soaked and that I wanted to get into Rotorua before dark. At Te Whaiti we picked up Sister Dorothy on her way to a *tangi* and eager to get to it before dark and so avoid an insult, almost a catastrophe, by Maori custom. Three miles from Te Whaiti, in blinding rain, the car broke down. MacPherson's only remedy was to grind at the self-starter until that gave out. Then we walked to the surveyors' camp and returned with the white cook. The cook, wet to the skin, worked heroically for an hour, and the contrast between his businesslike efforts and the amiable helplessness of the half-caste was saddening. But the cook had his troubles. The camp dinner would not be ready, and what did he care? He was going to clear out tomorrow. Was this a democratic country and those swine of surveyors turned up their noses at him and refused to eat with him, treated him like a dog? What was New Zealand coming to? I sympathized ardently – liked his face, and his voice, his patience with Mac, and the unconcern with which he allowed himself to get drenched in our service, and before he went off, defeated, he had infected me with strong indignation against the unseen surveyors.

Meanwhile we were getting wetter and colder, the deep wooded valley was growing more sombre, and Mac had some miles to walk to look for another car. There was, he thought, one other at Te Whaiti and for this he went. It was long hours after dark when we reached Rotorua.

Rotorua

I don't think I need say much about Rotorua. It is a place for the guidebook. . . . But what the guidebooks do not say is that, in spite of being on show, in spite of its marvels of geysers and seething mud, it is a sordid, shabby village, and the people lounging about in their little shacks look the same. The Maoris themselves told me that nothing less than a royal visit will make them clean it up and the results then would last only for a few days.

My guide, Rangi, supposed to be the best of her profession, had got back only that morning from a week of hockey matches and was still – rather incongruously – in her hockey blazer and skirt. She was a handsome woman, of the long-faced type. I never met a guide less corrupted by her profession. There was no hint of 'patter' in her descriptions; she discussed eagerly any points that arose; she made no attempt to hurry us on – though we were only three – but urged us to rest and to sit watching the play of the geysers. She showed us the famous stream where you catch your trout upon one side and cook it on the other.

I called to mind the Maori woman, studying anthropology, whom I had entertained one night in Oxford.[39] She had offered me many introductions, to the Prime Minister, etc. etc. Mentioning Rotorua, I had rashly said to her, 'Oh, thanks, but I don't think that I will bother with Rotorua. I understand that the Maoris are all spoiled by the tourists there.' I was horrified to find that this same woman had not only lived all her life in Whaka, but had been a famous guide there, known throughout New Zealand as Maggie Papakura. She had taken home to England a troupe of Maori dancers and in England had been wooed and won by a European.[40] All the Maoris were much interested to hear of her, they spoke of her, as did the whites, with a curious mixture of admiration and amusement. 'Ah, Maggie, isn't she marvellous? What will she do next?' I met her brother, as ragtag as most of them, and he told me that between them they practically owned the freakish bit of geology on which Whaka is placed. Thence comes the money for his sister's studies at Oxford.

At Ohinemuto, another Maori village on the lakeside, also steaming and gurgling (how do they keep their babies out of those awful cauldrons?), I saw something really funny – a statue of Queen Victoria, Maori fashion. Not the Queen herself – there are limits; she was as prim as ever with her crown and her bun, but the base and the canopy were the barbaric Maori design and colouring, looking very incongruous. The old Queen seems to put in an appearance everywhere.

On to beautiful Lake Taupo, blue and ringed with snow-mountains. Here I got off to call upon the Maori mother of the child I had seen at Ruatahuna. Her husband, the pastor, was away at a *tangi*. The child was left at Ruatahuna, as it was asthmatic. She was a jolly little thing, her house and garden looked quite nice, though perhaps not quite so orderly as a white wife might have made it. She said they could do little with the Maoris round Taupo, as they were all Ringatou, a religion of their own, with their own priesthood.[41] Ringatou means 'hold up your hand', which they do while praying, obeying, I think, some Old Testament injunction. I see the census of 1926 gives, out of 56,000 Maoris, about 4,000 of these, 569 Hau-Haus, 11,000 Ratana, another religion of their own. Thirty-nine denominations are given, among them the 'Seven Rulers of Jehovah', seventy-one, and Methusalites – one! Is he a very old man, or hoping to be one?

While waiting for a car to take me on to Napier, I got into conversation with a local worthy and discussed the Maori with him. It is a small town, a tourist resort in the fishing season, with several Maori *pas* around. Maoris and half-castes kept passing us. He pointed out from where we stood four or five shops, the owners of which had married Maoris or half-castes. There can be very little pure blood left in a place like that and all the time the Maori blood is spreading and thinning as it spreads. I made a point of asking New Zealanders of all kinds their opinion of the situation. In Auckland they told me of a handsome and talented young half-caste man who was accepted in society and was half engaged to a well-known white girl. There are half-castes descended from some well-known early settlers who are accepted anywhere. And if a Maori can rise to the top in politics, like Sir James Carroll, Sir Maui Pomare [and] Sir Apirana Ngata, he will be accepted socially in the highest circles.[42] But, in spite of all this, I gather that the upper-class New Zealander, if one can use such a word in a largely democratic country, would regard his daughter's engagement to a man with Maori blood with a good deal of disfavour. In the working, shopkeeping class it does not seem to matter, and, as always, it matters less, and happens most, when it is white man to coloured woman.

Napier

We went over some desolate plains, over which herds of wild horses could be seen roaming, and over high mountains to reach Napier. . . .

I saw little of Napier, except that in the night and early morning it looked a fine city built round a hill standing in the sea. In the morning at eight o'clock I got into another car and we drove through the prosperous downs of the east coast, round Hawkes Bay and inland to Palmerston. Sheep, sheep – pearls on velvet – I never imagined so many sheep, no one in years of insomnia ever counted so many going through a gate. I was very lucky. For the first part of the time I had one Mr Stuckey, Vice-President of the Farmers' Union, as my guide, and I got him talking hard about sheep and cattle, pasture, Maoris, etc. One or two points stick. He goes to England every other year and is shocked at the decline of sheep there in quality. The English do not believe you can breed for mutton and wool on one beast; the New Zealander has proved, after experiments upon which his livelihood depends, that you can. New Zealand no longer imports stud-sheep from England: England, he asserts, would be well advised to import from New Zealand. With his help I was able to appreciate the countryside – the kinds of sheep, the kinds of pasture, the co-operative dairy factory, the freezing works. As we passed from the richest and most developed lands we came to that which had recently been cleared or half-cleared, sheep almost invisible within a forest of tree stumps, sometimes the trees still standing, burnt and ashen coloured, the merest relic of bush still holding its own on some of the hilltops.

He added one item to my scant collection of Maori information. A Maori of his town had just returned from two years in America having an agricultural training, and had addressed the farmers of the district. This seemed nothing strange to him: (of course) they had all turned up, and (of course) the lecture had been a success.

Wellington

It was about half-past five that we climbed up an enormous hill from which we could see the west coast stretching back like a map (for we had now crossed from east to west), the straits between the islands and the rocky promontories and snow-gleaming mountain tops of the south island. A marvellous view of a glorious country. What a piece of loot for the British people!

Then down the hill until we emerged through a deep-cut pass in the rock to find ourselves in the basin of Wellington harbour. It lay round me, water within a complete ring, for we could not see the narrow entrance, steep, bare, with houses choking every bit of flat land and clinging to each foothold of the slopes. Expected to admire, I shivered instead. In the grey evening light, it looked extraordinarily grim. There was not a tree to soften the hard, steep lines; it was like being in a grey, metal basin. I hated the thought that the beautiful country behind would now hardly be accessible, that wherever one could stand there would be houses and factories. Indeed it must have been beautiful when the first settler came and saw it, lonely and clothed with rich bush from the waves to the heights.

My depression was deepened when we drove into the town, a dirty, industrial and commercial centre, almost a little Sheffield,[43] with narrow streets and old-fashioned offices built of brick, with decoration of yellow tiles, the streaky bacon type of architecture like Keble College, Oxford, with Gothic frills, the form in which, during the last quarter of the nineteenth century, the dignity of commerce was expressed. Towering among them, in sudden chunks, were the American concrete and steel frame buildings. The father of one of my Oxford students met me at the terminus and, being rather tired and hungry, I failed to disguise my disappointment with the capital, with unhappy results. I ought by now to have learned how a man feels whose grandparents came to New Zealand and who has never been out of it. No critical detachment to be expected there! The gloomiest thing of all was when he deposited me at a filthy old hotel, just where the trams met, bumping wickedly over the points all night.

Alone, at dinner, I felt I must have some distraction, so I had my first evening out. I went to my first 'talkie', supposed to be one of the best – *The Broadway Melody* – and that was the climax of my depression. If the restful silence of the movies is to be broken by those inhuman, uncoordinated, American voices, I shall never spend another half-crown on them. The only cheerful thing was a mail from home, with a cable that gave me to understand that my prophesy about my pupils' Schools results was correct in all points but one.[44] So I could comfort myself that though Wellington was grim and dirty, and that I must nerve myself to storm her tomorrow, yet Teresa had gained her first in History and would go on to do Modern Greats.

First thing in the morning I found new quarters in a clean boarding-house and then went to Parliament Buildings to find out why the

Prime Minister had not answered my letter from Auckland.

Parliament Buildings in Wellington are rather a joke. There is first a block of the original wooden buildings; another block of florid 1890 Gothic of the Albert Memorial style; and, lastly, a great half-completed block in grey granite of the new Georgian-classical style, quite simple and good.

At the Prime Minister's department I found that the Prime Minister, Sir Joseph Ward [was away, ill].[45]

I do not want to bore you with my first, half-baked ideas of New Zealand politics, but I must offer some framework upon which to hang anything I can learn about native policy.[46] I must therefore explain that Massey, after being in power all through the war, died and was succeeded by Mr Coates, who remained Prime Minister for six years, I think, until last year's election. In this Sir Joseph Ward, an old and ailing man whom everyone thought a mere ghost, and who was leader of the Liberals (which had consisted of one leader and about one follower) suddenly swept the polls and came in with about the same number as the Reform Party of Mr Coates. The Labour Party, about eighteen strong, decided to support the Liberals. So, to his own and everyone else's amazement, Coates and the Reform went out. I gather that the Reform party is more definitely the farmers' party, especially the big farmers, while Ward speaks more for commerce and industry and is of [the] opinion that the big estates have escaped their fair share of the national burdens. But the difference between them is not great. The Labour Party, too, is not so leftist as ours, since state socialism has long been in some measure an accepted practice; the difference is of degree, not kind. Sir Joseph made lavish promises to the electorate, including an enormous loan of, I think, 20 million, from England.[47] He is regarded as a good financier, though a bit of a scoundrel, and his sudden return to power at the age of seventy odd has amazed his own supporters and exasperated the Reform Party.

The Prime Minister being ill, seemingly a constant condition, I was handed over to the head of the Department for External Affairs, Mr Berendsen.[48] Here, I think, I must digress for a moment, for the name of Berendsen had a sinister familiarity for me and I expected to meet an ogre rather than a man.

The reason is this. Shortly before going out the Coates government, at their wit's end to know what to do about Samoa, appointed a committee of three, the Public Service Commissioner, Mr Berendsen, and two others, to inquire into the public service in Samoa. These three set off for that much investigated island and stayed there, I think, a fortnight. They produced a report of a most damaging kind. I have never read a more drastic public paper of the kind. The whole staff in Samoa, they said, inefficient and untrained to begin with, were now enervated by the tropics, were basking in lethargy and overpayment, were appropriating perquisites right and left, and a clean sweep should be made of the lot as soon as possible. The whole service was discreditable to New Zealand. Yet they supported the extraordinary rule that the officials, seconded from New Zealand, should not stay in Samoa more than two years.

This report was, of course, highly confidential; it damned the officials generally and individually, and it used some very hard words, such as 'discreditable'. I think myself that it was a cruel, ill-judged report, with a good deal of bureaucratic priggishness in it, and no understanding of tropical conditions. But the scandal is that the report, just made as Coates went out, fell into the hands of the incoming government, who immediately published it. The effect was devastating; in discrediting their opponents, the new government turned New Zealand herself into ridicule, and produced impotent rage and bitterness in Samoa. All the enemies of the administration, Labourites, and – worse – Nelson and the Samoans, quoted the report with their own annotations. As a result, heads of departments in the island had to carry on their work, in the face of subordinates and natives, after having been condemned as incapable, all but dishonest, as having made illicit use of government cars (what tropical service the world over would escape such condemnation?) and with the sword of dismissal hanging over their heads. 'What did we say?' chimed Nelson and the Samoans and the beachcombers.[49] 'We always said the New Zealand administration was inefficient and corrupt. Now, at long last, we are proved right.'

The Prime Minister's department is in the new buildings, handsomely appointed, and a solemn messenger led me along a royal red carpet between pictures of New Zealand leaders, Grey, Seddon, Stout, Vogel and Massey, to Mr Berendsen's office. Mr Berendsen was youngish, red and hearty, spilling over with confidence and vitality.

'Ah-ha, Miss Perham, we know all about you' (gallantly taking off my coat and posing an armchair). 'This department is entirely at your service. Anything you like to ask – information, papers – just say what you want.'

In the end we decided that he should tell me all he knew of Samoa and that I should take it all down. This was 10.30 in the morning, and my visit had been without any warning. He talked until one o'clock (which made me late for a lunch given by one of the women's clubs), asked me to be back as soon after two as possible. He then talked on until 5 p.m.

I must remark here that my experience of government offices has everywhere falsified all expectations. I approached at first in all humility a young and unknown female investigator, ready to await my chance to gather a few crumbs from some junior official, and looking with awe at the titles on the doors behind which the supermen of administration direct the world's affairs at high pressure. But I soon learned a secret that has made me bold as brass. No official in America, Samoa, New Zealand (and, as I insert later, in Australia), seems ever too busy to talk about his own work. The difficulty is not to get in to him, not to start, but to stop him. There is only one fatal mistake and that is to go to the junior man first. If you then go to Mr A., and interrupt him by saying that Mr B. or C. told you all about that, or has already given you such and such documents, then both you and Mr B. are out of favour. This may sound rather cynical, and I do believe that the many officials I have met have been actuated by kindness and courtesy, but that alone could not explain the time and talk that has been showered upon me, especially as the point has sometimes been reached when kindness and courtesy should have prompted my release.

Mr Berendsen's case was all the more remarkable as in the Prime Minister's absence he was virtually in charge of foreign policy, and the League of Nations was now in full swing. Secretaries with telegrams from New Zealand's representatives at Geneva demanding instructions about their policy, especially about 'the optional clause',[50] kept rushing in, and Mr Berendsen would rapidly draft a reply and then return to me.

I find it very difficult to maintain towards a man in the flesh the hostility I may have developed towards him on paper. As with Nelson, so with Berendsen, the man does what it is in him to do, he is the product of his conditions, and within his circle of possibilities he probably does his best. Mr Berendsen is too vigorous a man ever to see the wisdom of doing nothing, too self-confident to agree with me that what the Government wants is the service of the expert in Samoa; too colonial to admit that New Zealand could learn something from Britain's colonial experience. But he was very fair to his enemies, of whom he has many, and he is the sort of man who, unlike Richardson, will allow you to disagree with him, as I did hotly about his report, and its publication. 'Of *that*,' he replied, 'I can say nothing. I am bound by my relation to the Prime Minister.' Meaning, I assume, that the publication was as embarrassing to him as to the Reform Party.

Berendsen went up with the warships to Samoa[51] and Captain Godwin (the English plantation manager) had given me a picture of him rushing around, clapping Samoans on the back, and at the end of it all, crying out, 'Isn't it splendid, no one has been hurt.' The New Zealanders are humane, no doubt of that. He was aghast when I put it to him that a little firmness and severity then might have cleared the air. 'What, shoot down the Samoans? It would have been like shooting into a crowd of children – or a lot of collie dogs.' I had not advocated shooting. If only, with their humanity, the New Zealanders could have combined a little dignity and experience. Berendsen had returned on the same boat with the Chief Tamasese, leader of the Mau, who was being taken to imprisonment. 'Poor boy,' he said, 'it was a shame. He was absolutely miserable. I did my best to cheer him up. He and I became great friends. I called him Tammy.' Tamasese, high chief of a most punctilious race, to be 'jollied' by the man largely responsible for his arrest!

The next day I again, by orders, called on Mr Berendsen, in order to be introduced to Mr Nichols,[52] of whom I had heard in Samoa. He is a new kind of being, a British Foreign Office Liaison Officer, and the first of his kind. Quite what his duties are nobody knows. Is he there to create duties or to absorb them? Mainly, I imagine, to write reports for Whitehall on New Zealand affairs.

He was sitting, with his feet on his desk, smoking a pipe, a very young, straw-coloured, self-assured young Englishman, Winchester and Balliol. In addition to brains, games and breeding, he is an aesthete as well, brother, I believe, of Beverley Nichols. The impression given by such a young man is all the more overwhelming when one has long been in colonial society. One realizes as never before what it is the public schools at home offer and how much their traditions are those of an aristocratic country. There is no doubt that at the back, however far back, of young Nichols's measureless assurance, is the conviction that he belongs to the highest caste in the world. His assurance falls well short of being offensive; there is no doubt of his ability, nor is his mind closed; he will go on learning the things that he means to learn, he will accept instruction, even humbly, from those above him in his own hierarchy. But will any new revelation, any of the simpler emotions, get through the complicated mechanism through which he touches life? I may be wrong and he may become less complicated as he grows older. At any rate he was most interesting, civilized and attractive to meet. A very intelligent New Zealander told me that people out there were astonished at him: he was regarded as a marvel. Perhaps that is his function; a sample exported to show that, if England can produce nothing else, she still knows how to produce men of quality.

Mr Nichols and I found ourselves, naturally enough, very much in agreement about Samoa, so much so that I refused to read his report on the situation because I feared he might accuse me of plagiarism in anything I should write. But all we could do was to look at each other and say, 'The New Zealanders! They don't understand what can be done with natives by expert government, by a trained service, untangled by party politics.' We told each other how utterly the government in Samoa had lost prestige and how, in Africa, a single messenger with a slip of pink paper[53] can bring a chief two or three hundred miles from his own stronghold to answer to the government for his defaults. But the art by which that is done is unknown, could not be known in New Zealand. We found that we had both worked out schemes for exchange with the Colonial Service so that England could help and yet New Zealand save her proper pride.[54]

Mr Berendsen took me to the parliamentary library where I met the librarian, Dr Scholefield,[55] whose books on the Pacific I (fortunately) knew. He was most charming and gave me a private table in his staff room, as the Library is only for MPs. He, a man with his eyes open to the rest of the world, was very conscious of living in a backyard, a farmyard one might say. There was nothing too critical that he could say of New Zealand education and culture, of the ignorance and the complacency that block reform. Yet I was glad to see that, though he could criticize, *I* could not – one depreciatory word swung him into a position of hot defence. He was very kind indeed, and all through my stay at Wellington I spent odd moments at my table in the parliamentary library or chatting with him. His kindness was quite overwhelming; he personally looked out any books I wanted and set the staff at work hunting up references, etc.

The next day, being Sunday, Mr Nichols called for me early, and picking up two pretty girls, one a granddaughter of Prime Minister

Seddon,[56] he drove us at a steady fifty miles an hour out to the fashionable golf club. I, like a fool, keen for air and exercise, had pretended I could play golf, and with strange clubs and a strange course, not having played for a year, went out on to the keen and crowded course. By some miracle I hit at enormous length, but the direction! My drives inevitably landed upon some other green, and my second shots on the nearest tee. After imperilling the lives of New Zealand's leading politicians and industrialists, I had to expose my stranger's face at lunch and tea to a society in which everyone was on Christian name terms and nearly all related.

The two girls gave me some idea of the sense of limitation and isolation that clouds 'society' in New Zealand. Life is cut up by the trips to England, eagerly longed for, long dwelt upon. The more intelligent or socially ambitious they are, the more they feel and express themselves as exiles. Their own society is too small to give relief; they know each other too well. They complain that they have no drama, no music. Even clothes are a difficulty and they droop under the knowledge of being two months behind the fashion.

Yet to me, looking round, the scene seemed fair and animated enough. The course itself is beautiful: one of New Zealand's amazingly green rivers encircles it; snow-mountains in the distance; native bush still holding its own on the spurs; and the omnipresent glory of the willows, their green hair hanging over red-gold osiers. The girls, too, looked handsome and healthy, in their light golf-jerseys and caps. I wondered, looking round at tea, how one would guess that this crowd was not English. Not from the clubhouse, nor from the voices, nor from the look of the girls, but, perhaps, from that of the men. They are big men and red men, and there is a strain of coarseness in them – if that word can be used without any depreciation – the coarseness, not of mind but of fibre, that comes from a hard life in the open. For most of the men, even in the professions, began on the farm, are the children of farmers.

Back to tea at Nichols's house, perched on the very top of a ridge of hills, the house of the modern exquisite, restrained in ornament, the one Chinese jar and the one cubist picture, the selection of new 'highbrow' books on the table, a large divan, on which our host threw himself to cast epigrams at the ceiling. It was great fun. I could only hope he will leave New Zealand before he gets spoiled,[57] the girls were so hard at work burning incense to his charm, his brilliance, his decorative setting.

The next day, being in great need of a warm dress, I went shopping, and at once sympathized with the girls in their complaints. Not only is the standard of taste low and the selection small but the prices are simply appalling. I cannot believe that freight and tax should *more* than double the value of clothes. In the end I bought a disappointing jumper suit for seven guineas, reduced from eleven, which would have been three or four at Harrods.

I had lunch at another of the women's clubs. There are three in Wellington, all very strong. The editor of the woman's page of *The Dominion* was there and I felt not too kindly towards her for the awful hash she has made of an interview with me. She had reported me as saying, among other things, 'At one time it was feared that the natives might outnumber the whites in Africa in dangerous numbers, but the experts now say there is no fear of this.' I felt it was useless even to remonstrate. This must have been more than the kind of error made in local reporting of a lecture I gave on Somaliland: 'As Somaliland is almost completely desert, the natives are obliged to live upon grapes.'

In the afternoon I had appointments at the Departments of Health and Education. It was rather distressing to hear sketched out the conducted tours I might have had studying Maori conditions. It was the penalty I paid for landing in Auckland and of Sir Joseph Ward's being ill. However, they told me all they could and plied me with reports. There was a charming woman doctor in the Health Department. The New Zealanders pride themselves much on all they do for health and for children, and indeed with justice.

In the evening I went to the House of Representatives and had my first taste of New Zealand politics. There are about seventy members, about twenty-five of the former ruling Reform Party; about the same of the United (Liberal) Party and about sixteen Labour on the cross-benches.

The Prime Minister, Sir Joseph Ward, who with his reddish nose and waxed moustaches looks like a prosperous bartender, did not come in until late. Then he lay down on the sofa – the house is arranged with sofas to hold two – and apparently went fast asleep with his bowler hat over his face, leaving his two lieutenants, Messrs Wilford and Forbes (both expecting the reversion to their aged leader's place and reported to be mutually hostile), to keep things going.[58] Meanwhile two ministers, for Health and for Industry and Commerce, men who had never been ministers before and had never even been in Parliament before and were obviously in the last stages of panic, had to stand hammering on the estimates, it being House Committee of Supply. They have a way here of making the minister under examination sit at the table beside the Chairman. This gives him the appearance of being in the dock and also removes him from his colleagues of the front bench; very important disadvantages, it seemed to me, for these two miserable men. Both were quite demoralized; they looked, agonized, at their recumbent Prime Minister and kept plucking backwards with nervous hands to the permanent officials on the bench behind, who fed them with facts and papers. I could not have believed that any parliament in the world could display such an exhibition of indignity, almost buffoonery.[59] One minister even said that if his tormentor would let him off now he would talk to him in private and give him every satisfaction. The whole ruling party, mostly new in the House, could give no support. Then a great broad-shouldered man, with a suggestion of swagger, came into the House, a youngish, vigorous, red bull of a man. He helped the ministers out, encouraged them, decided a point of order over the Chairman's head, wandered about the House, sitting down now on the Labour leader's sofa, now actually going across to sit with one of the Government. This was Gordon Coates,[60] the ex-Prime Minister, and, as most people told me, the next Prime Minister after an interval of lunacy. He shared his sofa with Mr Downie Stewart,[61] Member for Dunedin, the Edinburgh of this hemisphere, and Finance Minister in the Reform Government. He, quite young, is a helpless cripple as a result of the war and is carried in and wrapped in a rug before the House meets.

Quite suddenly, when one of the Reform members was speaking, Sir Joseph Ward, looking a ghastly colour, toppled his hat off, swung up in his seat, and shouted furiously at the Speaker, 'Get on with the vote.'

'Hullo! have you woken up?'

'I wasn't asleep.'

'Oh yes you were, or you would have known that what I was saying was exactly on the vote. And now you can go to sleep again.'

Yet they bear very well with Sir Joseph's irascibility, knowing how ill he is. He comes in, step by step, like a man in the last stages of decrepitude and it is known that he has diabetes. The standing orders have been remodelled to suit his invalid habits. The Labour Party barks and baits but it will not vote against the Government and I got the impression that Mr Coates was helping them out because he does not want to force the issue and bring on another election just yet. He and his party want to wait awhile, to lick their sores and find out the reason for their totally unexpected defeat.

I picked out the Maori minister, a very dark man, on the front bench, Sir Apirana Ngata, Minister for the Cook Islands and Native Affairs. There were two other Maori ministers, one on the Government side, one on the Reform benches (one of the fat, jolly kind). The most brilliant of them all, Sir Maui Pomare, ex-minister in the Reform Government, is lying seriously ill.[62] These men represent the four constituencies into which the Maori population is divided.

I thought the general level of debate was extraordinarily low. I went nearly every day this week. The Labour Party, which did most of the talking, are beneath contempt. They don't keep their demagogic business for the hustings; they unload the most nauseating of it in the House. They were perpetually lashing themselves into a fury of moral indignation by distorting what the other fellow said and going off into the deep end about the idle rich. On the subject of introducing paying wards into the hospital they nearly broke their hearts over the downfall of democracy.

After the debate I went along and knocked on the door of the room labelled 'Private Secretary to the Leader of the Opposition' in order to pick up Miss Montague, the woman who lives in my hotel. I thought it was pretty safe at that moment, but I had no sooner settled down to wait and to warm my toes by her fire than someone burst into the room next door, stamped along the floor and flung into our room. It was not difficult to guess that this was Mr Coates, the leader of the Opposition. He did not seem to mind my being there, discovered by a series of rapid questions who and what I was, and put himself at my service in the most generous manner, arranging an interview for 9.30 the next morning.

9.30 next morning saw us sitting over his fire. The first thing you feel about Mr Coates is that he is a powerful animal, a great big healthy man, with a vast spread of shoulder, a farmer's son with a soldier's carriage. It is easy to believe that he enjoyed the war and distinguished himself at it. When you first encounter him you shrink a little for fear that he should bellow at you; to your surprise his voice is very soft, and when he has spoken, he says thoughtfully, 'Yes – yes – yes' in descending scale. I think at one time he must have bellowed and has now learned to restrain himself.

I began a little nervously – for two weeks ago I still had an awe for prime ministers – to cross-question him about Samoa. He replied with the utmost frankness, and made no difficulties about giving himself away.

He had no opinion of Richardson – he knew too much about him in the war – a man who listened to the complaints of NCOs over the heads of his officers. (I might have pointed out that Coates did exactly the same thing by allowing Nelson, in the very first contact, to complain to him about Richardson.) Richardson talked too much. When he had to appoint another man he thought, 'Who is the most silent man I could find?' and thought of Colonel Allen,[63] under whom he served during the war, and for whom he has almost a schoolboyish admiration. Nothing seems to make a man more popular with men than a combination of great military prowess and great modesty. He told, and told well, a story of the war – very bloody sorties, and the two Allen brothers engaged in different ones, of Colonel Allen retiring with a quarter of his company alive, and calling up Coates. 'Have you seen my brother Wobert?' he asked (he cannot say his r's). 'Because I happen to be particularly interested in my brother Wobert. If he dies intestate, I am his next heir.'

It was, apparently, for these, or kindred reasons, that he made Allen governor of Samoa.

Asked about the extraordinary Civil Service Committee, he said, 'What could I do? I chose perhaps the ablest man in New Zealand, Verschaffelt,[64] and two others, the best I could find, and asked them to clean up the mess. It is not the report, it is the publication of the report, that is scandalous.' He used very strong language here about his political opponent and grew very red in the face. But he was very angry, too, with Sir James Allen[65] and Sir Francis Bell,[66] who, in the Legislative Council the week before, had attacked the report as well as its publication, although they belonged to the government that had appointed it.

When I brought out my usual remarks about the need of studying the Samoan, of the danger the administration is in through its absolute ignorance, its lack of contact with the native, he showed no comprehension of my point. Like all, or nearly all others with whom I talked here, he knows nothing of our Colonial Service methods, has no respect for the expert, thinks anthropology is cranky, and is unaware of the 'new thought' in native policy now being hammered out in Africa.[67] And yet, as I have become tired of pointing out to them, when the present Secretary for Native Affairs[68] retires (and he is condemned in the famous report as a missionary) there is not, I believe, a single man in the Samoan administration, except one clerk, who can talk the language, still less anyone who understands the customs and psychology of the Samoan. Like all pioneer countries, New Zealand has not learned the value of the expert.

Mr Coates has a fixing eye and he hit back at me in a way that made me realize what his capacities in debate might be. But I was disillusioned then and after about his intelligence. I am conscious of the dangers of intellectual priggishness; I know that a rough-and-tumble politician cannot be expected to debate with the 'cleverness' of Oxford dons, who at least know how to arrange arguments and employ words. I know too that for some purposes a blunt instrument is better than one too sharp. But – here, I know, I may be giving myself away – to tell the honest truth, and to my own amazement and dismay, for I wanted to admire, I felt that I had a better brain than he. (Of course, power of pure cerebration is only one of the qualities a political leader must have and, perhaps, not the most important.) I was the first to abandon the subject of Samoa, because I saw it was no good: he was out to make points, not, with complete honesty of mind, to argue himself a little nearer a solution. The New Zealanders pride themselves upon their understanding of the Maori and their ex-Prime Minister should have got beyond the stage of saying 'They're lazy beggars, those Samoans, you know.'

Conversation swung back to the personal. What, he asked, was the Prime Minister doing for me? When I said he had not answered my second letter he nearly jumped out of his chair. I became a party matter at once. He stamped round the room calling Sir Joseph names – he seems to hate him – and regretting that he was out of power or he would have done this and that for me. 'Never mind, the Reform Party will do what it can.'

It certainly did. Mrs Coates called on me that same afternoon, and they gave a supper party for me in the House as soon as the evening sitting ended at ten o'clock. I there met a number of politicians of all parties, including one of Ward's ministers, but spent most of the time talking to Mr Coates, whom I could not help liking very much for his kindness and frankness and who certainly showed off well in the House by his common sense and his courtesy to his opponents. He motored me back to my hotel, and, in short, took complete charge of me for the rest of my stay, arranging something for me every day. I passed, at a step, into the fascinating atmosphere of politics, and as the Opposition ministers discussed very freely in front of me their ideas and their plans, I began to feel very much one of their party. All went well until it transpired one evening that, in Britain, I was 'Labour', when they all turned and rent me for a traitor in their midst and I found myself very much with my back against the wall.[69]

My days during this time were long series of appointments with people interested in Samoan and Maori affairs. I dashed from one to another, nearly always twenty minutes behind time because the breakaway was always so hard to make, and generally battling through the howling wind which seems to be Wellington's speciality in weather when it is not providing a very remorseless kind of rain. I was too tired at night to make notes, so I will pick out from memory the more interesting meetings.

I went to a luncheon party at Mr Nichols's and there met selected very Anglophile New Zealanders, men who had been 'home' to university and school and who discussed New Zealand with almost cruel detachment. There was a master of the Wanganui school, 'public' in our sense, not theirs, where a staff of completely English masters endeavours to maintain English public-school traditions on New Zealand soil.[70] We talked art and literature; I defended America and Oxford and women at Oxford. Then Nichols drove me back from his eyrie to meet one Matheson, selected as New Zealand delegate to the meeting of the Institute of Pacific Relations at Kyoto. He wanted to meet me and pick my brains about Samoa which was on their conference agenda. (The English delegation consists of Lionel Curtis, Eileen Power, young MacDonald and Lord Hailsham.[71] I wish I could be there.)

Mr Matheson proved to be a thin old man with a bearded face, scored with lines of an unusual mixture; the weathering of hard, physical struggle as a farmer and the later scoring of thought, for he is a self-made scholar. He tackled me and the subject very directly and, almost for the first time since I left home, I met someone more interested in making me talk than in talking himself. He agreed with all I said even when, once or twice, I said rather critical things about his country.

Then I drew him out and learned something of the struggle he and his wife went through, when, for years, they barely wrested £100 a year from their farm and this with a growing family to keep. Then, inevitably, this old man, into whose character struggle and thrift are woven, turned upon the Labour Party and the unemployed, the sapping of initiative and responsibility under the system of state socialism. He ridiculed the plea of unemployment in New Zealand; it was not unemployment but softness of fibre. When the weaklings on the farms heard what the rate of unemployment relief work was in Wellington they flocked into the city, abandoning the farms. To this the socialist can only answer by allowing much truth in it, especially in a country like New Zealand, but by pointing out that in England and elsewhere the fight between man and modern labour conditions has ceased to be a fair one. I found universally in New Zealand an almost savage attitude to the new unemployed, natural among men who have borne the burden and heat of the day and now regard the unemployed as wasters, frittering their own hardly earned surplus. But the Labour Party now holds the political balance between the two older parties.

I liked Mr Matheson very much, not only, I think, because he paid me the compliment of listening to me, but because of his great simplicity and his rare union of qualities. His brother, I understand, is a senior Fellow of New College.

With Colonel Hutchen,[72] Secretary to the Samoan administration for six years, until his recent dismissal, I drew blank. Berendsen, with his buoyant optimism, had promised to get me an appointment. This was rather too much to expect of the man whom he had damned and displaced and who now holds an obscure position in the War Graves Department. As Mr Berendsen rather naïvely explained, 'He would hardly speak to me. He simply said "Do you imagine *I* know anything about Samoa?" and turned on his heel.' I had, expecting this, made my own independent approach. So I found Colonel Hutchen and found him quite a young man, sitting in a minute office, surrounded by plans of New Zealand cemeteries. I could get nothing out of him; he was too much embittered to speak of the island and he clearly suspected my connection with Berendsen.

But I did see Dr Ritchie, Chief Medical Officer under General Richardson and responsible for the vigorous policy pursued in Samoa in health matters.[73] He, too, was quite young: he was keen to talk and hit out vigorously against 'the other side'. He told me how the traders had tried to discredit him with the Samoans by saying that in New Zealand he was only a rat-catcher. This was because, owing to fear of plague, he made them unpack cargoes in lighters and catch the rats before landing goods on the wharf. He had saved the traders hundreds of pounds by examining the tins of beef and making the exporters compensate for those condemned. But this was a difficult thing to run because the traders tried to get him to abet them in cheating by not condemning their own old and surplus stock.

He sketched in eagerly all he had done and tried to do. I was particularly interested in what he told me of the women's committees he organized throughout the islands with the help of the wife of the American consul.[74] To him these committees were more than an education for the women, they were a revolt against the sanctified domination of the men and as such they probably played their part in inducing the general unrest. He admitted this in the end. 'But I would do it again. What else could I do? I regret nothing.' And this raises one of the most difficult of all problems – the problem of pace. How fast dare the administrator outrun the prejudices of a people for their own good? I fear the answer is given by Samoa today, stewing in its own diseases, with the Health Department largely helpless. But then again, maybe, health policy alone would not have produced this result. If enthusiasm had been tempered with more discretion in all other departments, perhaps it might have been allowed to run free in this. I have just read a book on medical research in Polynesia, recently published by the School of Tropical Medicine.[75] It made me understand dimly, with a layman's mind, the horrors of some of the diseases, above all the frightful, obscene, fantastic distortions of elephantiasis, for the worst is hidden beneath the man's *lava-lava*. I wondered whether moderation is not out of place in the war against disease. I hope to learn more of this in Africa.

That same evening I spoke at one of the womens' clubs. There is great enthusiasm among the women to improve themselves, to keep abreast of things 'at home' under their adverse conditions. My talk, sandwiched between the reading by a fat woman of the 'Mercy' speech from the Merchant of Venice and some parlour music, led to a rambling discussion. In this I was nearly lynched – verbally – for an apologia for America and had to listen to all the old clichés from people who enjoy hating America because they are half afraid of her.

On Saturday afternoon Mr Coates took me out to see a football match. He and his wife came to the hotel in a luxurious looking *American* two-seater. For this he apologized and told me how he went as a matter of course to an English firm, of their lethargy and the way he had to do all the work himself in order to find out what they had offered in conditions of sale, spare parts, etc. In contrast, the American firm had heard about his quest as soon as he entered their rival's shop and had literally plucked him out of the one showroom into the other.

'We would like to do business with *you*, Mr Coates. We have no doubt we can meet you as to make and price.' And so, I imagine, they cut their price and so caught the leading propagandist of 'British goods'. It is the same story, the same apology, everywhere. British cars are unsuited to colonial conditions and the salesmanship is even more unsuited. I met a fresh young New Zealander in the train, who, after real searchings of heart, for the New Zealander really cares politically about the Empire, and also desires exchange with his best customer, had transferred his services, as salesman, from a British to an American firm. Morris[76] was out here the other day, and while I was in New Zealand his posters were going up. 'Morris keeps his promise. He has designed the car for you.' And the new 'Isis' is a six-cylinder, about £600: New Zealand (much as she likes to buy British) simply laughs, though a few plutocrats may buy. What answer is this to the new Ford? Or the Chevrolet? It is all the worse because everyone goes for a car in New Zealand today on the instalment system: it is becoming one of the biggest businesses, with a proportionate importation of American oil. It has also very unfortunate psychological or political effects, as an industrial country is mainly judged by its cars. The car, cherished in the garage, is almost part of the family: advertising itself on the road and in every car-park, it is in itself a political and commercial agent of a most insinuating kind. And in the cinema American influence is also dominant.

Coates's progress to the football field through the crowds was a triumphal procession. The best seats were given to us and he followed the game with a breathless interest which, unfortunately, made it quite impossible to interpolate politics. Mrs Coates is rather pretty, fashionable and very nice. She is not much interested in politics; she simply moulds herself round the domestic side of her husband's life and concentrates on keeping him happy and healthy, obviously with a good deal of success.

I was due to tea at Mr Downie Stewart's and the Coates decided to come too. Did I say that Downie Stewart had been Coates's Finance Minister, said to be the brains of the party, and a cripple as a result of the war? I was told that he was one of the most able men in New Zealand. I liked him enormously. He is said to mark the very highest index of intelligence in the community, which opinion is a comment on the general standard. One has to remember that this is a small population, the grandchildren of pioneers. Perhaps their greatest man was their colonial governor who, astonishingly, became Prime

Minister, Sir George Grey. He was a great expert on the Maori. I tried to draw opinions about him, but ideas were rather hazy in this generation. He seemed to be remembered mainly for his moral delinquencies. I can't quite remember what they were and in this high-minded society I hardly dared to ask. I believe he kept something like a harem in his island retreat in the north.

I found my contacts fascinating. Stewart and Coates talked politics and I gathered that Stewart's political scruples were cut a shade more finely than Coates's. Not that Coates is unscrupulous; far from it. In the Parliament his moderation is astonishing; he not only loses every chance to score but seems to do all he can to help the limping ministers over the stiles. If half I hear of Sir Joseph Ward is true, he must be an almost complete rascal.

The attitude towards England revealed in these and many other conversations is interesting. It is such a mixture of envy and independence. They will break off in the very sentence in which they are acclaiming something English to assert New Zealand's capacities in that line and to resent the possibility of English tutelage. I, of course, noticed it especially in Samoan affairs, with reference to the respective ability of England and New Zealand to run a coloured dependency. It is rather moving, this wistful look cast so far away towards England and deeply at odds with their necessity to maintain their own self-confidence. You can see the two elements merging and then dividing in their minds. They rage against the rest of the world, above all against America, and, rather sad to say, against Australia. This is a summary of what almost every New Zealander has said to me, often in the same words: 'Don't you find New Zealand very English? The people, the life we live, the accent? You will find things very different when you go to Australia. They are getting Americanized, but we remain more English than the English. You won't like Australia: things are in a very bad way there. It is a pity you could not go to our South Island. Christchurch is just an English town: you would feel completely at home.' And so on. One man told me what a relief it was to come back from America and read newspapers written by gentlemen for gentlemen. It is naturally an article of faith with such people to believe that all their unemployment troubles are due to the latest immigrants, whose quality is universally condemned.

I have just had a very jolly evening with the politicians and we agreed to forgather again tomorrow after dinner. New Zealanders, under their domestic conditions, are chary of giving dinner parties, but they make up for it by lavish 'teas' in the middle of the morning and meeting after dinner. With women the invitation to morning tea is the usual thing.

I had an interview with Sir Apirana Ngata, Minister for Native Affairs and the Cook Islands, New Zealand's other dependency. I was ushered in through a waiting-room full of people, white and Maori. Sir Apirana was sitting in a room, and at a desk, of ministerial proportions. (I could almost work out to the cubic footage the amount of space proper to all the different functionaries, from the minister to the messenger.)

He is an ugly man, of the broad-faced variety of Maori, and very dark. He is not one of the forthcoming, genial Maoris. He presents a hard surface, cool and self-contained. This, when all the circumstances are considered, is impressive as well as suprising. I could not help delighting in the picture presented by this 'native', the dignity of his reception of myself, the white secretaries and under-secretaries coming and going with their deferential 'sir', but also – or did I imagine it – with something warmer than deference in their attitude.

I explained myself. He is not a great talker. I knew that his great work has been to wean his own people from their inertia, to make them take hold of civilization, but in their own way. He has obtained land for them on the east coast and there made settlements where the communism of the people (or so-called communism, for the analogy is really false, and the cause of endless misunderstanding),[78] is employed in co-operative dairies. He has been very successful; their products have been passed as being in the highest class, but it has meant a vast amount of work and leadership on his part. Though he wishes his people to embrace the new, he is equally anxious for them to keep their pride in the old, and he encourages and helps research into Maori customs and art.

From him I learned that there is practically no adequate material upon the Maori as he is today: the very full, but not always reliable, information attached to the 1926 Census which he gave me was the best available. But he warned me that the proportions given there of half-castes, 11,000 out of the Maori total of 63,000, was far too low, and that it is becoming increasingly difficult to be sure which of them are full Maoris, so much is the white blood infiltrating.[79] He spoke sadly of Sir Maui Pomare, the other leading Maori and one of Coates's ministers, and said that there was little hope of his surviving his present illness. Sir Maui is, of course, the leading Maori in the

Opposition party. 'It is a pity,' he said sadly, 'there are so few of us.'

Yes, it is true that there seem to be few leaders. In spite of their supposed civic equality and of the ability the Maori is held to possess, very few reach the university, and you can count the really big men on one hand. The reason is not far to seek. Political equality and even official social equality are not enough. I was told of Maoris going hopefully to college or to take some training, and coming away disheartened and embittered. They could not compete on equal terms as doctors or lawyers with the white man, nor yet as parsons. Yet to work among their own people, where the idea of payment for services by a member of your tribe is still foreign, and where the population in any case is poor and scattered, gives little scope. It means a life of sacrifice and obscurity. This is in contrast to America, where the educated negro is learning to find increasing scope among his own people, with their growing standards of education and wealth.

Of Samoa he spoke sadly. As a Maori he knows too well the easy confidence with which the white man asserts that he 'knows the native'. In his opinion it was a great mistake to put Samoa under the newly created Department of External Affairs instead of letting his own ministry, with its experience of Maori matters and of the administration of the Cook Islands,[80] take Samoa too.

Not that he considered that experience of the Maori gives one the key to the Polynesian. These kindred peoples have been long separated and the future of the Maori, a minority among the whites, must be different from that of the islanders. When asked, tauntingly, in the House to go and straighten up Samoa himself, he declined the honour, saying, with effective irony, 'It would take a Maori years of study to understand the Samoan.' He agreed with me that there had been far too much idea of making a new heaven and earth in the mandated territory for display to the League of Nations.

I did not keep him long, as his ante-room was full of suitors. Afterwards he most kindly sent me a present of some Maori books.

On Sunday afternoon Mr Coates called for me and motored me out into the country to Sir Maui Pomare's house. Sir Maui had been Sir Apirana's predecessor in office, which he had held from 1913 to 1928 when Coates's party had been defeated. On the way, in the car, I got Mr Coates to tell me about the last Imperial Conference, and he told me, in confidence, what he thought about it.

'It was scandalous. I don't know what is coming over you English.

You just smile and say nothing and give everything away with both hands. There was Baldwin and Balfour letting South Africa and Canada say and get whatever they liked, and leaving it all to me to defend the Empire. And I did, too. I took Hertzog aside and talked to him like a father. I said "*What* do you want? What *do* you want? If it isn't secession, what is it?" And I pointed out there was a very different point of view, ours. And I think I influenced him, too, though he relapsed as soon as he got home. But why didn't the English stand up to him? He'd have climbed down. And what is going to happen in the future? Canada and South Africa will want more independence, and we think that already things have gone too far.'[81]

I shouted something back about the American Revolution and the Liberal tradition, but he was well launched, and said what he thought of Ireland and railed against the new fashion of the dominions' having embassies and legations. He thought it was all damned nonsense and bound to lead to trouble, not counting the expense. New Zealand would have nothing to do with it. There was some sense in Canada being represented at Washington, but Ireland in Paris!

Now we drove in to the very fine house and garden where the Pomares live. They were expecting us and Lady Pomare was at the top of the steps, leading down to a terraced lawn, with roses trailing from the pergola behind her. She was indeed a lady, dignified, kindly, cultured. She is, I think, half- or quarter-caste, very handsome, with fine black hair, excellent features, soft brown skin, and very black eyes. She is slender and tall and was very well dressed in black, with a raised Medici collar. Her reception and entertainment of us was more that of a woman of the world than I had hitherto met in New Zealand. She made even Mrs Coates seem almost provincial. Her one fault was a tendency to talk too much and too fast: this I guessed was due to the nervous strain of her husband's illness. I turned with great interest to the family and was not disappointed. They told a dramatic racial story. First, Lady Pomare's old mother, hardly able to speak a word of English, a full-blooded Maori, with tattooed face, her eyes always having at the back of them the bewildered stare of the savage up against civilization which marks the older generation. The man's tattoo goes all over the face, the woman's over the chin, in ink-blue pattern, very hideous, too. . . . Sir Maui often says that he has Scotch blood in his veins, and when this causes surprise he explains that his father ate a Scotchman! I might add here that the Maori often makes jokes about cannibalism. Twice when I went out with Maori men, they turned to me on the threshold and said 'You're not frightened, are you? We're not cannibals any longer, you know?' . . .

To return to the Pomares, we have the old mother seated in silent state, the gracious Lady Pomare, and her three children. Her eldest boy, handsome, with perfect manners, would yet be known as a half-caste anywhere. The daughter is a real Maori, more Maori than her mother, not so much from her darkness, but from her fat, jolly roundness, her infectious good humour. She gave us a delightful sketch of the ball that week at Government House and one gathered that she had had no lack of partners. She did not look as though her colour had ever given her a moment's perplexity, and, though frankly Maori, she was so jolly and attractive that I can well picture her marrying a white man. The youngest, a son, was exactly modelled on the English public-school boy, and would have been taken anywhere for one. In colour no more than a healthy looking tan, with excellent features, dark hair brushed back and oiled, perfectly cut tweeds, Oxford accent, he seemed just a very good-looking, dark-haired English boy. He is at that Wanganui public school that I spoke of before, second head of the school, and captain of games. He showed us some photos, games groups with himself in the middle, himself in the choir, or arm in arm with a group of friends. I am told he is enormously popular: he is certainly most attractive.

At Mr Coates's request Lady Pomare allowed me a very brief interview with her husband. His bedroom, beautifully kept, was like a garden of flowers. He was propped up in bed, looking much lighter in colour than his wife, in spite of the white bed-linen. It is a fine head, of the Caucasian type, good aquiline nose, deep-set eyes, skin like parchment. He looks like a patriarch now, with his long, silvery hair and beard, though generally he is clean-shaven. Lady Pomare told us that he is enough a Maori to find it impossible to put up with a white nurse. They had a splendid nurse, but he fretted against being looked after by her, and was going back in health, so Lady Pomare and her daughter now do it all.

Sir Maui has tuberculosis, the great enemy of the Polynesian. He was very weak, talked in gasps, but laughed as much as he talked. His eyes lighted up with the joy of battle when his political chief came and he questioned him eagerly about events in the House. Meeting these Maoris after the New Zealanders is like meeting Latins after Teutons. The New Zealanders may be the civilized part of the community but the Maoris have the sunshine in their blood; theirs is the humour, the wit, the poetry and the art. Sir Maui, ill, ghost of himself, shed a new radiance on the political situation which I had seen only in a New Zealand light. Nor is he afraid to give authoritative advice to his chief and former Prime Minister. Of Sir J. Ward's opposition cabinet, speaking as much with his expressive eyes and hands, he said, 'Don't prick them yet. Blow a little more air into them, a little more, and then – pouf! bang! – they'll explode by themselves.' Speaking of Samoa, he looked up straight at Mr Coates. 'I didn't agree with what you said, Chief. That the Samoans would not be ready to govern themselves for a hundred years.' Mr Coates flushed a little and denied having put it like that.

Again, speaking of Samoa, 'No, of course Ngata refused to go to Samoa, not only because he would not understand them, but because they would not receive him. He has not the blood.'[82] Explaining to me, he said, 'You know the Polynesians keep their genealogies for many centuries. The Maoris are divided, not into tribes, but canoes, all being descended from the dozen or so canoes which came at different times before about 1500.[83] If a Maori can trace his genealogy back to a common point with the Samoans, then they recognize him as a high chief and he at once has caste, even authority, with them. But Ngata is of an obscure and broken line. They would not recognize him at all.' (Coates told me afterwards that Sir Maui has 'the blood' himself.)

But Sir Maui was most amusing about the League of Nations. 'Of course Samoa is, according to the Covenant, a "backward" nation, and must be put under the tutelage of the civilized nations of the League. Samoa, as it happens, is 100 per cent literate, and has been for fifty years. She is completely Christian; she is monogamous; prostitution is unknown; her people are orderly, self-supporting. But that is not enough. She must be taught to be civilized under the League of Nations. Consider some of the members – oh! I name no names, that would be invidious! – here is one where slavery is recognized and the slave-trade not unknown – here is another, not 20 not 10 per cent literate – here is another, Mohammedan, polygamous – here is another where brothels are recognized publicly by the State – here is another, just 2 per cent literate, and rejoicing in child marriage and other customs I will not mention. Are these the blessings of civilization? And I could go on. I have not finished, but I do not want to be tedious.'

I cannot reproduce the sparkle of humour and malice, the vitality of eyes, lips, hands, voice. There was much more than I can exactly remember and all of it gave me a view of the West from the East, of the civilized from the 'savage's' point of view, in itself an education. If only there were more men like Sir Maui who can interpret one race to another and if only they could be heard! For such men are not intransigent, they recognize the hard facts of life and race and they value the best we can give. But they prick the bubble of our dangerous self-complacency; they touch those two elements, so sluggish, so necessary in this relation, our imagination and our sympathy.

Loaded with flowers, we drove away down the Hutt valley to emerge into the iron bowl of Wellington harbour and to run along the rim to the rather drab city.

I invited to dinner with me in my hotel a Canadian who for six years ran the Meteorological Station founded, characteristically, by the Germans in Samoa. He had to leave at the first warning fevers of elephantiasis. Now cured, he longs to go back to the island. From the detachment of a scientist and a Canadian he had observed acutely all the Samoan events and we went through the points in sequence, finding ourselves largely in agreement. Then we wandered out and paid a surprise visit upon an ex-Chief of Public Works in Samoa, who the meteorologist told me was a most brilliant man. We found him alone, at about 10.30, slightly drunk, but studying higher mathematics in a room full of books, bottles and Samoan decorations. He talked well at first but, as he went on drinking, he became personal and began to tell us exactly what he thought of his wife, so I departed. Sometimes I feel quite dazed with the variety of human beings set before me and the contradictions a single personality can encircle. Individually they are all so likeable; it seems that it is only in the mass, where one quality, or one opinion is multiplied into a force, that men become stupid or dangerous.

Next day Mr Coates took me to the rooms of his opponents, the Labour Party, and introduced me to Mr Holland,[84] the Leader. I did not want to see him, as I had read all the New Zealand debates on Samoa, and thoroughly disapproved of the intrusive, politically self-seeking part he had played. He has a dangerous half-knowledge of Samoa, has written mischievous pamphlets upon it and, having deluded himself into a pose of self-righteousness, uses the Samoan question as party ammunition. Each speech of his has an echo in Samoa, thanks to the activities of the 'Beach'[85] whose gentry see that it reaches the Samoan leaders. More than that, when I visited that whisky-sodden Irishman in Apia, upon whom Nelson's mantle has fallen, the descendant of the Plantagenets, he waved in my face, to prove his own importance, bundles of letters, and telegrams too, from Mr Holland, to prove how closely they were working together. I think Holland is one of the few men whom I did not feel inclined to make allowance for when I saw him in the flesh. A short, fat, compressed, white-haired little man, with the fanatical, preaching strain of the demagogue, a man beyond all reason or argument. I felt that no possible exchange could take place between us, so I listened to his speech and promptly departed.

I went back to Mr Coates's room and had morning tea with him. Then he sent for a very jolly Maori who took me over to the Native Land Court Department to see the Chief Judge. A tiny, snow-headed, red-faced little man, he was a mine of information but could give me little or no printed material on the general situation of the Maori with regard to land. The way of him who wishes to investigate the Maori of today is hard. He will meet a hundred men who fancy themselves as authorities on the Maori and who will talk by the hour in a jumbled, contradictory way. But I increasingly learn in Maori affairs (but not only in them) a respect – though even that is tempered – for the printed word, put down with some care and supported by some evidence. And this is seldom to be had.

Judge Jones confirmed my view that the famous Treaty of Waitangi made with the Maoris in 1840 is still the base of all legal operations.[86] He emphatically contradicted a view widely held that the Maori regards land litigation as a good game, a speculation, and makes frivolous or even false claims just to see what he can get. He said he never treated a Maori claim with anything but respect. But he also said that disentanglement was now impossible. The conflict of customs, the maze of claim and counter-claim, the complexity of Maori law, made anything more exact than honest arbitration impossible. He also said that all the time the land was passing from the Maori and would pass until he had none. Questioned on the possibility of inalienable reserves, he said that, even if possible, the reserve system was not really desirable. I think he is probably right. The danger of the reserve is that the Maori will simply bind himself to customs from which the vitality has departed and, like a creature in a zoo, live a life of pensioned deterioration. This has been the fate of the Red Indian. After what I had seen during my visit to the Maori lands in the north I could have little hope for the 'protected' Maori.

The Judge and the Maoris in his office, when questioned as to the possibilities of my having one more look at their people, urged me to go up to Otaki, about sixty miles up the west coast. One of the Maoris wrote at once to his brother, and the Education Department wrote to the Maori school there to warn them of my visit.

From the Native Land Court I went to see Elsdon Best,[87] said to be the greatest living authority upon the Maori, so old and so valuable that funds have been raised, mainly by the Maoris, to keep him alive and writing until the last possible moment. I found him in a highly warmed room at the top of a tall building. Here, surrounded by books and papers, he was engaged upon still another work on Maori religious thought. He is an enormous man, with an attractive multiplication of wrinkles produced by a life of exposure, with a little pointed white Vandyke beard and moustache and set in his old face, eyes brilliant with intelligence and vitality.

He told me of his early days, fighting the Maori, of how men of his generation who had fought the Maori loved him. He told me stories of his own knowledge, similar to some I had heard, of the Maoris sending out ammunition to the soldiers, when theirs was exhausted, in order to make the fight even. After the wars he determined to live with the Maori and after many years they adopted him and treated him as one of themselves. The white man imagines he knows the Maori; they are friendly and apparently frank, but Best knows that not until you have fully understood their customs and ideas and even got their vast genealogies by heart will they let you into the innermost secret of their thoughts. He talked so that I could see what a tragedy the white invasion had been to the old generation of Maoris. He could appreciate their pride, their sensitiveness and their spirituality. But the whole system of their life, the circle of their ideas, were highly specialized to their conditions and so brittle that they broke almost at a touch by the white man. All the elaborations of *tapu* and *mana* which Best himself can hardly understand, but whose framework made the pattern of their lives, were as delicate and complex as a cobweb and were dislocated by the gun, money and Christianity.

'With the coming of the white man our sacred life principle of man was defiled,' said one old chief to him, as nearly as he can translate the words. There was nothing for the Maoris to do but to watch helplessly and to die, one by one, in absolute despair, dimly hoping that, not their children but their grandchildren might learn to become *Pakehas*[88] and find a new kind of happiness and success.

He told me how, squatting over a camp-fire at night, a dirty, tattooed old man would explain to him the difference between the spirit of a man which dies with him, the soul of a man which lives after him, and that force by which all life and form is given and which man shares with birds and stones. And picking up a stone this old man would question, almost in Socratic fashion, asking how its substance could hold together unless some spiritual force existed within it.

Mr Best analysed their attitude to things material; that quality, or lack of it, that makes us say, impatiently, that they are hopeless at business, unreliable in money matters. He, nowadays, will get a letter from some old Maori:

Oh Best, I have no blanket. Give me one immediately.
                    [Tuhoe]

or:

I want three shirts, Oh Best! Send.
                    [Rangi Te]

And he does what he is asked. It may be six months or two years when (after no acknowledgement) they evidently have a windfall in the tribe, and a five-pound note comes to him:

Oh Best! This from our love and friendship.

But when I tried to draw him on the Maori of today, he became less interesting. He is living in the past, re-creating it in his books. One of these he gave me and, promising to come again if I could, I went on to see another writer, Andersen.[89]

He was a long-haired man, dreamy, with a funny, precise manner. It was he who told me about Best, how he could not get his books published until the Maoris subscribed and the Maori Board of Ethnological Research was founded. He, Andersen, knew more than Best of present conditions and he spoke bitterly of the way the Maori had been treated with regard to land and labour. He gave me to understand that among whites there was some of the 'nigger' attitude and that in Gisborne, where Maoris are numerous, an attempt is being made to keep them out of the best cinemas, etc.

At night I went again to Downie Stewart's, having agreed to meet Coates there. It was there I let out that, in British politics, I was Labour and I annoyed them by calling them Tories. They took it quite seriously and denied that there was such a thing as Conservatism in New Zealand. They were only mollified when I said I doubted if I should be Labour in New Zealand. They were very critical about Snowden.[90] Indeed, these leading politicians positively glowed with jingoism. Why hadn't we stood up to the European governments long before instead of following our mawkish, self-sacrificing policy?

The problem of how to spend my last day in New Zealand was seriously discussed and was interesting because Mr Coates, having been so long in power, gnashed his teeth at the rare experience of being out of it and so unable to help me more. Had he been in power, he said, he would have provided a Government car to Otaki and arranged it all in style. Had I yet seen the Prime Minister? I replied that he had written asking me to come at 11.30 tomorrow, and that I had said I would if I could, but that my plans were still uncertain. Stewart suggested that Coates should use his influence to have my journey to Otaki arranged by the government. 'Ngata is under obligations to you. You could do it. If you won't, I will.'

Coates burst out, 'I'm not going to ask any favours from that bunch. I'll do it some other way.'

Stewart was determined to work it through the Government, but I saw it was going to be very awkward and was – apparently – almost making them quarrel about it.

Mr Coates walked all the way back to my hotel with me and he told me what a blow his defeat had been to him and yet what a relief to be relieved of responsibility. He spoke, too, of his hopes and plans for the future.

The next day I got up very early, and, not to bother my friends, I slipped away on the eight o'clock service car, leaving a message behind for Mr Stewart and Mr Coates. It was a marvellous day and I drank in for the last time the colours of New Zealand and the character of the country. I travelled with a man who, having asked me where I had come from, where I was going, said, 'Well, I never believed they employed women in the Secret Service, but now I do.'[91] All New Zealanders find my being alone very hard to swallow. Their conception of women is still very much of their domestic role, quite different from America, where almost no one was surprised about my mission.

I reached Otaki at 10.45 and arrived just as the master of the school[92] was sitting down to his morning tea. It is a Church of England school, quite old-established, to cater for Te Rauparaha's people when they settled here. Many of the older boys were away in camp but we went and looked at the school. There we found a brother of the man I had met in Wellington and his sister, both teaching. The Maori men, at my request, gave us some singing, conducting beautifully (I have already described how very affecting their singing is.) The white master's daughter was sitting at a double desk with a Maori boy, and the Maori master lived in the house with him. Mr Ellis's father had been a master at the famous Te Aute Maori School and he himself had been educated there. It seems that to know the Maori really well is to love him. Mr Ellis is almost passionately devoted to him and he suffers proportionately to see the bad effects of our civilization. In Otaki there are more pubs than the place can maintain: they therefore resort to every device to increase the sale of drink among the natives, with only too much success. They are becoming increasingly mixed in blood, and, too often in the process, decadent.

He showed me the Maori church. They built it in 1840, and it is the oldest church existing in New Zealand. I have added a picture of it, but it does not bring in the height of the three central pillars and the enormous length of the ridge-pole in the centre. An engineer who passed when these materials were lying on the ground laughed and said they would never go up. It was a technical impossibility without special gear. When he passed a week later they were up. The decoration inside is in the usual rich black, white and red; the walls have woven panels, and the altar is beautifully carved.

We passed where two tennis-courts were being made, and a very dark Maori, filthy with his work, called out to the headmaster, 'I say, Steve, come and let me show you something.' Mr Ellis and I went over. He was another brother of the schoolmaster and had been at Te Aute with Mr Ellis. He was extraordinary attractive and very witty. We had a long talk. He told us some of his war experiences in Gallipoli and how the Maori war-cry frightened the Turks. He told us that when the captain of their (Maori) company was mortally wounded, he called them all round him, Maori fashion, and chose the chief next in blood to succeed him in command. And succeed he did. Maori tradition cut military red tape.

I was back again in Wellington by the middle of the afternoon to find Mr Coates had arranged tennis for me, but I was too late. I rushed along to the Prime Minister's office to apologize for having cut his interview and to leave a note. However, he said he would see me now.

Sir Joseph looks rather less ghastly at a close-up. But his face is a mask, the mask of a bartender but a very shrewd one. I could not resist hinting that an appointment on the day before I left was not much use for me, also that Mr Coates had been extremely kind to me. But he blinked that on one side without any trouble.

On Samoa he was as disappointing as possible. Let us hope that the presence of Ngata in his cabinet may bring some wisdom.

'We have been very lenient with the Samoans,' he said, 'very lenient. But now we must uphold law and order. The prestige of a white government demands that. We are waiting to see the results of this policy.'

I could have told him of some of them but he did not want to hear. So I made a few compliments about New Zealand and retired quickly, finding my way to Mr Coates who had secured Sir James Allen for me.

Sir James Allen, ex-High Commissioner in London, ex-Minister for Samoa and responsible for it in the early days of the mandate, and now member of the Legislative Council, is a courtly gentleman. He took me down to tea and into the rather dignified second chamber. We discussed Samoan affairs for an hour or two there. He put most of the blame on Nelson and some on the present government for publishing the famous report.[93] Then he and Mr Coates arranged for me to see Sir Francis Bell in the morning. He has just come out with a great tirade in defence of Richardson and against the recent report. I parted from Sir James with great regret to rush home and get ready to go out to the theatre with Mrs Coates. We saw the *Desert Song*, a mushy affair, though well produced considering the expense of bringing all the outfit so far. Back to spend the night writing letters and packing. In the morning rushed down to Parliament to say goodbye to Coates, Berendsen, Nichols, etc. Nichols had the bright idea of picking me up in his car and driving me out to a picnic lunch on the cliffs, rather hazardous as the boat sailed at 2.45, and I still had to round off my packing. Then I went to say goodbye to Mr Pearce, the Acting Treasurer whom I had met in Samoa, the funny, awkward, ugly man whom I had come to like very much before I left.[94] He insisted upon my going in to see his chief, the Civil Service Commissioner, the notorious Mr Verschaffelt, head of the Committee of Three which had made their devastating official visitation to Samoa.

He had a very magnificent office, in spite of which he agreed to see me at a moment's notice. He had a fine, intellectual face, and was the sort of man with whom you could immediately get down to business. This was the more necessary as I had so little time. So I said at once –

feeling that to him I could say it – that I disagreed most emphatically with his report. He defended it, but he made no pretence to defend the present government for publishing it. I think he said their action was damnable. He even admitted that he was ignorant of tropical conditions. I liked him enormously: he has a strong brain, quite the best I had met in New Zealand, and I thought it was all the more sad that he had just missed the point in Samoa and that his rather ruthless intelligence had not made its potential contribution. I think it is lack of sympathy: there is no window open in his mind on the native question; he showed this by remarks he made on the South African problem when he heard I was going there. So, thinking it worthwhile, and having little time, I flung my ideas at him as hard as I could and he certainly caught the ideas I threw, though he may not keep them.

I hated leaving him; I would have loved further talk. However, I dashed out to Mr Pearce, who was delighted with the impression his chief had made, and then I ran along to Sir Francis Bell's office.

Sir Francis Bell, also ex-High Commissioner, and ex-Minister in Coates's Government, much mixed with Samoan affairs, acting Prime Minister under Massey, is an old war-horse. A great, big, powerful head, one eye bleary and half shut, a man of the great world, he advanced upon me with much benignity and told me that General Richardson had written to him about me, warning him that I knew how to make old men talk. (Good for the General! I flattered myself that he thought *he* was in control.)

With Bell I touched a new line, one of the greatest interest to me. He had been several times to the League of Nations as delegate for New Zealand; he had also been before the Mandates Commission (as had Sir James Allen) to speak for Samoa. He is a bitter opponent of the mandates system, which was very good for me, as I had never yet met any of the enemies of the system, at least open enemies.

He spoke vehemently in favour of downright annexation, for which Massey had contended at Versailles.[95] Their task in Samoa was hard enough without the added embarrassment of a mandate. And then the Mandates Commission took upon themselves to catechize, to condemn, to suggest policy. Who, in Heaven's name, were the Mandates Commission? A group of private gentlemen and one lady, utterly obscure and irresponsible.[96] (What about Lugard?) Interference had never been intended when the system was founded. They were merely there to *advise* the Council. Yet the minutes of their discussion were published – most mischievous, most inquisitorial. At the famous incident at the Council in 1926, when Briand and Sir Austen had rapped the Mandates Commission over the knuckles when they asked for further powers, he had been there, representing New Zealand, and had abetted the Council with glee. He held forth about the sovereign state – he is a lawyer. I joined issue with him here and we wrangled about sovereignty. We had a regular ding-dong fight and I managed to gain a little ground from him. He, like Sir James, was full of plans for further discussion and it was with the deepest regret that I contemplated my immediate departure just when so many fascinating vistas were opening for me in New Zealand.

Down below, through the window, Nichols, in his beautiful Armstrong-Siddeley, was evidently getting impatient. (Lately, in Wellington, I had been at least a quarter of an hour late for every appointment.) I joined him and we dashed off, picked up some food in the town and ran out to one of the hills, where, hanging over the harbour – it was rather nerve-racking to see my boat, very small and far below, steaming up – we contemplated the blue water in the basin and all the cheerful little red tin-roofed houses encrusting the rocks like limpets. Nichols, in mellower mood than usual, admitted he had learned something from New Zealand; it had made him appreciate the value of his own type and some – very few – of its limitations. It was with great difficulty that I got him to hurry his lunch and come back to my hotel. Result, of course, that I was nearly late for my last appointment in New Zealand and simply flung myself on to the boat at the last possible moment.

I nearly wept as we took the corner out of the sunny harbour and through the gate, and finding many flowers and an enormous box of chocolates in my cabin did not make me feel less sentimental. I really loved New Zealand, the beautiful country, and the great kindness I had met with and I hated to break off all those deeply interesting and instructive contacts I had made in Wellington.[97]

4

Australia

I think I ended my last batch of diary and posted it just as I was leaving New Zealand and feeling very sad at saying goodbye to so many interesting people, with whom I was just beginning to make friends, and also to develop a fuller appreciation of their country, which makes me regret some of the hasty generalizations made in the earlier sections of the diary.

But sad sentiments were soon engulfed in self-pity. I generally do find myself a little uneasy for the first two days on any ship, especially if it reminds me too often that it is travelling over waves. The second day out from Wellington we ran into a storm. Our ship[1] carried no cargo so she danced like a bubble. My cabin was on the top deck and for'ard so it was very exposed. The seas swept right over our deck and soon a very big wave smashed the outer door and the water began to bang angrily upon the inner one. It broke right into the cabin next door and its occupants, so I heard, were got out with some difficulty. My cabin was saved because the gangway was tied up along the rail near us but the gangway itself was smashed up and the sea took a bundle of deck-chairs and champed them to splinters outside our door. It burst open the big double doors of the main saloon and rushed in hurting several people. Even the teak and iron seats clamped to the deck were broken up. It was astonishing that nobody was seriously injured. I lay cowering in my bunk with my companion while our baggage slid and crashed between us. It was maddening to see through the window the gulls calmly sailing over the mountainous waves.

The storm subsided: the sun shone: passengers emerged on deck. I now remembered that Mr Coates had given instructions to me and to a certain Captain B., MP (English),[2] to make each other's acquaintance. This had now become possible and when at last I staggered out of my cabin and went out upon deck it was to witness a strange performance. A young, square-shouldered man, later identified as an English ex-

180

batman, came on deck carrying a large embroidery frame which he set up complete with high-backed chair. Followed an obvious Englishman with many skeins of coloured thread bursting out of his pocket. He sat himself down and began to work on the tail-feathers of a magnificent bird. Looking up, and seeing me, he guessed who I was and introduced himself as the English soldier MP. 'Can you beat it!' exclaimed the male passengers, to each other and to me, after watching their operations.

Captain B. was Byronic in appearance, with something about the collar and tie which seemed—deliberately?—to deepen the suggestion. He was an extremely elegant, indeed aesthetic-looking, youngish man. He was very much a man of the world yet with something feminine in his impact (not to be taken as depreciatory!). Being with most New Zealanders is like eating very wholesome food without quite enough salt and pepper. It is in the old continent that men have learned the detachment, the critical (including the self-critical) faculty that gives the spice to human contact. I knew the Captain MP possessed this quality as soon as, almost before, he spoke and I was hard put to it not to join in his commentary upon the two dominions and much else. For I think that in my final phase in New Zealand I had come to enter a little into the essential character of a colonial state, its achievements and its inevitable differences from the historic nation which it had left half the world away. He told me he had been six years in the House of Commons but professed the most engaging ignorance on all major political topics. Whatever appropriate subject I started, he would say, with a charming smile, 'Ah, you see, that's not my line of country.' He had one line of his own, however. He seemed to be very rich – and he had a valet-batman travelling first class with him. . . .

Sydney

Benedicta, my friend from Samoa, met my ship but as she was working against time to prepare an exhibition of her paintings she had to hurry away. But she left a letter in my hand and [told] me that Ava was ill in hospital with elephantiasis, and that members of his family were camped round his bed, Samoan fashion. Thank Heaven there is a truly humane naval doctor there! I expect that the family will see to it that Ava does not actually die in hospital. The letter was from Kalamete, my blood-brother in Tutuila. She also told me that the new governor and his wife were doing well but that the harmony of the station had been marred by a row between the Captain of the Yard and my *bête-noire*, the civilian judge.

It was a great joy to learn that Kalamete had not forgotten me. I think his letter is worth quoting in full, though it must lose its full flavour without his strange writing and paper.

Laulii
August 23rd

How to do:
Dearest Miss M.F. Margery:

I am very, very Sad Dear, on the days of 'Our' Departing in the Custom house.

And our meeting before at Laulii; or at the Station the place where the Governor's Inauguration held. Now, Dear, I think that you have forgotten me but myself, I cannot you in sometimes or in a months and years – too. I write this letter with a crying eyes. And my Best Regard is upon you. I am very very disappointed.

I have always wait and pray each night for you till we meet again.

May God with you and myself too. I think you are all alive in this sickness. Ava is sicker and we are all in the Hospital.

I want to know the place which you place. And I want you to write a letter for me.

I've always remember the name that you have given me before. Christapha. Dear will you come back to my own country I will, want you to be my own marriage. 'I think you will might accept.' Answer if you please.

Good Bye. God Bless You.
Mr Kelemete Christapha

I replied at once:

Dear Kalamete,

It was a great joy to get your letter. But I am very, very sad about Ava. Do give him my love and my hopes that he will get better. Thank him and his family for their kindness to me.

It is sad our time together was so short. But we shall always be friends, you and I, and remember the happy hours we spent together. I am glad that you like me so much that you want to marry me but you must marry one of your own people, someone young, beautiful, good and healthy.

Kalamete, dear friend, I want you to promise me something. You remember how we threw stones on the beach, and how far you threw and how strong and fine your body is. You must look after your health. As soon as you find anything is wrong, go at once to the American doctor. If you have something wrong with your eye, do not try Samoan medicine, do not let them scrape it with coral, but go at once to the doctor for ointment. And as soon as you have the fever that makes the body grow big and ugly, go to the doctor. And when you grow up, try to make all your friends and relatives do the same. The Samoans have many good and beautiful customs – but the white doctors are the best for health.

My very dear friend, Christapha, I am glad that you pray for me. I shall be very happy to have a present from you and I, too, will send you a present from my own country. That will not be for a long time, but I shall not forget.

Now, dearest Kalamete, goodbye. If you want to write to me again, send it to Governor Lincoln or write this yourself on the envelope (Address).

God be with you, dear, and keep you and your family safe and well.

Your loving friend
Margery Perham

Tell me how to spell my Samoan name.

Benedicta had to work hard painting Samoa out of her memory. So I left her in her studio, which was full of her vigorous, almost violent, interpretations of the coloured life of Samoa and, with Kalamete's letter in my pocket, I walked off in a state of the deepest depression. Sydney seemed terribly jarring. Besides, I was alone. Everything seemed very flat after the way I had been spoiled in New Zealand. In this travelling one has intervals when you are nobody and have no claims, no position, a mere ordinary unit among a strange public, as at first in Fiji. Then there are other times when you are in the charge of the people at the top and you have a magic wand to wave to summon help and open doors, and your main problem may be to get any time to yourself to rest and to think.

I am really rather ashamed of the way I am treating Australia. I can't pass through her without sending any diary to my friends. I can only ask them to make allowance for the superficial and perhaps prejudiced remarks I may make upon this hurried rush across this vast country.

My plan for Australia was to visit her main cities and move by quick stages across to Perth and there catch a boat to South Africa. I did not plan to do more in the time than to learn a little about Australian attitudes towards the dependency of New Guinea and the mandated territory of Papua, with some inquiry into the state of the aborigines clinging to the fringes of the white man's world.[3] I found my next ship, SS *Demosthenes*, in a dock close to ours, so I had my heavy baggage sent over to her and faced the unknown climates of Australia with only a suitcase.

Immediately an immense Australian porter seized this and carried it the few steps to a waiting taxi. I gave him what I thought was a much more than adequate tip, upon which he broke into curses. The taxi-driver joined in and they agreed that this was almost a matter for the police. This was clearly a technique of robbery by intimidation. Knowing nothing of Sydney, and after being again defrauded by the driver, I found myself at the obvious hotel, the Australia. It was as big and pretentious as an American hotel but there was no 'service with a smile', only indifference in all matters but tips. When you gave a shilling to a hotel newspaper boy for a penny-halfpenny paper he walked off without so much as a thank-you for the enforced tip.

Thinking that I might have a look at a State Parliament, I rang up the secretary to the Governor of New South Wales[4] and asked if he had had a letter from the Colonial Office about me. He denied having had any such a letter and was clearly not interested. I went out to a meal alone in a very bad and very expensive restaurant – labour laws mean that you must dine very early – and came to the conclusion that Australians had worse manners than any people I had met; that the girls looked hard and fast; that the men were either tough and stringy, or red and fat; that Sydney was a big, commonplace city that had absorbed the worst of America. After this I went on, in a deluge of rain, to find the public library in order to read something upon New Guinea. Drunken men reeled, yelled, and even snatched at me in the road, and I saw some of the most criminal faces I [have] ever met at street-corners and looking out of doorways. Finally I reached the public library, where an incompetent staff produced an out-of-date report on New Guinea.

I had been met on the ship by a letter inviting me to stay at Government House, Canberra, but it also informed me that His Excellency would be away in Western Australia. It was signed 'Sydney

Stonehaven'.[5] I later learned that not only the Colonial Office but my friends the Max Müllers[6] had written to the Governor.

I could not make out if 'Sydney' was wife, daughter or son of the Governor-General. I consulted *Who's Who* at the central library but this gave the wife's name as Ethel. I then consulted the library staff but drew blank. However, one of them kindly brought me a local book on etiquette. I consulted it. 'Although you are not likely to meet members of the nobility in Australia, yet it is just as well, should such visit your country, that you should know how to address them.' I then learned a great deal about etiquette but nothing to my purpose. Benedicta told me that Lady Stonehaven was regarded as a terrible snob and the whole family, it was said, spoke cordially only to the dozen leading families in England. Disregarding this absurdity I wrote and thanked the writer but said that, as I was arriving at five o'clock in the morning and staying only two days to interview ministers, it was not fair to bother her.[7]

The next morning I was feeling very rotten, so lay late in bed, then went out to explore Sydney. It seemed to me the Roman Church rather dominated the city, having crowned the highest point with a huge yellow sandstone cathedral, fronting on Hyde Park; across the bay on one side the big stone buildings of their girls' convent catches the sun, while far away on the other side the cardinal's palace makes an arresting block on a hill beyond the water. The English Church, to the casual view, is nowhere to be seen. For the rest, the shops are good, in a different class from anything in New Zealand. The streets wind, having been built early enough to escape the American squared pattern. It was most refreshing at last to find an old, weathered red brick English church, with stained green copper spire, on Wren lines, built by Governor Macquarie.[8] I saw, too, the solid blocked-stone jail, reared by convicts for their own worst delinquents. The grass of the parks looked untidy, worn and littered, and scattered with sprawling dockers, etc., whose facial expressions seemed to explain the perennial labour rows which make so much of the news from Australia.

But at last gloom lifted, trees doing for me what men could not. The Botanical Gardens are wonderful! They must have been long in loving and expert hands. . . . [There follows a long description of the Gardens.]

The palm trees made me feel better and ready to admit the beauty of Sydney's natural position. One has only to go a mile or so through commonplace streets to find oneself out on one of the bays, with water

radiant in the sunshine and people swarming on the sands and, across
the water, gay with white sails, more bays between the promontories.
The houses all peer across the water and, the nearer they are to it, and
the higher the land, the better the houses – yet I saw few houses big by
the standard of a prosperous English suburb and as soon as the view
out to sea was lost there was an outcrop of little bungalows with
unattractive iron lace-work on the verandahs.

Any view of Sydney is today dominated by the new £7 million trans-
harbour bridge, now sticking up into mid-air, dramatically incomplete.
It is throwing everything else out of proportion, even the Roman
Catholic buildings and the skyscrapers. They were a brave firm
(Dorman Long) who dared embark upon such a huge contract in
Australia.

I went back to Benedicta's studio in pursuit, not of Samoa, but of my
present inquiries, in order to go out with her and Professor Radcliffe-
Brown.[9] He is reckoned, I believe, about the leading anthropologist in
the world, at least the English world, and is in close touch with New
Guinea and Papua, about which I hope to learn something from him if
only at second-hand.

Benedicta had been rather cryptic about the Professor and he
certainly was the last man in the world I should have associated with
his profession. I should have put him down as an actor. He is one of
those people intensely aware of himself and alert to you. Benedicta
introduced us in a way that must have been brutally businesslike to
him, telling us to talk shop and make the most of my time. The
Professor did not seem to welcome this advice and things were rather
halting at dinner, until we were joined by one Roy le Maistre,[10]
Australia's leading artist (I am told), and an authority on art, at least of
the modern school. He plunged with Benedicta into talk about her
show and left the Professor to begin on me. I had some difficulty in
getting him to talk seriously upon his subject and just as I was
succeeding it was time for him to go off and read *Hamlet* at the
Repertory Theatre. What he was saying was becoming so well worth
hearing that I went with him and we carried on as we walked to the
ferry and crossed the harbour, starry with lights, and went right under
that terrific bridge, just springing on its semicircular curve into the
sky. My anxiety to hear the Professor again was not quite equal to
sitting through unabridged *Hamlet*, with a caste of mixed ability – I
need not say the Professor was excellent – and I stole out in the dark
and went back to my hotel.

Business and shopping consumed my next morning, and a second interview for the Sydney press (the first had been on the dock). This time the journalist was a very charming woman. Then I lunched extravagantly with the embroidering MP, who was more than ever amusing and flower-like and who had chartered his own aeroplane in which to get about.

I had a great blow when I learned that the aeroplane service was no good to me, as it went once a week and would give me six days in Perth. Then, to my horror, I found that it was impossible to get a berth on the train, as every one was booked owing to the centenary celebrations in Western Australia.[11] This meant that my stay in Australia was much curtailed, as I must dash down to join the boat at Adelaide on the 5th.[12]

Next day I rang up the Professor and he came down to the hotel at three o'clock and we talked until four, when he took me out to tea and we talked until six. The Professor is undoubtedly a great man in his line and it is one of the puzzles of human nature that a big mind is sometimes attached to a character not quite on the level with it. He was at his worst when discussing the work of his fellow-scholars, all the big names of anthropology. I noted all these opinions and, by the end, the only conclusion to draw was, not that the Professor was the best anthropologist in the world but that he was the only one with any claim to that title at all and that all the others were on entirely wrong lines, with the possible but doubtful exception of Malinowski. As for Oxford and Cambridge, I gathered that they were merely a joke.[13] But I found him stimulating and generous with his time and he taught me a lot of what I needed to know.

The Professor's line is social anthropology. He is not of the antiquarian type. He studies the extant cultures and social systems of peoples and is only too anxious to produce results in a form that can be of use to administrators and to develop a school for officials. But, as a scientist, he says it is not up to him to tell the officials what to do. In South Africa he organized the anthropology at the Cape, went into the Transkei and lectured to the service there, which, it seems, was at first contemptuous and then enthusiastic. He is now building up – my information is all from him – one of the best schools in the world, with a whole flying squad of young men and women doing research work in the Pacific. He is head of the course for officials in training for the Papuan and New Guinea service and generally has them back after they have been a year in the island. He handles large grants of money from America from the Laura Spelman and Rockefeller funds.[14]

I ought to have studied more anthropology; I still ought to study it more.[15] But the next best thing, and what I can do now, is to talk deeply with a man of this experience. In this way one can learn the training of mind necessary before one can attempt to understand a primitive people. Otherwise it is like pretending to read the Koran without having learned Arabic. It is only by such a training that any dim idea can be got of the motives that are actuating the people. . . . The answer may be that the interests and ultimate purposes of the white are so paramount that it does not matter what happens to the inferior system so long as white prestige is kept, order maintained and 'progress' achieved. But is it not better that the material, which after all is human, should be understood, that the player should know the stops instead of everything being 'jangled, out of tune'. In all other enterprises, the material *is* studied; the scientist or experimenter is called in, whether it is chemicals, metals, plants or animals. But this is *man*, and it is assumed that anyone can understand man and, if it is inferior man, it does not much matter whether he is understood or not. Perhaps it did not when the object was to frighten, displace or extinguish him. But these are no longer the professed objects. Apart from idealism, and Article 22 of the Covenant,[16] these are the people who are to work for us upon our tropical farms and enterprises where white men cannot work, and whose products are now regarded as being absolutely essential to us, fruit, rubber, metals, timber. How can any untrained, ignorant man get this mysterious human mechanism into good running order and keep it so? It may be easy in the early stages when it is simply their brute strength working under the fear of ours, which is directed by our intelligence. But what of the next stage? When they become aware of us and themselves and, stripped by us of their sanctions, of the religion and customs that have moulded them for generations, they are yet refused the best of ours, or given them clumsily, grudgingly? How difficult and dangerous will that stage be! There are Government anthropologists, or their equivalents, in Papua and New Guinea, also in Java; there is one on the Gold Coast.[17] But we want anthropologists by the dozen, part of every Colonial Service, recognized by the governments and used by them.[18]

The Professor is very dubious about New Guinea. It is a difficult proposition. The people are very mixed, some very primitive, and infinitely divided by language. In some parts each village has its own language and pidgin English is the lingua franca, even in education, with not very good results. For pidgin English has to be learned by the white master and already misunderstanding has arisen through the newly arrived white men thinking they understand it. The other difficulty is the country itself, unhealthy and full of natural barriers, swamp and mountain. The crevasses are so deep that in some places men shout across to the next village to say a party is on the way that will take two days to cross.

The Government has failed in somewhat the same way as in New Zealand. Can a young colonial democracy produce the type that can govern natives? It would not be impossible to find some men of the kind wanted but there is no tradition in a new country that carefully selected, highly educated men should enter such a service. It is true that in Papua, handed over by the British to the Australian Government in 1906, things are better than in New Guinea. But this is partly because she was taken over as a going concern, if only in an elementary stage, and partly because Australia has had the luck to have, for a long period of years, a first-rate governor, Sir Hubert Murray.[19] Already those responsible are saying 'What shall we do when he goes?' And it has been suggested that Sir Hubert, pleased and proud of his own Territory, may not be too anxious to help much with the new mandate, especially if it meant transferring any of his own men, trained with so much care. I wish I could meet him. His brother, Sir Gilbert,[20] has talked to me of him in Oxford.

Inadequate men, it seems, have been sent to a supremely difficult task; inadequate money is being spent upon it. It was reported in the New Zealand papers, with some relish (as Australians have thrown stones at their own mandate), that the Mandates Commission reported this August that they were dissatisfied with Australia's conduct of New Guinea and refused to comment until further information was given. The newspaper article in which I read about this was so ill-informed about administration that I could not evaluate its case. The Professor tells me that someone is privately supplying information to the Mandates Commission about New Guinea; that he himself is suspect, and the government has laid traps to try and find out if he is really the culprit.

Of Samoa he said that he was in favour of much more self-government. He said emphatically that the New Zealanders were more woefully unaware of their own incompetence and ignorance than even the Australians and got an even worse type of official. He would like to send one or two of the best anthropologists obtainable – preferably his own pupils – and get them to study the situation and report and remain there to go on studying and reporting. He would also like to train young men in his own school.

I dined at the Italian café that is in Sydney's Quartier Latin, with young artists and would-be artists shouting at each other and the proprietress telling us to wait on ourselves because she wanted to go to the theatre. Result, I caught my train to Canberra with only three minutes to spare.

Canberra

Australian sleeping compartments are good. I had a long talk with the conductor who said Australia was going to the dogs and would go all the quicker if Labour got in at the present election. Yet he dare not reveal his views or life on the railways would be unbearable.

I have not spoken of the election. Mr Bruce,[21] rather unwisely and abruptly, it is said, raised the problem of the overlapping powers of the Federal and States Governments. His contention is that the powers belonging both to the States and the Federal Government make for confusion and weakness, also that the workers flout the Federal awards. But some of his own party, including Hughes,[22] who was supporting the Government, voted against him, and so he appealed to the country. Hence an election. Much to my disappointment, as I had counted on finding Parliament sitting at Canberra and politicians accessible.

All the people whom I met were anti-Labour and full of gloom and apprehension about the election and the future of their country. Granted that there is a wild and even criminal element in Australian labour, I find it difficult to believe that half the population of Australia, educated, shrewd men, can be bent upon a policy of suicide. But I have not got much grip on the political situation. It seems that Australians of all parties are trying to build a high wall round the portion of the earth they have got hold of and rigidly monopolize its benefits for their own small population. Hence 'White Australia', and hence the tariff policy. They now discuss dealing New Zealand serious blows by keeping out her pork and dairy produce because their own cannot compete in quality. And they have put a prohibitive duty upon the import of bananas from one of their best customers, Fiji, in order to protect the miserable fruit produced in Queensland, that is said to go bad as soon as bought and costs more. With this jealous attitude towards the world there is naturally growing jealousy within as to the sharing of the proceeds. Labour seems to have safeguarded its position pretty well; employers talked bitterly of their situation. They give one example which I find incredible. Workmen's compensation covers a man from the moment he shuts his own door until he opens it again. Thus, *they say*, if he slips on the mat or has a smash when driving his car, drunk, the employer is liable. The whole atmosphere seems to be one of grudged service, of resentment against the employer. And even the customer. Not only did I get indifference verging on rudeness when, at the official Tourist Bureau, I asked for advice about my journey, but they could or would tell me nothing beyond the borders of New South Wales. Cook's being sensibly situated next door to catch those thus turned away, I went in there and had an interesting talk to the English manager, whose views of Australia and Australians were withering. Presumably he is on temporary appointment here or he would hardly dare express such views.

To talk politics in Australia is to invite a series of stories to illustrate the insolence and suicidal policy of the unions. You will be told fantastic tales of overtime charged on a ship because a flag was run up to salute a passing warship; of my next ship, the *Demosthenes*, being declared 'black' and having to miss all her cargo because a union man had been caught and charged with pilfering; of ruinous, paralysing strikes on sheep stations by shearers over some detail; of the graft that reigned in Queensland while the Labour Government was there. But when you ask questions and try to find out the causes of these symptoms it is impossible to get reasonable answers: the speakers simply fall back upon abuse in order to excuse thought and put the whole situation down to 'Red' agitators – from England, of course. So that when I ask whether anything is wrong with, for instance, the educational system, I get a resentful assertion that the Australian system is the best in the world.

It is impossible to spend even a flying week in Australia without being aware of uneasy economic and, one might almost say, moral conditions. The fierce contention between the parties, as reflected in election speeches, appears to be an unreasonable, class-directed, personal and almost wholly materialistic contention. The Australians either live out on the farms or sheep stations, where conditions and the capriciousness of the weather have made for a hard character, or in the few main towns which are full of the restlessness that comes from their economic uncertainties and from the angry discontent on the docks. The contrast between the almost feverish industry of the Americans and the 'go-slow' Australians, with their passion for sport, mainly horse-racing, struck me forcibly. Perhaps it is not altogether fair to judge Australia at a moment when, relying so much upon two or three major products, she has, after the boom of the war and after-war, to see their value declining. Wherever you go you see posters urging you to wear more wool and eat more Australian fruit in order to be healthy. As far as Western women are concerned, I doubt they will ever carry more wool than they do now, having learned [of] the convenience and cheapness of artificial fabrics. For fruit, the Australian's standard of efficiency and of co-operation cannot touch those of California. From London to Auckland I have eaten nearly every day an orange or a grapefruit, stamped 'Sunkist', and every one was good. Once in the range of Australian oranges you never know what you were going to get: some are magnificent, others uneatable. It is the same with tinned fruit. The woman in Putney who buys a tin of fruit salad wants to be perfectly sure she will find an exact, unvarying proportion of good quality fruits inside. From California she gets it, from Australia she does not.

It may have been bad luck, but every Australian manufacture I touched was inferior. Chocolates travel so badly that one would have thought here there lay an opportunity, yet Australian (and New Zealand) chocolates are almost uneatable and the market is dominated by Cadbury, who either export direct from home or from their Tasmanian factory. As for silk stockings, I bought a pair of a much advertised brand and they were in holes two hours after I put them on. It makes one realize how much knowledge and skill go to successful manufacturing; and, one might almost say, character. The last point is illustrated by Japan. She had a marvellous chance during the war to flood Australia with manufactures and she took it. I am told there was a time when you could get only Japanese electric fittings, etc. But not only were they not good enough; the Japanese forfeited their customers' confidence by various tricks and lapses, and now the market is largely lost. . . .

I believe that all this long and probably superficial comment arose from my discussing politics with the guard on the train to Canberra. I got to sleep rather late and awoke to find my carriage stationary and alone in a siding, and no sound to be heard but the loud singing of birds. It took me a long time to remember where I was. I lay in this placid, blessed somnolence for about an hour. I got up, dressed and looked out of the window in order to get my first view of Australia, since so far the town of Sydney was all that I had seen. I found that my carriage was sitting in the siding of a very new little station set in a shallow basin between low hills. The earth was Devon red, showing in every path and shining through the scanty grass. The hills, almost bare of trees, found their beauty in the brilliant gradation of blues made by a sequence of ranges. At half-past six a car came from behind a low shoulder of hills and crept up to the sleeping station. A very good-looking young man got out of the car and found me. This was not difficult, as I was the only occupant of the only carriage. He was dark and good-looking and when he came up to my carriage and spoke he revealed himself as very shy, very Irish, and very much a soldier.[23] He told me he had come with an invitation to stay at Government House. I did not refuse! We drove for about five miles along the hardly made roads of the projected capital to Government House. In contrast with my last three hotels it looked like Paradise. It lies shut away in a fold of the ground in its own low valley, smiling out of a lovely garden. It was once the house of a big sheep station, the land of which has been taken over by the Federal Government for its new capital. The house, begun about a century ago, and skilfully remodelled, is restful and domestic with its low walls and soft green roof. I was taken to a charming suite of rooms of a luxuriousness which reminded me of my last ambassadorial setting, in Washington. The room led on to a wide verandah, looking over a curve of river beside which was a file of willows, admiring their reflections.

At last it was breakfast-time. I came down to find my hostess, a handsome woman in early middle age with short reddish hair.[24] I was delighted to see that she was in a riding-habit, side-saddle, in grey whipcord. Secretaries, aides and her two children made up the breakfast-table. Though I was sorry to miss the Governor-General I doubt whether he would have felt able to talk very freely about Australia. As it was the whole atmosphere was free and friendly, with the two little daughters making a gay contribution.

Immediately after breakfast a car appeared to take me over to the government offices. I now had a chance to see the layout of Canberra.[25] The skeleton city is in the wilderness, its empty and reputedly inconvenient site made necessary, I was told, by the jealousy between the states. An expensive luxury, it seemed, to build a city in this arbitrary way. The plan is grandiose and most of the central buildings, parliament, government offices, etc., are still only temporary. I could see the lines of street after curving street pegged out on the plain. In four corners of the natural basin were the beginnings of four suburbs, of different classes, each house built to plan by the commission in whose hands the design and control of the city has been put. Here one of the hotels; here the cinema; and here, right on the main road, very brand-new and public, the Prime Minister's house, the tenancy of which is at present uncertain. Meanwhile there seems to be a general sense that the whole project is a bottomless sink, a grandiose capital for a country that can ill afford it. Much of the time in Parliament is spent grumbling about the domesticities of life that must fill the minds of men removed from the world – the size and standard of house meted out to A, or the outrageous decision to allot only one bathroom to the Minister of Defence.

I selected the Ministry of External Affairs as my goal and was able to make contact with one or two officials about New Guinea and to fix further plans. Coming back to Government House I was delighted to see some beautiful horses waiting at the door. Soon, in a borrowed habit, I was cantering along the green ridges and looking sideways to admire my hostess on a tall grey mare with flowing mane and tail. We rode for two hours through the reddish grassland scattered with sheep and the bones of sheep, and cut here and there with deep nullahs, almost dry. In the afternoon Lady Stonehaven took me for a drive up the highest nearby hill, where we had a more extended view of the country. It was all of the same character, its beauty given by the sense of space, the depth of colour made by distance, and the scattered, graceful eucalyptus trees, standing at intervals. In the evening I went [on] another ride, this time a long one with the Irish aide-de-camp, and by the evening the riding and the glorious spaces had made me understand why people can love this rather barren country.

In the evening Lady Stonehaven invited the Secretary of External Affairs to dinner to meet me.[26] Afterwards he and I talked for nearly two hours while poor Lady Stonehaven made desperate attempts to entertain his rather unresponsive wife. The Secretary was a fat, pale man, rather slow, but thoroughly sensible and, I should think, honest and well-meaning. We did not get finished that night, so he asked me to come and see him in the morning.

Today the Secretary showed me at his office the whole of the correspondence he has had in the last month or two with Geneva during the sessions of the Mandates Commission and the Assembly. It was deeply interesting and evidence of the honest effort made by

Australia to meet the wishes of the Commission as to information. Each point that came up in the minutes of the meetings has been picked out and questions sent to New Guinea to obtain the necessary information. He is therefore deeply aggrieved that the Commission are still hinting that something serious is wrong and that they have private information. But they won't come into the open and say what it is. I could not help sympathizing with him about it, and seeing the work of the Commission through the eyes of the officials concerned. I am going to take it upon myself to write to Lord Lugard on the subject.[27] The Secretary pointed out the huge expense of this constant, long telegraphing to Geneva. I shall not really get hold of the business until I see the minutes and report of the last Mandates Commission. When pressed to admit that the Mandates Commission did keep his department and the administration of New Guinea up to scratch as nothing else could, he agreed, and agreed, too, that the Commission had acted in most matters with moderation and ability.

I got back in time to have another lovely gallop with Lady Stonehaven, and then the Lane-Pooles (he is head of the Federal Department of Forestry)[28] came in to lunch. After lunch, as I had expressed a wish to see a sheep station, one of the staff motored me for about twenty-five miles to a station which was all the more interesting as shearing was in process. There was a pleasant, oldish, substantial house, nothing very impressive. The owners were very English Australians; they play polo and have old prints and etchings on the walls and old furniture in the house. There was a rugged old grandfather who had obviously borne the burden and heat of the day. There were several cars before the front door; it is difficult to imagine the loneliness of these sheep stations before the invention of the car. There was an attempt at parkland round the house, and close by ran a river, with its attendant nymphs, the willows. After tea we went down to the shearing sheds. First we saw the packing in the enormous square, jute bales that come from India. This was demonstrated by the son of the house, hard at work in greasy overalls.[29] It takes thousands of men in England to disentangle the splintered jute threads from the wool and they are now experimenting with paper linings. Then we saw the grading. . . .

On to the shearing, the comb-like knives driven by machinery like a dentist's drill. The shearers look hard cases and the speed at which they work is amazing. They concentrate almost with desperation for two hours, then knock off for a half. The sheep which lands struggling into their hands is so handled that it becomes powerless; a pinch of the right muscle and out shoots the leg, straight for the clipper. The contrast between the covered sheep, fat, dark grey and rather dignified, and the diminished, naked, white object, scored with scarlet cuts, that emerges from the fleece, is almost comic. Finished, the shearer throws it head over heels down into a pen below with what seems quite unnecessary violence and drags the next victim from the other pen. The sheared sheep walk through a one-at-a-time pen and a tarry substance is dabbed on to their wounds. Truly, the lot of the Australian sheep is not to be envied. . . .

Back to Canberra, where I had a late appointment with the head of the department administering the Central and Northern Territories.[30] These are still under the Federal Government because the remnants of the aborigines now survive in these almost desert margins of White Australia. He was very angry when I suggested that Australia's present record with her aborigines was not much better than her past. But, when pressed, he could give me very little evidence of public interest in the matter and he admitted that the distances made effective supervision impossible. I even managed to get out of him a very damning report recently made on the subject.[31]

I rushed back just in time for dinner and feeling very sad at leaving this comfortable and hospitable house with its kind people, not to speak of the horses. The Irishman motored me to the station to catch the night train to Melbourne.

Melbourne

On the train I met the English MP again and we had a cheerful breakfast together. He was as insouciant as ever and, in spite of his damning reputation as an embroiderer, he seemed to have had an extraordinarily good time.

Between breakfast and 1 p.m. I had my first chance of seeing Australia from the train. I understand that it was at its greenest just after good winter rains. Even so it was not very green. There is brown and gold in the green and my impression of Australia is of extreme barrenness, low rolling slopes in the foreground and always a range of blue hills in the background. It is woe to the scenery in a land given up to sheep. The great, omnipresent feature of Australian landscape is the gum tree. . . . But, like the aborigines, these trees seem to be the remnants of an unwanted species. . . .

Everywhere the country is intersected by the stock routes, which are anything from a quarter of a mile wide and over which the statutory pace for driving sheep is eight miles a day. Approaching Melbourne the land is dead flat, and agricultural, and the plough reveals it a deep purple.

In Melbourne I had from 12 a.m. one day until 4 p.m. the next. At Lady Stonehaven's request I was most kindly entertained by Mr Norman Brookes, the tennis player, and his wife.[32] I fear I have nothing of interest to say about Melbourne. It is a big, rather murky-looking town. Mr Norman Brookes took me to the Town Hall and introduced me to the Lord Mayor, then to the Parliament House, where he introduced me to the Prime Minister, Sir William Macfarlane.[33] I tried to draw him on the aborigines. He looked puzzled. 'They don't do much harm now,' he said; and then, 'They're dying out quickly, and the sooner the better. If they're no harm, they're no use.'

I saw the red-plushed upper house – red seems the fashion for senates – and the green lower house. I wondered how it was possible to furnish all these seven Australian legislatures with suitable human beings. I was taken to the university and had to admire the not very admirable buildings. I find that it is much harder work to be the admiring visitor than the showman. It throws a great strain upon one's inventiveness and sometimes, I fear, upon one's morality.

I had lunch with one of the professors, an Englishman with a Wycombe Abbey[34] wife and not too happy, I guessed. Then I caught my train.

Adelaide

On through the night to Adelaide, to which we came through rather charming hills, crowned by the houses of wealthy South Australians. From the hills one got rather a good view of Adelaide, red and white dots on flats beside the sea. The Governor's ADC met me at the station and motored me the few yards to Government House, where Lady Hore-Ruthven took me in to breakfast.[35] Government House, a low, old, Georgian, whitewashed building, stands in the very heart of the city, its gardens open to the view of the passing public. The unexpected here was in the form of an earnest and indomitable young man with fiery red hair, his face all blotched and half swathed in bandages. He was travelling round the world by himself instead of going to college. He had just got a Baby Austin almost across the central desert, when he got stuck and burned with the sun. I discovered that he was young Goldman, son of our neighbour at Walpole House on Chiswick Mall. An earnest, eccentric and resolute youth. With the son of the house stealing a year away from Eton with his tutor, and an aide-de-camp we were a very cheerful party.

After lunch an ethnologist took me round the anthropological museum. This was really excellent, as was this man who had worked in the north and in New Guinea. He, like a few others I have met, is devoted to the 'abo', as he is called here, and insisted that there was no more generous and affectionate people in the world. It is just because they are so primitive that they need such expert handling, and get the worst possible. Their social and economic life is so elaborately specialized upon their conditions and localities that they can hardly live when displaced. They are very vulnerable to disease, especially venereal and pulmonary troubles. Wonderful horsemen and stockmen, the prosperity of the big farmers in the interior is largely based upon their work. But, even as a labour supply, there has been little effort to conserve them and the first hint of defiance met – and indeed often meets today – with bloody retribution. As the sheep invaded the interior, one to fifteen acres, it was said there was plenty of land. So there was, but not plenty of water, and when a tribe struggled to get back on to the springs from which it had been driven, a force was sent out to 'disperse' it. Many Australians have told me that the 'abo' is barely more than an animal, yet the large and growing number of half-castes witnesses that the white man is not above mating with an animal. Meanwhile, almost the only people whose job it is to look after the natives are the police whose care is mainly of a penal nature. These 'protectors' have on two occasions lately shot down their wards, in one case to the number of forty, and then burned their bodies, presumably to try to cover up their work.[36] The problem is, of course, difficult: it demands patience, knowledge and money and these will not be applied until public opinion is aroused. Meanwhile there is a division of authority. Queensland has some natives, South Australia a few, West Australia many, while those in central and northern territories come under the Federal Government in Canberra.[37]

In the afternoon my hostess took me for a long drive all round Adelaide. A wind full of sand was blowing, yet the sun was brilliant, and the effect, not pleasant to feel, was rather charming to see, as if the country was wrapped in some golden-green iridescence. We visited marvellous old gardens with the flowers and trees of all countries meeting in them, palms and pines, azaleas and wisteria, Japanese maples of all colours and patterns. I liked Adelaide, a placid, dignified, sleepy kind of town in contrast with the two others I had seen.

After dinner we talked and about eleven o'clock the three young men drove me the sixteen miles to Fremantle[38] to catch my ship. We were all very dry – we could blame the sandy air – so they came aboard and we had drinks and at midnight the *Demosthenes* drew out into the Great Australian Bight.

Perth

Of the Bight the less said the better. I took one long look at the passengers, who all knew each other by now,[39] and seemed to draw together against the stranger like sheep at a dog, and decided that I was in for a thoroughly miserable voyage all the long way to South Africa. After my usual first two days of retirement I emerged to find we were nearing Perth and was much cheered to get two wireless messages. One was from the Conservator of Forests to say he would meet me at Perth and the other from the Governor to invite me to spend the day at Government House.

I woke on the third day to find we were already in the estuary that is the port of Perth. The youngest of the Australian states was now celebrating her hundredth birthday in an orgy of speeches, official centenary histories, self-congratulation on her material achievements, bunting, parades, and fat-stock shows.

An English official, Mr Stephen Kessel,[40] ex-Rhodes Scholar, came aboard early and took me off. Fremantle is just nothing particular; the only outstanding building I saw was the jail, built of huge blocks of sandstone by the convict labour which Western Australia used, and even solicited, years after the other states had purged themselves of it. We drove on to a high neck of land, looking down one side on to the brilliant open sea washing the pure white sandhills, while on the other a wandering chain of river curved in and out of big shallow lakes as it found its way up to Perth. It was a glorious day, and the place charmed the eye, with its little red-roofed houses rimming the sweeps of water and winking out of the wooded slopes. We looked down on Perth from the height of a big park full of beautiful young trees and saw the city built along the edge of a shallow, brackish lake of clear water which was spotted with numberless water-birds.

I drew Mr Kessel on forests and he told me of the glorious harvest of timber recklessly squandered by the young state and with how much difficulty they had at last got through a measure of conservation and reafforestation. It is from here that sandalwood comes, a small tree whose twisted, golden stumps I saw piling the docks and filling the trucks at Fremantle. It is imported by the Chinese as a necessity in religious rites and as it is now extinct in their country Western Australia makes use of the monopoly to spoil the Oriental. From here, too, comes jarrah wood, an immense gum tree, whose purple-red is seen everywhere in this state and which planks the floor of St Hugh's College Common Room.

We drove through the squared, white, hot town, into a glorious garden beside the lake, to be confronted by a colossal pink sandstone baronial castle, rather on the lines of St James's Palace, but seeming even bigger – Government House. It looked ludicrously out of keeping with the exotic garden, full of Mediterranean pines and palms. Many of its windows were stained glass of those crude colours peculiar to nineteenth-century churches. I thought it was immensely kind of the Governor[41] and his wife to have bothered with me, as they were distracted and exhausted by the celebrations. Both of them, plus three aides, kept dashing in and out opening this or laying that, reviewing Girl Guides or Boy Scouts or parades of veterans. Finally the Governor came in quite shattered after reviewing the Australian Air Force, the 'Wapitis', who had come over to escort the great air race from Adelaide to Perth and whose method of saluting, to his consternation, was to nosedive all together right on to the unfortunate Governor's stand. There was a roar and we found the devils had followed him home and were doing terrible stunts over our heads in the garden and all round the pink turrets of Government House.

I could not help wondering, as I dried my hands on the crowned towel and ate off the crowned dishes, whether there is a special factory in England for furnishing government houses all over the Empire, not to speak of embassies and legations. I wonder how many acres of portraits of Their Majesties there are all over the world and how many artists, and of what calibre, do the copying. It must represent a considerable industry. These representatives of the King and Queen, my hosts on this – for them – exhausting day, were rather simple, genial, cheerful people, and, I should imagine, very popular in Western Australia. Lady Stonehaven ought to have been here in all the glare, brass bands and bunting, instead of riding and reading philosophy in the green bowl of Canberra. The Governor-General, too, why did he hardly land in Perth, staying on the warship in the harbour? This does not do in a country with an inferiority complex, especially when, conscious of financial stringency, they ask questions about the cost of furnishing Government House. The selection of aristocrats for export to the dominions must be a difficult business, and the politico-psychological losses on a mistake quite considerable.[42]

From the point of view of acquiring information Government House was, unavoidably under the ceremonial circumstances, unproductive. It was with great difficulty, however, that I got away. On the strength of a journey to the north HE and his son wanted to instruct me upon the aborigines and, with the kindest intentions, and in spite of their own exhaustion, almost blocked my way to my main objective, the Chief Protector – revealing title – at the Aborigines Department.[43] However, I got there at last and found that the offices of a department in a state were very much humbler than those of the Federation at Canberra. I found my way in to the Protector past a queue of girl half-castes. I had to admit that among them were some of the ugliest human beings I had ever seen – my standard being that of the white Caucasian, of course.

In a stifling, congested office, I found a polite, weary, disillusioned Englishman. We talked at length. He confirmed all my impressions: that public opinion in Australia was indifferent on the question of aborigines; that there was no chance of getting anything constructive done; no sense at all of any obligation that should be fulfilled, especially if it should cost a little money. For the missions he had nothing but condemnation; the same for the police. I took down all he said, and intend, when I get time, to write it up with the help of other documents and will send it along to him for comment. Also to contact the Anti-Slavery Society.

I went to tea with the Forest Officer in a little bungalow at the water's edge, a house in which Australian and Oxford tastes met,[44] and then we went off to the royal show to see his samples of West Australia's mighty timbers. We passed stall after stall at the show – the cramped *broderie* of half-castes working under Roman Catholic tuition; gold nuggets; fat sheep sweltering under oily fleeces; golden fruit luminous in glass jars; bales of kangaroo skins and many other proud achievements of the 60,000 West Australians.

Then back to my boat to find that I had mistaken the time and that a

humane second officer was desperately trying to hold the boat back for
me, with all the passengers hanging over the taffrail to see the fun. I
raced up the gangway in great embarrassment. We moved softly down
the estuary and soon the Australian continent looking flat and pink and
green, and canopied by a glorious evening, faded slowly away to the
east.

As I stood last night gazing back at a disappearing continent and then
at the turbulent wake of the ship, I took myself to task for the rather
unfavourable views which, I found, Australia had printed upon my
mind. Were they not due to my own lack of imagination and
sympathy?[45] Had I been long enough in the continent to form a
judgement at all?

The mind cannot be restrained from acting upon what is presented
to the eye. But I can ask myself whether I had not luxuriated too much
in the congenial society of the exported British who had entertained or
instructed me – not that any of them had by word of implication
criticized their host country. In any case, had I been long enough in the
country to judge? And were there not many things to admire – the
sense of freedom, the hacking and fencing of the wilderness in less than
two centuries into such large productiveness? The civic pride
expressed in clean streets, spacious parks, avenues, ambitious
buildings? Yet I cannot argue myself out of the sense that there is
something wrong with Australia, and that she cannot turn away
criticism by vaunting her material successes. There is a concentration
upon the material aspects of life, a lack of sensitivity towards its deeper
issues, its spiritual and aesthetic elements. But, again, I asked myself
whether this was not both natural and necessary in a young nation
developing a raw continent? Was it not enough to found a state in
which few, if any, have to go hungry or bow to a superior class, where
nearly all are well housed and fed? On this foundation, with continuing
inspiration and protection from the parent state, even though she is
half the world away, the good stock planted in fresh earth is, surely,
certain in time to grow into a healthy nation.

For historical and other reasons I could not accept the view that the
elements Australia had earlier sucked in through her five mouths, the
convicts, the rapacious exploiters of the Pacific islands and the gold-
diggers, had tainted the colonial society. And if a casual visitor such as
I feel that this is a people which has not yet developed a national ethos,

allowance must be made not only for the time factor but also for the wide scattering of the people through their states.

One matter, however, could give rise to doubt. A test I was bound to apply in view of the purpose of my journey was the attitude to the original inhabitants of the continent. As far as I had had time to inquire, it was only to meet a widespread ignorance, lack of interest, or something worse. Should the strong appropriators of his vast island not feel more sense of responsibility towards the weak, scanty and vulnerable people they had found in possession?

5

Facing Africa

Australia having sunk over the eastern horizon, and Africa being so very far across the great triangle of the Indian Ocean, I realized that this little world of 10,000 tons is likely to loom very large for a few weeks.[1]

The most impressive thing about the ship is that it is English. Since I disembarked from the *Homeric*, about which, dominated by the size of my undertaking, I had no mind to be critical, I had been upon ships and on lands belonging to Americans, New Zealanders and Australians. Now I was under the British flag, with an English crew and officers. I realized at once the great difference in discipline. The stewards do not settle down to the tables to eat long before the passengers have cleared from the saloon as on the *Sierra*; nor do they barge about on deck or flirt with the girls in the music-room, as on the *Sonoma*; nor are they filthy and rowdy as on the *Tofua*; nor, as on the *Lady Roberts* . . . but I won't insult the SS *Demosthenes* by coupling these two ships in the same sentence.

I asked myself what was the quality of these English working this ship. Meeting them after an interval which has been filled by Americans and colonials, I ought, if at no other moment, to appreciate them justly. I think there is a kind of philosophy about them which enables them to take life for granted. The stewards do not assert themselves in any way. They do their work adequately and quietly. They do not resent their position and face it out with bravado and familiarity like the Australians. Admittedly they do not show the grace and enthusiasm for their work that continental waiters show, which is half natural gaiety and half cupidity, and of course they are not blatantly efficient like Americans. In fact you hardly notice them until you realize with a start that, for the first time since you left England, you are being called Miss or Madam, and are in a community in which people 'know their place', one in which class divisions are recognized. I

made inquiries and learned how completely the discipline of the White
Star crystallizes this: the authority of the officers who have little pay
but much prestige, the prohibition against stewards and stewardesses
setting foot on any deck used by passengers. None but the captain, the
chief engineer and the doctor are allowed into the public rooms or
permitted to play bridge with passengers. It is a concession, carried on
from the Aberdeen days of the line, that officers are allowed to play
outdoor games; on regular White Star boats, I understand, this is
forbidden. The conception of status, the belief in discipline, a
readiness to accept facts – these I seem to find when I get back under
the Union Jack. What underlies this sense of discipline and gradation?
Is it a shared, unspoken, perhaps unconscious, reliance upon our
British nationhood which, especially in a foreign context, is status
enough?

I soon found our world well-peopled and was not forced to seek
diversion by going to the third class to watch a man[2] training kangaroos
to box (there are only first and third class on this boat which is no more
than half full). My table seemed dismal at first sight. It contains a silent
Scottish chief engineer; an even more silent, indistinguishable, mouse-
coloured female; a great Australian beef-eater next to me; an enigmatic
foreigner on my right; and two gauche and callow-looking dark young
men further round. . . .[3]

On my right is one Underberg, Doctor of Philosophy of the
University of Cologne, student of economics and history, an
immensely rich young man on a four-year grand tour for his education.
Good-looking in a German way; intellectually as old as the hills, or the
Rhine, courtly, critical, subtle, intellectual, a brilliant conversationalist,
but detached and very supple in the exercise of living. His eyes are
always alertly travelling the saloon and he murmurs to me his
appreciation of that he sees – a frock, a neck, a gesture, the tone of a
laugh. His qualities? Imagination, sympathy, humour, intellect, *joie de
vivre* – these are all arts rather than parts of his character; *that* remains
something withdrawn that enables him, so it seems, to know and to
experience at no cost to himself. Perhaps, for this freedom, he has paid
once and for all? He has been in the German Navy part of the time, I
think, on a submarine, and he gave us a most vivid account of the
German revolution and the experience of being arrested and
imprisoned by his own men on his own ship. Such is his intelligence
and discretion that he does not scruple to open discussions of the war
with men who have been soldiers or sailors on the other side or even to

discuss its origins. And it [is] his skill and broad-mindedness, not ours, which saves us any tense moments. He represents, one hopes, the new Germany, disillusioned with the past, finished with militarism, rather cynically amused to find how forcible disarmament has saved them expense and diplomatic complications and basing all their future hopes upon economic greatness. In travelling about the British Empire he has learned a great admiration, almost affection, for the English. His tolerance extends even to the French, although they quartered Senegalese upon his family in their beautiful house outside Cologne which, of course, was ruined. They also condemned his father to prison for sending a postcard to the Kaiser wishing him many happy returns on his birthday.

Poor Underberg! Distressed at a possibility of getting stout, which no one else can detect, [he] has endured for three weeks the most drastic dieting scheme, one sent him from Hollywood. So he sits beside me, sucking half a grapefruit or eating an oatmeal biscuit, with one eye upon my plate. Meanwhile he plays all games, including bridge half the night, and delights the ship with his animated conversation. The doctor engaged me to play Eve by choosing little delicatessen off my plate and putting them into his mouth. So, by slow degrees, I have broken his resolution and we have celebrated his final defeat by a champagne dinner.

Poor Underberg, again! He has had an unfortunate accident with me. A cricket net was put up on the boat-deck for the officers and, as a great concession, after fagging balls hopefully for them for two days, the Captain allowed me to play.[4] One day Underberg came up and with childish excitement at the idea of a new game he picked up a ball and rushed in between the bowlers, and threw the ball with all his strength from half-way up the pitch. I was playing against the early sunset and never saw it coming. Everyone shouted, but when I saw it, it was too late, and it caught me right on the point of the elbow, full pitch. Everyone was very excited and very furious with Underberg, who was in a terrible state, nearly sick, as he told me after. At the moment, with the idea of reassuring him, I said I was all right and told the next man to bowl. My left arm, however, proved to be quite powerless, and the bat therefore swung out of control and I crashed my own left ankle. So I was taken down to the doctor with two hurts and appeared limping, with elaborate bandages, to enjoy being fussed over at dinner. Underberg wrote an agonized letter and sent with it a large bottle of '4711' eau-de-Cologne. My arm has recovered but not the leg, so I have had to drop out of the finals of the sports and still have a rather misshapen ankle. . . .

Another striking character on board, and a very different one, is little Joey Marks, an American-Jewish music-hall comedian. He is so Jewish that anyone with an anti-complex must have recoiled at the very sight and sound of him when he came aboard, all nose, gold teeth and plus-fours. He has a Jewish wife. Low, knockabout stuff is his speciality, and climbing like a monkey up the plush curtains. There are plenty of sticky English people aboard, including a lieutenant-colonel and a naval commander, and yet, before the end of the trip, little Joey has become the most popular man on the ship with everyone, and the whole of the first class have arranged to take the front seats for his first night in Durban if the boat stays long enough. . . . He has spent his whole life on Broadway; he is quick as a sparrow and frank as a child, and his New York slang is infecting the whole ship.

Joey is taking round with him one Melville, a young American actor, mainly I imagine for his looks, a tall, slender creature of the cinema-idol type with golden hair and blue eyes, oft-married though only twenty-eight but, it seems, momentarily unattached. About the fifth day on board he introduced himself to me, explained that he had learned who and what I was, and proposed in the most businesslike way to engage me as his companion for the voyage. This, on the grounds, I gathered, that an artist must have a succession of new experiences and that an affair with a woman of my type would be a complete novelty. It was so barefaced, so unsentimental, that it was impossible to refuse in anything but the same spirit. He was rather puzzled by this (as he professed) first refusal, but after brooding over it for a day he made a second choice, a little South African who had been to Australia to get married and had returned by the same boat, after one interview with the betrothed, this experience making, presumably, for a pliant condition. From that moment she has gone about the ship in a state of ecstasy, like a sleep-walker . . . until, to insert a later note, the boat heaved away from the dockside at Durban, and the long streamer of coloured paper which was all that remained to attach her to Melville, snapped and floated down to the water.

One more character, the First Officer. Age thirty-two, he stands out as the essential type of Englishman.[5] Disciplined, efficient, unassuming, it was only by accident that it came out that he had done all sorts of grand things in the war, been torpedoed three times, and had played for the United Services in both cricket and football. It was splendid to see how, without much education and little social training, he has stood up to the brilliant Underberg and got the better of him on war topics. He also takes down Melville, the actor, when necessary. He is always on the look-out for Cinderellas and lame ducks, bringing them into the games or cheering them up. He gave me some insight into the mercantile marine, especially in the passenger service, including the way in which the tip-receiving people have to share their tips with the folk behind the scenes, especially in the kitchen, paying the cooks for special items demanded by the passengers, and the storekeepers for any such extra not on the menu. He gives a pretty gloomy picture of his profession, too. The Cunard and White Star are the aristocracy of the sea, but when you do get into them it is more for prestige than pay, for promotion is slow. The officers have to watch the stewards making much more than themselves, especially on the Atlantic run, where the chief stewards and deck stewards have cars, sometimes with chauffeurs, to meet them at the home port while junior officers can hardly pay their train fares home to see their wives and families. . . .

I also have at my table a South African vegetarian, very silent and delicate, owing to [his] having a German bullet in his lung, [and] a Scottish veterinary science lecturer leaving New Zealand in disgust after – so he said – a two-year struggle with ignorance and complacency. He confirms my opinion that they do not yet know how to use the expert. He is now going to Uganda to try his hand in the Colonial Service. There are two Scots, one Englishman, one South African, one West Australian and one German. All this makes rather a good diversity for conversation and as, upstairs, we are generally joined by a Rhodesian tobacco farmer, a mixed Belgian-Polish musician on his way to Brazil, the Marks and the chief officer, who is the illegitimate grandson of Louis-Philippe, we do pretty well.

Apart from Melville there are only two people aboard whom I have any reason to dislike and that only for a single incident. We have had, of course, a ship's concert provided by the passengers, the Marks company being the main performers. I did my best to avoid conscription but in the end was cornered. I have no parlour tricks. But as a child I was forced to provide what were called 'recitations'. I could remember one of these called 'Lasca', about a couple in South America on a cattle ranch.[6] It is *very* dramatic! It recounts how the beautiful, horse-riding Lasca and her man were caught in a cattle stampede and, mounting one horse, raced for their lives. When their mustang fell just in front of the rushing herd, she spread her body over his and so saved his life at the cost of her own. I decided to burlesque this highly dramatic and tragic poem, which I did with the help of a chair in place of a horse. This I mounted and rode until the tragic denouement, when I flung the chair upside-down on the floor.

> Then came a thunder in my ears
> As over us surged the sea of steers,
> Blows that beat blood into my eyes
> And when I could rise (here my voice broke into a sob)
> Lasca was dead!

I thought the applause was a little more restrained than I had hoped for, and as the interval supervened at once and we were thronging out of the saloon, I heard one Englishwoman, to whom I had never been attached, say to another, 'Well, and what did you think of *that*?', evoking the obviously expected condemnation, 'To tell you the truth, I thought it rather overdone.'

Our voyage is now drawing to an end. In a matter almost of hours, after this long isolation in our little society on this ship, we shall see the south-eastern rim of the vast continent of Africa, so much more populous and variegated than Australia. . . . Now, before it appears as a grey smudge upon our so long unbroken horizon, I brace myself physically and mentally for a longer and deeper encounter with the problems of race than any I have encountered upon this almost frantic rush across America, the Polynesian Pacific and the dominions of New Zealand and Australia. For me this will be the really serious part of my journey round the world and probably the most serious subject of my future work.[7]

Notes

1 THE UNITED STATES

1   The full odyssey of this Travelling Fellowship is now covered in four separately published diaries. In chronological sequence, these are: *Pacific Prelude* (July–October 1929); *African Apprenticeship* (October 1929–February 1930); *East African Journey* (April 1930–January 1931); and *West African Passage* (November 1931–April 1932). She wrote up for publication neither the diary for her visit to Uganda (March 1930) nor that for Eastern Nigeria (May–June 1932).

2   Margery lectured at Sheffield University from 1917 to 1920, following which she spent a convalescent year mostly in Africa with her sister and brother-in-law in 1921, returning to Sheffield from 1922 to 1924. She was then elected Fellow and Tutor in Modern History and Modern Greats (Philosophy, Politics and Economics: see Sir Norman Chester's history of the Modern Greats/Social Studies Honour School at Oxford, *Economics, Politics and Social Studies in Oxford, 1900–1985*, 1986) at St Hugh's College, Oxford. She had graduated from St Hugh's (1914–17) with First Class Honours in Modern History.

3   This was the White Star Line's 'ugly' SS *Homeric*, of some 40,000 tons, sailing from Southampton to New York on June 25, 1929. Margery was placed at the purser's table.

4   Under what she read as the terms of the Travelling Fellowship, Margery was required to do no more than examine ('look at rather than study', according to her interpretation) 'native problems', principally in the United States, Australasia and Africa. Perhaps to underline the awesome thought of this 'getting around the world', the original version of the opening page bears the subheading 'First Day of the Circumnavigation'.

5   While in no way controverting the force of her argument about the daunting nature, intellectual as well as physical, of the undertaking ahead, Margery was to show herself neither as helpless nor as hesitant as she felt on the eve of embarkation. In her phrase 'little experience in travel' she overlooks the best part of a year she spent in Somaliland in 1921, at an age which, with possibly pardonable approximation, she underestimates when, as a single white woman in the small British community at Hargeisa, she was indeed a *rara avis* – and rarer yet, as the first white woman to accompany the District Commissioner on a unique trek along the Somali–Ethiopian border (*The Colonial Reckoning*, 1961, p. 31). Nor does she take into account her visits to Geneva in 1927 and again in January 1929, to study the Permanent Mandates Commission of the League of Nations in action.

6   The youngest of eight children, Margery had only one sister, Ethel (b. 1887

?). In 1910 Ethel had sailed to East Africa to take up missionary work, but by the time the ship reached Mombasa she had become engaged to Henry Rayne. At that time he and 'Karamoja' Bell, author of *Wanderings of an Elephant Hunter*, had just become the first European settlers on the Juba river. Later Rayne was to be decorated in the war (there is some confusion in Margery's accounts of his exact decorations) and then join the Colonial Service as a District Commissioner, first in Somaliland and thence to Tanganyika. He wrote two books about his African years, *Sun, Sand and Somals* (1921) (wrongly cited by Margery as . . . *Somalis*) and *The Ivory Raiders* (1923). It was with the Raynes that Margery had spent her convalescent year in Somaliland, an episode that served as the basis for her novel *Major Dane's Garden* (1925). After the death of her youngest brother, Edgar, killed at Delville Wood on July 25, 1916, Margery's favourite sibling was Ethel: it was a close relationship that was to last over sixty years, for much of which they shared a house.

7   Dr Abraham Flexner (1866–1959) is particularly known for having, as a non-medical researcher, stimulated major reforms in the system of medical education in North America through his outspoken critique, *Medical Education in the United States and Canada* (1910), followed two years later by his *Medical Education in Europe*. Since the book referred to here, *Universities American, English and German*, which denounced the subordination of scholarship to functionalism, was not published until 1930, one must assume that Dr Flexner had mentioned the imminence of his study. Shortly after, Flexner became the founder of Princeton's premier Institute for Advanced Study, which he directed from 1930 to 1939. It may be conjectured that Margery had met Dr Flexner when he held the Rhodes Memorial and the Taylorian Lectureship at Oxford in 1927–8.

8   Unlike Chicago, which has retained its famous (and no less 'fiendish') 'L' and its Loop (as the central part of the city was called after 'elevated' trains were introduced downtown in 1897), New York dismantled its elevated railway soon after the Second World War.

9   Her lectures, given in 1928 and 1929, were on 'British Policy towards Native Races' and 'The League of Nations Mandates System'. Margery used to attribute the motivation for these two courses to her year in British Somaliland, which had 'aroused a strong interest in the problems of colonial government'. By 1928, as she saw it, 'any hope of returning to Africa seemed dim' (*EAJ*, p. 12). The lectures formed part of Oxford's new Imperial History syllabus devised by Sir Reginald Coupland (1884–1952), the Beit Professor (1920–48), and Lionel Curtis (1872–1955), the Beit Lecturer (1912–13), subsequently Fellow of All Souls College and a force in the Round Table movement (see Deborah Lavin, 'Lionel Curtis and the Idea of Commonwealth' in *Oxford and the Idea of Commonwealth*, eds Frederic Madden and D.K. Fieldhouse, and her forthcoming full-length biography of Curtis). On Oxford's leading role in the teaching of colonial government, see Richard Symonds, *Oxford and Empire: The Last Lost Cause?*, 1986, p. 245 and *passim*.

10   Sir William Johnson (1715–74) was a distinguished and thoughtful

Indian agent who became the leading planter in Mohawk Valley, NY, which lay in the domain of the Iroquois. He commanded a Mohawk levy in the French–Indian war of 1754, and in 1759 he led a combined force of Six Nations levies, British and colonial troops in a successful attack on Fort Niagara, thereby defining the future north-western boundaries of New York State. It is clear from Margery's early MS notebooks that she had it very much in mind at one time to make a close and possibly major study of America's Indian administration (see, for instance, MSS 78/19 and 79/20, with their extensive documentation on 'Sir William Johnson and the American Indian Problem', including draft lecture notes; and again MSS 35/2, complete with historical brochures and coloured postcards bought on the spot in July 1929).

11   It was not until 1967 that the Public Record Office, the official repository of Britain's governmental archives, moved from Chancery Lane to Kew. At this time, too, it was a fifty- and not a thirty-year rule which was in force for access to official documents (earlier, it had been a hundred-year rule).

12   It was her *Native Administration in Nigeria*, not published until thirteen years after Margery was appointed to Oxford and twenty past her first academic appointment, which was to earn her public recognition as an authority on colonial administration, especially the policy of indirect rule. This reputation reached its climax in the second volume of her biography of Lord Lugard (1960), himself the architect of the administrative policy of Britain in her African possessions, and in her Reith lectures in the following year, *Colonial Reckoning*. A combination, over thirty years, of Margery's writings, teaching Colonial Service cadets at Oxford and from time to time at Cambridge, organizing Summer Schools on Colonial Administration, working hand in hand with the Colonial Office Training and Recruitment Division, visiting one-man-and-a-dog stations up-country as well as headquarter Secretariats, and camping out in bush rest-houses besides being invited to stay at Government House, together brought her recognition, respect and friendship from countless members of the Colonial Administrative and Sudan Political Services.

13   In the event, she never did turn to writing about British colonial administration in the eighteenth century nor about Indian administration in North America. Although a comparative consideration of America's policy towards its Indians was meant to be part of her Rhodes Trust research project in the United States, nowhere outside the poignant reflection on p. 40 does it form a major part of her diary or in her subsequent publications. Indeed, she retrospectively was to accept that all she had time for was a superficial 'looking at the Negro problem in the United States, with a glance at the Amerindians' (*EAJ*, p. 12). Given Margery's pre-eminence in the post-war growth of African Studies (underlined by her election in 1963 as the inaugural President of the African Studies Association of the United Kingdom) and the high regard in which she was held in American universities, which throughout the 1960s were pace-setters in the establishment of a notable record of Africanist resources and research, it is something of a surprise that Margery never revisited the United States in a scholarly capacity after her month there in

1929. That there was no lack of welcoming invitations is not to be doubted. Perhaps she did not find America all that exciting – implications of cultural boredom and rejection are recognizable in many of the American pages of the present diary. She did make a brief return visit towards the end of the war, as part of Britain's team dispatched to the United States in 1944 by the Ministry of Information 'to try and correct distorted views of the character of our empire' (*Colonial Reckoning*, p. 51). But it was Africa that was to become her principal focus of research for the next fifty years. And she did, once, get back to her 'beloved' Somaliland, for the country's independence celebrations in 1960.

14   The convention of writing Negro with a capital N was not widespread in the 1920s.

15   From the evidence of the hotel stationery on which she wrote up much of her first round of the American experience, this was the Van Eyck Hotel, Albany (see Perham MSS, Box 35, file 1).

16   The reference to '159 years ago' (=1770) is puzzling. Perhaps it was a *lapsus calami* for 153 (=1776).

17   It is not clear what the celebrations were for, but one may surmise they may have marked the 160th anniversary of the building of Sir William Johnson's home, Johnson Hall. He began this in 1762, just to the north of what from 1771 became Johnstontown (*sic*), NY, some forty miles north of the State capital at Albany.

18   This is but the first of several manifestations of Margery's resigned but resolute reaction, 'There was nothing for it but to . . .', as she encountered logistical problems on her travels. From cosmopolitan San Francisco through remote Samoa and on to up-country New Zealand, Margery came up against a series of 'No Room at the Inn' rebuffs, somehow confident (through now and again, one suspects, only just) that all would work out well in the end.

19   The quotation is possibly taken from the copious notes Margery had been making from the Public Record Office files on British administration of the American Indians before 1776.

20   Margery was to go on pondering 'this race business' throughout her academic career. She was the anonymous author of a hard-hitting *Times* leader of March 14, 1942, in which she blamed some of the British disasters in Malaya on 'the habits of self-indulgence' of the resident white community and the 'stratified spirit of inequality and discrimination' that characterized colonial society there. In 1944 she published her important if controversial correspondence with Elspeth Huxley, *Race and Politics in Kenya*, and when ten years later the Roan Selection Trust endowed a Chair in Race Relations at Oxford University, Margery, although not one of the electors, took a personal interest in what she felt its activities ought to be.

21   Miss Fishback sounds very much like one of the fanciful names that Margery uses freely in this diary.

22   Sir Esmé Howard (1863–1939), later Lord Howard of Penrith (cr. 1930), was British Ambassador in Washington. Resigning in 1892 after seven years in the Diplomatic Service, he served in the Boer War and then in a variety of consular posts from 1903 to 1911. He was Minister in Sweden throughout the Great War, being appointed Ambassador in Madrid in 1919 and to the United States in 1929. His wife, whom he married in 1898, had been Lady (Isabella) Giustiniani-Bandini (hence, perhaps, Margery's feeling about there being Italian blood in the sons' features). The Howards were, as Margery notes later, a Roman Catholic family. A biography based on Sir Esmé's private diaries is currently [1985] in hand by Dr Brian McKercher of the University of Alberta.

23   Margery seldom fails to record, whenever she fell on her feet during this trip, her sense of 'luxuriating in luxury', whether as a house guest of the British Ambassador in Washington or as guest of the Governor-General of Australia.

24   Howard University received its charter in 1867. In accordance with the vision of its founder, General Oliver Otis Howard, Commissioner of the post-war Board of Refugees, Freedmen and Abandoned Lands, of a university for newly emancipated slaves, it has long been a leading centre of Negro scholarship. As part of the expansion of African Studies in the 1960s Howard developed a major programme, in which its Jesse E. Moorland Library collection of over a hundred thousand items on Negro life and history became a prominent national resource.

25   Dr Mordecai Wyatt Johnson (b. 1880), Baptist minister, pastor and scholar, became President of Howard University at the age of only thirty-six and went on to hold the office until he was seventy.

26   In the United States lynching is prominently linked with violence and vigilante law in the Southern States after the Civil War, and is often associated in the public mind with the reign of terror exercised by the infamous Ku-Klux-Klan. To give an idea of its prevalence (not quite as horrifying a total as Margery was given but none the less appalling), records compiled at the Tuskegee Institute on behalf of the activist NAACP show that between 1882 and 1962 no less than 4,736 persons were lynched in the United States. Of these, 3,442 were Blacks and 1,294 Whites. Five out of every six lynchings took place in the South. In the 1890s, the figure averaged as many as 150 a year, a total which had declined to six in the 1950s. In the year of Margery's visit, Walker F. White's important *Rope and Faggot* appeared, following on the closely documented study commissioned by the NAACP of lynching in the United States between 1889 and 1918. The notorious Scottsboro Case, when nine black youths were indicted in Atlanta on charges of having raped two white girls in a railroad fright car, occurred shortly after Margery's visit (1931). It can be read about in *Scottsboro Boy* (1950) by Haywood Patterson (the alleged ringleader, he had been sentenced to seventy-five years' imprisonment but escaped in 1948) and in Dan T. Carter's *Scottsboro: A Tragedy in the American South* (1979).

27   To some extent this feeling had likely been rekindled by the popular

Marcus Garvey movement of the past decade, with its emphasis on African institutions and terminology to promote its 'Back to Africa' ethos.

28   In the original, Margery unwittingly reveals how she had been misled by the American pronunciation of DuBois and has 'De Bose'. William Edward Burghardt DuBois (1868–1963) was an American educationalist who, having thrown off his earlier support for the gradualism of Booker T. Washington as expressed in his famous Atlanta speech of September 18, 1895, assumed the leadership of the more radical but still biracial movement, the National Association for the Advancement of Colored People (NAACP), which urged full and early equality. As editor of its influential journal, *Crisis*, Du Bois emerged as the effective leader of the American Blacks in the period 1910 to 1934. He was also an active promoter of the various Pan-African Congresses. From 1934 to 1944 he taught at Atlanta University, and in 1961 accepted an invitation from Kwame Nkrumah to settle in Ghana. Du Bois died in Accra two years later. His best book is probably *The Philadelphia Negro* (1899), but it was his semi-autobiographical *The Soul of Black Folk* (1903) which made his name as a writer.

29   For her visit to Hampton, see p. 55. Unfortunately, a 'severe heat wave', coinciding with fatigue brought on by such a full programme, caused Margery to cancel her planned visit to the celebrated Tuskegee Institute. This was to be the first of several bouts of illness throughout the Fellowship.

30   Anson Phelps-Stokes (1874–1958), clergyman, educator and author, made at least three across-the-globe journeys. These included Africa (Cape to Cairo) in 1932–3, from which emerged his *Education, Native Welfare and Race Relations in East and South Africa* (1934). At the time of Margery's visit he was Canon of Washington Cathedral (1924–39). Officer and trustee of numerous foundations and associations, his father had been a wealthy banker and later chairman of the board of directors of the Phelps Stokes and Co. family bank. The family house in Washington was No. 3040 Massachusetts Avenue.

31   The Phelps-Stokes Fund was established in 1911 and became the major agency in seeking to implement the philosophy of the Hampton-Tuskegee approach, through both research and publication, in the education of Negroes, 'both in Africa and the United States', as envisaged by its founder, Miss Caroline Phelps-Stokes.

32   Soon after the Second World War the Fund made its first major move to fulfil its responsibilities in the African field. As a result of a joint initiative from the American Baptist Foreign Mission Society and the Foreign Missions Conference of North America to the Phelps-Stokes Trustees, two landmark inquiries were carried out under its auspices in 1920–1 and again in 1924. These were published respectively as *Education in Africa* (1922), covering West, South and Equatorial Africa, and *Education in East Africa* (1925) covering East, Central and Southern Africa. Their very important reports (they are widely credited with having prompted the British Government to issue its milestone *Memorandum on Education Policy in British Imperial Africa* in 1925) have been admirably abridged by L.J. Lewis in his *The Phelps-Stokes*

Reports on Education in Africa (1962). From her contemporary notebooks, we now know that the recommendation to the Phelps-Stokes Fund came from Dr J.H. Oldham, to whom Margery was introduced at All Souls College, Oxford, on February 9, 1929 (MSS 80/21).

33 Edward Mandell House (1858–1938), always known as Colonel House because of his appointment by Governor James Hogg to his staff in the direct rank of colonel, was a Texan diplomat who became a confidant of President Woodrow Wilson until an irreparable break came about during his handling of the Peace Conference at Versailles in 1919.

34 Margery had made two visits to Geneva, the last in January 1929, where the League of Nations Permanent Mandates Commission had its headquarters.

35 This was at Richmond, Virginia. Jackson Davis (1882–1947), educationist, was from 1915 to 1929 general field agent and, from 1929 to 1933, associate director of the General Education Board of New York City, whose programmes for Negro education received a substantial subvention from the Rockefeller Foundation. He visited Africa in 1935 and subsequently played a leading role on Liberian education commissions. He was also secretary of the International Education Board from 1923 to 1938. In 1940 he became Vice-President of the Phelps-Stokes Fund.

36 Patrick Henry (1736–99) was the first Governor of the Commonwealth of Virginia, from 1776 to 1779, and then again from 1784 to 1786. The quotation given here was contained in the resolution put by the First Continental Congress from Virginia in 1774.

37 The 'Jeanes training', named after Anna T. Jeanes who left a large bequest for training visiting teachers for Negro schools in the Southern states, envisaged a community approach to education. At this time it was considered a model for the needs of Africa. Among the Jeanes schools that impressed Margery on the African leg of her Travelling Fellowship were those at Hope Fountain and Domboshawa in Southern Rhodesia (*AA*, pp. 245–6 and 252–3) and at Kabete in Kenya (*EAJ*, p. 35). The last-named enjoyed a special reputation in Britain's mass-education programme in colonial Africa.

38 Margery was not quite clear of the distinction in the United States between university, college, institute and school.

39 The Petersburg National Battlefield, associated with the siege of Petersburg by Ulysses S. Grant lasting from June 15, 1864 to April 2, 1865, heralded Lee's surrender and the end of the Civil War a week later. The Battle of the Crater, fought on June 30, 1864, commemorates the day when a regiment of former coal-miners from Pennsylvania tunnelled 500 feet under the Confederate lines and detonated 8,000 pounds of black powder. The blast left a crater some 170 feet long and 30 feet deep. But the ensuing Union attack failed to seize the city.

40 The Hampton Institute (not Institution), Virginia, was a private, non-sectarian and coeducational college founded in 1868 as a training centre for Negroes on the initiative of General Samuel Armstrong. In 1920, by which

time it had earned the reputation of being probably the most successful institution for Negro education in the world, it changed its name from a Normal and Industrial Institute and advanced to college-level programmes.

41   The Tuskegee Institute (not University: the name changed in 1937, and in 1943 Tuskegee offered graduate instruction for the first time), Alabama, was formed in 1881 as the Tuskegee Normal and Industrial Institute, under the leadership of the notable Negro educationalist and social reformer, Booker T. Washington (1856–1915). He remained its President until his death. His strategy was that of gradualism, arguing that the Negro's best way of improving his lot in the United States was through advance in education and employment rather than his seeking to achieve instant social equality with the Whites. His autobiography, *Up from Slavery* (1901), attained the status of a minor classic. Louis Harben has written a notable biography (1972) as well as editing Washington's copious papers. It is curious that while on the Eastern seaboard Margery did not visit Lincoln University, Pennsylvania, the oldest university in the United States dedicated to the education of Blacks (founded in 1854).

42   Unerringly, Margery puts her finger on the crux of the emergent African nationalism: the 'excluded' feeling of the urban intelligentsia, that generally despised educated class whom Britain herself had helped to create. It was a theme she was to return to thirty years later in her analysis of the end of empire and the impact of discrimination on the aspiring class of educated elites (*Colonial Reckoning*, p. 39). She foresees, too, at the end of this paragraph, several of the events of the Civil Rights movement in the United States twenty-five years later: the black boycott of buses in Montgomery, the Little Rock incident of 1957, and the freedom marches, rides and sit-ins of the early 1960s, culminating in Martin Luther King's inspiring leadership and tragic assassination in 1968.

43   Once again, Margery's perceptions are justified by subsequent events. This very Americanness of the US Negro was often to prove a stumbling-block, for both parties, in the initial exuberance of what was later to become the 'Roots' syndrome of the 'Back to Africa' imperative of the late 1950s and early 1960s. A spectacular example was Richard Wright's huge sense of disenchantment with his 'native' Africa, so poignantly expressed in his account, *Black Power* (1954), with its significant subtitle of 'A Record of Reactions in a Land of Pathos'.

44   General Samuel Chapman Armstrong (1839–93), whose tenure in command of the 9th Colored Regiment, US Army, stimulated a profound interest in the Negro, was, as noted above (note 40), the founder of the Hampton Normal and Industrial Institute for Negroes.

45   This, of course, was the classic item of division among American Blacks: emigration *versus* integration. For a summary of the whole debate, see Peter Duignan and L.H. Gann, *The United States and Africa: A History* (1984).

46   Marshall Field (1835–1906), businessman, millionaire and philanthropist,

was a major benefactor of Chicago, the city in which his departmental store – after he had bought out, in 1881, the self-made dry goods millionaire Levi Zeigler Leiter, whose daughter Mary Victoria was to become Lady Curzon in 1895 and then Vicereine of India – was a byword for innovative customer service, e.g. a restaurant for shoppers, tickets displaying the price of all merchandise, and a system of allowing goods to be returned by dissatisfied customers within a reasonable time. The full title is the Field Museum of National History, originally called the Columbian Museum (which Marshall Field had built for the World's Columbian Exposition in 1893) and subsequently resited and redesigned in accordance with his will. His grandson, Marshall Field III (1893–1956), founded the *Chicago Sun* (later the *Sun-Times*), while Marshall Field IV (1916–1965) was the publisher of the *Chicago Daily News*. It would presumably be Marshall Field III whom Margery met in Chicago, though he was educated at Eton and Cambridge, not Christ Church.

47   Carl E. Akeley (1864–1926) was a leading American taxidermist of his generation, who spent twenty years with the Field Museum in Chicago before moving to the American Museum of Natural History in 1907. He made no less than four big game hunting expeditions himself, for studying and the collection of wild animals. The depredations of the famous lions at Tsavo brought the construction of the Uganda Railway to a standstill in 1898–9 – see J.H. Patterson, *The Man-Eaters of Tsavo* (1907) and chap. 9 of Charles Miller's *The Lunatic Express: An Entertainment in Imperialism* (1971).

48   The British Consul-General in Chicago was G. Haggard, with Vice-Consuls W.H. Gallienne and W.J. Sullivan.

49   Prohibition was surely a powerful stimulus. For Chicago's gangsters, prohibition opened a whole new source of potential wealth, and it was there that the first 'professional' liquor robbery took place when six men hijacked $100,000 worth of liquor from two boxcars. For an authoritative history, see Thomas M. Coffey's *The Long Thirst* (1975).

50   North Platte, Nebraska, lies 300 miles west of Omaha, and fifty years later still boasted a population under 25,000. Better known than the fracas reported there is its claim to being the home of Buffalo Bill Cody and the site of a commemorative rodeo going back to 1882.

51   The British Consul-General in San Francisco was G. Campbell. Unfortunately we do not know which of the three vice-consuls was Margery's young Oxford escort – probably E.S.R. Cawley, who hosted the outing to Chinatown later on in her visit.

52   Prohibition, which was not lifted for another four years, did not of course apply to diplomatic missions on American soil. However, it did extend to American ships outside territorial waters.

53   From internal evidence, it seems his real name could have been May. In other manuscript and typescript versions he appears confusingly as Jay, D. and A.D.

54   The historic town of Orange in Vaucluse, Provence, is the site of a Roman amphitheatre.

55   This was probably Laura Foreman, who married a Mr Brode.

56   The history of Samoa's imperial overrule is more than a little complicated – hence, no doubt, the apt choice of title in Paul Kennedy's *The Samoan Tangle: A Study in Anglo-German-American Relations, 1878–1900* (1974). Other helpful guides through this colonial maze are Sylvia Masterman's *The Origins of International Rivalry in Samoa, 1845–1884* (1934) and the chapter 'The Partitioning of the Islands' in C.H. Grattan's *The South West Pacific to 1900* (1963). Samoa was earlier known as the Navigator's Islands, just as Tonga was for long charted as the Friendly Islands. Under the pressure of commercial rivalry in the region between Britain, Germany and the United States, the 1880s were characterized by what Deryck Scarr has called a decade of 'Samoan anarchy presided over by three Consuls with different masters, interests and aims – and no revenue' (*Fragments of Empire*, 1967, p. 69). On June 14, 1889 a joint agreement was signed whereby a German, an American and a British consulate ('all at loggerheads with one another', as Robert Louis Stevenson described the scenario in a letter dated July 13, 1890: cf. Lord Salisbury's apophthegm of a *furor consularis*) was each established in Apia, the capital of Samoa. The principal German interest was that of the Hamburg firm, Johann Godeffroys, while the main American presence was exemplified in the Central Polynesian Land and Commercial Company. Ten years later, in 1899, this tripartite agreement was revised following the Berlin treaty of April 10, 1896, to allow for a 'Final Act of the Conference on Samoan Affairs' which now provided for an international supervision of Samoa. Control over the islands of Tutuila and Manu'a, along with the smaller ones of Rose, Swains, Ofu and Olosega (amounting to less than a hundred square miles in all), was now vested in the United States, with her important naval base located at Pago Pago. The two larger islands lying some seventy miles to the west, Savaii (660 square miles) and Upolu (430 square miles), together with seven smaller islands, passed to Germany, an apportionment subsequently adjudged by Margery to have been the lion's share (*The Times*, April 11, 1930). As compensation, Britain received Tonga, Germany's island possessions in the Bismarck Archipelago (mainly the eastern portion of the Solomons), and the western portion of that zone of West Africa recognized as neutral by Germany and Britain in 1888. This involved the Mamprusi-Yendi area of the Northern Togo-Gold Coast marches, plus the renunciation by Germany of her extra-territoriality in Zanzibar. When war broke out in 1914 New Zealand promptly occupied the German territory of Western Samoa, after an unopposed landing by some 1,400 troops on August 29. When Germany's former colonial possessions were redistributed among the victorious powers at the end of the Great War, Western Samoa was declared a Class 'C' mandate by the League of Nations on December 17, 1920, a charge conferred on Great Britain but to be exercised by New Zealand. Whereas a Class 'A' mandate was a category exclusive to the former Turkish Empire territory in the Middle East and Class 'B' was devised for the ex-German colonies in Africa (other than South-West Africa, for which a Class 'C' status was secured by Smuts), Class 'C' was used

for territories which it was considered could be best administered as an integral part of the mandatory power's territory. These were principally the ex-German islands in the Pacific and, unlike Class 'B', 'C' mandates required no 'open door' policy. Following the reclassification of League of Nations Mandated Territories as United Nations Trust Territories after the Second World War, the first UN Trusteeship Council missions visited Western Samoa in 1947. She became independent in 1962. American Samoa remains (1985) an unincorporated territory of the United States and since 1951 has been administered by the US Department of the Interior, replacing the naval administration that had existed since 1900. Margery made a neat, contemporaneous, comparative judgement: 'If lovers of round statements can say that the rule of New Zealand has been the right thing being done in the wrong way, they can also say that American Samoa shows the wrong thing being done in the right way' (*Colonial Sequence, 1930–1949*, 1967, p. 31). Newcomers to the Samoan imbroglio may thus tend to sympathize with W.P. Morrell's assessment of its being 'the most troublesome problem in the partition of the Pacific' (*Britain in the Pacific Islands*, 1960, p. 238).

57   It is interesting to speculate on Margery's good fortune in having 'no terms', and how in the event, having once 'settled her conscience', the impetus of much of her fifteen weeks of pre-Africa research (and hence the whole burden of this diary) emerged from this 'one-day-in-Washington', small newspaper item. Elsewhere she has described this discovery of a project in even more casual terms: 'Hearing there was some kind of trouble among the natives [in the two Samoas], I visited both these beautiful and deeply interesting dependencies' (*AA*, p. 12). In the original manuscript there is even room for some doubt as to whether Margery was really aware that the United States actually had a colony in Eastern Samoa, for 'it reminded me' is a latter-day gloss on the earlier 'it appeared that America possessed a colony'. However, the apparently impromptu nature of her 'new' research project is to an extent mitigated by her subsequent admission that Western Samoa had 'long fascinated' her as an integral part of her interest in the mandates system. Despite this momentary agonizing over her possible terms of reference, in her second report to the Rhodes Trustees, dated August 22, 1929, she simply narrates her visit to Pago Pago, wisely making no attempt to rationalize it.

58   On Mau, see pp. 104 ff.

59   Stephen Victor Graham (b. 1874, retired 1931 with the rank of Rear-Admiral) was Governor of American Samoa from 1927 to 1929, succeeding Henry Francis Bryan (1865–1944). Because of the strategic importance of the harbour at Pago Pago (in Samoan, this *g* is pronounced *ng*), which had been first exploited by the mission of A.B. Steinberger, as special US agent, in the 1870s (he was deported in December 1875 on board HMS *Barracouta*), the governorship, usually for a two-year appointment, lay in the gift of the US Navy until 1951.

60   It was not until February 1924 that the US Congress formally accepted the deeds of cession agreed twenty years earlier.

61 A notable instance of Margery's conscious determination to go straight to the top in pursuit of her quarry. Elsewhere she confesses that this cutting out of juniors and middlemen, and getting the top brass to talk about their own work and themselves rather than listening to her, was the secret of her success in research interviews.

62 This was possibly the leader of Mau on American Samoa. If so, his name was Ripley. It was certainly not Mr Nelson, Mau leader on Western Samoa, who was a Swede and whose wife was not 'white' but a Samoan. It was typical of Margery to want to track down at once even those who had tangled with the law, regardless of the risk of becoming so entangled herself.

63 Despite the grandiose description of General Headquarters, this would be no more than the Californian branch of the Kuomintang (KMT), which under Chiang Kai-shek controlled the government of China from 1928 to 1949; and thereafter in Taiwan.

2 THE PACIFIC ISLANDS

1 There is some confusion here. The Vice-Consul had been her host for the evening, but the only possible 'academic' acquaintances she had met in San Francisco were Mr March whom she had 'picked up on the train', or the 'young Oxford man whom I picked up' in the British Consul's office (Elwyn Cawley ?). It may thus be that they were one and the same person.

2 The Matson Line's SS *Sierra*. Her cabin companion, whom Margery did not immediately like, was an Australian woman called Bent.

3 They turned out to be two Colonial Service officials on their way to taking up posts in the Western Pacific. The elder, whom she christens 'Petronius' in the diary, was probably A.E.P. (later Sir Alan) Rose, a Cambridge graduate recently appointed to Fiji as Chief Police Magistrate. He was transferred to Northern Rhodesia in 1931, becoming Solicitor-General of Palestine in 1936 and later Chief Justice of Ceylon. This 'Petronius' is of course another of Margery's *noms-à-clef*. To confuse matters further, in another fragment she calls him Mark Antony (MSS 36/614)! Margery quickly cautions the reader that she nicknamed her new friend Petronius without rhyme or reason. 'For some now-forgotten reason,' she wrote forty years later when preparing her script *Samoa: Trouble in Paradise* for a radio talk, 'I named him Petronius.' The younger man, an administrative cadet or junior DO, may have been G.W. Bishop.

4 The Governor at this time was still drawn from the US Navy. The Governor-designate was Gatewood Sanders Lincoln (1875-1957).

5 The island of Alcatraz, which served as a barracks from 1849 to 1904, became first a military prison and then, in 1934, a purportedly escape-proof federal prison. It was closed in 1963 and then reopened in 1972 as a public park and tourist attraction.

6 *Major Dane's Garden,* based on her observations while spending a 'gloriously happy' year (*AA*, p. 22) with her sister and brother-in-law, Major Rayne, in Somaliland. She variously used 1924, 1925 and 1926 as the date of publication: the correct date is 1925. It is worth quoting Margery's own evaluation of her venture into fiction, in view of the fact that it was not until the early 1970s that she gave up her general reluctance to claim the authorship of the book among her list of publications (e.g. the long list attached to the two volumes of *Colonial Sequence* and to *East African Journey*). Balked, as she saw it, of the modern alternative of writing a PhD, she 'wrote a novel and poured into it the problems of Somaliland as well as the adventure and the harsh beloved setting. . . . The story has been forgotten for about half a century but, astonishingly, it has been resurrected [it was republished in 1970]' – *AA*, p. 26.

7 The British Consul in Honolulu was G.H. Phipps and the Vice-Consul W.H. Baird.

8 The Institute of Pacific Relations, founded in 1925, was composed of a number of autonomous national councils having a major interest in the Pacific region.

9 From time to time we are involuntarily reminded that Margery was travelling on a limited budget.

10 Her first British colony was the barren and impoverished Somaliland, where she had spent nine months in 1921/2.

11 The American constitutional commission, which visited Samoa in the summer of 1930, consisted of two senators, two Congressmen and two Samoan chiefs. In Margery's opinion, Congress set it up so as 'to clear the little islands from sin and itself from a long reproach' (*The Times*, April 11, 1930).

12 In an attempt to prevent native societies succumbing to the pressures inherent in too abrupt a contact with the Western way of life (the underlying theme of Alan Moorehead's related account of Europe's invasion of the South Pacific between 1767 and 1840, in *The Fatal Impact*, 1966), the League of Nations incorporated into its mandates the tutelary message about literally helping people to stand on their own feet (Article 22 of the Covenant). One of the accusations made against the New Zealand administration of Western Samoa was that its vigorous policy of commercialization could not possibly be reconciled with the mandate's fundamental principle of preserving *fa'a Samoa,* the Samoan way of life, by isolating it from the disruptive forces of the outside world.

13 This would probably be Dr Margaret Mead (1901–78), who had published her classic text, *Coming of Age in Samoa: A Psychological Study of Primitive Youth for Western Civilization,* only the year before. In her own amusing description (in the preface to the 3rd ed., 1961), she looked at it as 'the first piece of work by a serious professional anthropologist written for the educated layman in which all the paraphernalia of scholarship designed to convince one's professional colleagues and confuse the laity was deliberately laid aside'. For Professor Franz Boas, doyen of American anthropologists and

her mentor, Mead's superb fieldwork confirmed what the profession had long suspected, namely that 'much of what we ascribe to human nature is no more than a reaction to the restraints put upon us by our own civilisation' (Foreword, 1928 ed.). Though recently under revisionist attack (e.g. Derek Freeman's *Margaret Mead and Samoa*, 1982), *Coming of Age in Samoa* remained a basic textbook for anthropologists for over fifty years. Mead herself was also to declare, in retrospect, that the book was welcomed by the anti-nationalistic America of the 1920s as 'an escape in spirit that paralleled an escape of body to a South Sea island where love and ease were the order of the day'.

14   *Tapu*, the Polynesian term for prohibition or interdiction, has now established itself in the English language in the form of 'taboo'.

15   'The first love, the first sunrise, the first South Sea island, are memories apart and touched a virginity of sense' – R.L. Stevenson, *In the South Seas* (1892), p. 2.

16   The *fale* is the characteristic oblong, thatched Samoan house.

17   The *fita-fita* were members of the local Samoan marine corps, who virtually constituted (to use Margaret Mead's classification) 'the police, hospital corps men, and interpreters for the [US] naval administration'. Service in this unit was considered an honourable profession for the able and ambitious.

18   Another example of Margery's insouciance over accommodation. In this particular instance of the kind of accommodation on offer at Pago Pago, there is a distinct echo of the plight of the missionaries *en route* to Apia in W. Somerset Maugham's celebrated play *Rain*, set in Pago Pago. This first appeared as a short story called *Sadie Thompson* in the collection *The Trembling of a Leaf: Little Stories of the South Sea Islands* (1921) and later in the collection *Love and Tragedy in the Seductive South Sea Islands*. Recalling some forty years later her arrival in American Samoa, Margery's remark, 'I had some difficulty in disembarking at the American naval base of Pango Pango [*sic*]' (*Colonial Sequence I*, p. 1), coming as it does after an allusion to her investigating the Samoan troubles and to having met some of the Samoan dissidents in San Francisco, had long seemed to me to refer to problems of the kind associated with officialdom, but her diary now makes it clear that they were primarily related to matters of accommodation and not of immigration or bureaucratic hindrance.

19   The trader's name was possibly Reed. On Nelson and his partners, see p. 105 and note 67.

20   This was the disguised 'Benedicta' of Margery's diary. Her real name was probably Aletta Lewis (later Mrs D.C. Dunlop). Born in 1904, she had studied at the Slade and went on to teach at the Sydney Art School. She held a number of exhibitions between 1924 and 1931.

21   The *Emden*, one of Admiral von Spee's Pacific command of five cruisers at the outbreak of war, enjoyed a brief but brilliant history in the first months, largely thanks to her captain's skill in recoaling and her false fourth funnel

which gave her the appearance of a British cruiser. She was eventually destroyed by the Australian navy's *Sydney* on November 9, 1914 (cf. *H.H. Asquith: Letters to Venetia Stanley*, ed. M. and E. Brock, 1985, pp. 252–4).

22   This important South Seas drinking ritual is described on p. 85.

23   *Taro* is a wider, Polynesian term for the Fijian *dalo*, the tuberous root *colocasia antiquorum*, a member of the arum family which forms the principal crop and staple diet.

24   *Taupo*, usually *taupou*, was a ceremonial virgin, hence any village maiden. Many more vernacular terms are used in the original diary.

25   *Matais* are heads of families.

26   *Malai*, properly *malae*, is a village meeting-place or public square.

27   To quote a note attached to the original typescript: 'All the more serious information – not that I am pretending that in the rush around these Pacific Ocean territories my studies can be very serious! – goes into my notebooks.'

28   For this reference to a US visiting mission, see note 11 above.

29   After looking to the Imperial Institute, London, from the turn of the century the Colonial Office formalized its training programmes at Oxford and Cambridge Universities in 1926 with the establishment of the Tropical African (subsequently Colonial Administrative) Service courses. The University of London's School of Oriental and African Studies and the London School of Economics were also to become involved. These courses lasted for fifteen months, reduced later to an academic year. The average annual recruitment of colonial administrators was over one hundred from 1926 to 1929, but as the slump hit Britain the numbers dropped to a mere twenty in 1931 and only twenty-five in 1932. They did not begin to recover until 1935, and by the eve of the Second World War they were back in the nineties. Margery was to be closely associated in the reconstruction of post-war Colonial Service training at the universities, renamed the Devonshire Courses in 1946 – see the memorandum written by the Registrar of Oxford University, Sir Douglas Veale, in the papers of Sir Ralph Furse, Director of Recruitment in the Colonial Office, and the unpublished paper by R.E. Wraith, both in Rhodes House Library.

30   The articles appeared eight months later, in *The Times* of April 10 and 11 1930. Entitled 'Difficulties of the Mandate' and 'The American Method', they were accompanied on the second day by a leading article headed 'The Art of Governing Samoans', which referred to 'the impressions from the pen of a Rhodes Travelling Fellow'. Margery always believed that this accolade of writing for *The Times* had something to do with the Rhodes Trustees' offer of an extension to her Fellowship, cabled to her in Africa shortly after publication. They certainly constitute, with the exception of her two 'unrecognised' novels, *Major Dane's Garden* (1925) and *Josie Vine* (1927), her first appearance in print. Nearly forty years later, *The Times* was still glad to publish letters from her, e.g. 'The Nigerian Civil War', September 19, 1968.

Forty years earlier, Robert Louis Stevenson wrote the first of his letters to *The Times* (March 11, 1889) – and, likewise, the forerunner of many more – also on the subject of the maladministration of Samoa. The student of colonial administration might reasonably have expected Margery's side-by-side analysis of the American and New Zealand governance of the two Samoas in *The Times* articles to take account of the initial cloud at the time when New Zealand was awarded the League of Nations mandate. Whereas American Samoa had escaped the ravages of the notorious influenza epidemic of 1918, its severest impact was experienced by Western Samoa. Nearly 10,000 people succumbed, perhaps as much as 25 per cent of the population. The inferences drawn locally were far from favourable to New Zealand's incipient image as a colonial power. Significantly, the dread memory of the nature of the disaster was evoked on the islands during the outbreak of infantile paralysis in New Zealand at the end of the Second World War.

31   She has not. There is a hiatus in the diary here, but my rearrangement of two *non sequitur* pages in the original gives us what is now at least a coherent text. Fortunately, the journal in the *Lady Roberts* was of only twelve hours' duration.

32   Margery's nightmare of a tourist invasion came a palpable step nearer when the facilities of Tafuna Airport were improved and a large hotel was opened at Pago Pago in 1965. Today there is a 100-room hotel overlooking Pago Pago Bay, 'built in the style of a traditional Samoan village', and package tours operate: 'Ride the tramway up to Mt Alava for a breath-taking view. . . . Attend a Samoan feast . . . sit cross-legged on a straw mat . . . try delicious suckling pig on a banana-leaf plate while watching marvelously skillful and energetic Samoan dancers' (from a US Travel Service advertisement, 1985).

33   Despite what her family and friends have labelled 'occasional crises', in her later years, especially after being influenced by Dorothy Sayers's *The Man Born to Be King*, Margery abandoned her agnosticism and began to enjoy a deep faith. She also became a strict observer of Lenten observances, as unthinking hosts quickly learned.

34   Forty years later, the narrative on pp. 83–91 was relived by Margery in a condensed version given as a talk on BBC Radio 4, reprinted in *The Listener*, September 9, 1971, 333–5.

35   On the eve of the First World War German's Pacific possessions (principally Western Samoa, New Guinea, Nauru and Micronesia) comprised some 96,000 square miles, with an indigenous population of 640,000 and approximately 2,000 Europeans, out of her total colonial empire (predominantly in Africa) of over a million square miles and a population of 12 million.

36   Margery had first been introduced to Lord Lugard in April 1929. Later on in her journey, when visiting the ex-German Cameroons, she noted in her diary, 'several points that I might supply to Lord Lugard at the Mandates Commission'; and again the entry, 'Thank Heaven that through Lugard, if I can win his confidence, I can hope to have some indirect access to the Mandates Commission' (*WAP*, pp. 151 and 181; see also p. 200).

37   The only two New Zealand representatives who appeared before the PMC in this period and could testify with first-hand knowledge of Samoan affairs were General G.S. Richardson (appointed at the end of his governorship of Samoa in 1928) and C.A. Berendsen, appointed to attend the 21st Session of the PMC in 1931. Berendsen had been Secretary of External Affairs in Wellington during the Mau rebellion. Others to present the New Zealand case at Geneva over this critical period in their country's exercise of the Mandate were Sir Francis Bell, Sir James Allen and Sir James Parr (whom Margery had found so helpful in London earlier in the year) in 1929 and again in 1935, by which time Mau had finally failed to earn recognition as an alternative government of Samoa. In that year, one of his final sessions as a member of the PMC, Lugard castigated New Zealand by declaring that there must be something basically wrong with an administration – probably, he hinted, in the recruitment and training of its officials – that was continually reporting unrest and trouble (28th Session of the PMC, 17th Meeting, October 30, 1935). He went on publicly to express the hope that the next administrator would, for the first time, be 'a man with experience of native races'. For a good commentary on how New Zealand had to face the music before the PMC, see J.V. Wilson's chapter on New Zealand's participation in international organizations in T. Larkin (ed.), *New Zealand's External Relations* (1962). Wilson concludes that, despite the PMC being before pretty much in the dark over the true nature of affairs in Samoa, especially after the outbreak of Mau, 'there was hardly a single weakness' in New Zealand administration to which the PMC did not apply 'a sure if somewhat feline touch'. One may arguably suspect a Lugard initiative here.

38   A useful history of Samoa up to 1960, the eve of independence, is J.W. Davidson's *Samoa mo Samoa* (Samoa for the Samoans) (1967). A history don at St John's College, Cambridge, and a distinguished Pacific historian, Davidson had in 1947, on the invitation of the New Zealand Government, submitted a detailed but unpublished report on the past and potential administrative policy of Western Samoa. His mission and report were designed to provide a reliable brief for Governor Voelcker and his staff against the imminent arrival of the first UN Trust Territory Visiting Mission. At the back of one of her field notebooks (MSS 80/21) Margery listed a number of authorities whose writings she obviously had it in mind to consult. The most widely known writer on Samoa at the time was of course Robert Louis Stevenson, and Margery took along as an essential vademecum a copy of his *Vailima Letters* (which she mistakenly refers to as *Vai'lima Papers*), covering his years on the island from November 1890 to October 1894. These journal-letters, she commented in a manuscript note, 'cover in passionate detail every move in the conflict between the two royal houses of Samoa . . . and the intrigues and interventions of the [three Western] Consuls'.

39   HMS *Calliope*. The German ships *Adler* and *Eber* were sunk in the storm, together with the American vessels *Trenton* and *Vandaha*, while the German *Olga* and the American *Nipsic* were beached but later refloated.

40   Margery has a similar story of non-Western magnanimity. The New

Zealand Government once arrested a large number of 'rebellious Samoans and held them in a wired enclosure. The next day they discovered this camp had been broken into, not to facilitate a mass escape but to allow more Samoans to come in and keep their friends happy' (note attached to one of the revised versions of the diary).

41 The reference is to the Maji Maji war in German East Africa (1905–7) and to the Herero war in German South West Africa (1904–7). For further details see, respectively, John Iliffe, *Tanganyika under German Rule, 1905–1912* (1969), especially chapter 2, and Jon M. Bridgman, *The Revolt of the Hereros* (1981).

42 Wilhelm Solf (1862–1936) was the first Governor of German Samoa (1900–11). He was opposed to the appropriation of land by white settlers. Arguing that the colony was, like Togo, too small to depend entirely on a European plantation economy, he advocated partnership with the native producers in an integrated agricultural economy. The son of a Berlin industrialist, a scholar and an authority on Sanskrit, Solf went on to head Germany's *Reichskolonialamt* from 1911 to 1918 and then became Ambassador in Tokyo from 1920 to 1928. He was generally an Anglophile and specifically an admirer of Lugard, whom he visited in Nigeria on behalf of the German Colonial Office in 1913 and who presented him with a copy of his *Political Memoranda*, the confidential instructions to his political staff on native administration. These were, as it turned out, not made public until 1970! Solf was succeeded in Samoa by Erich Schultz-Ewerth, who was Governor when war broke out. His territory was at once occupied by New Zealand forces. It is relevant to recall Felix Keesing's judgement on Samoa's first governors, made twenty years after the German administration came to an end, that their rule had been 'experienced and scholar-guided' (*Modern Samoa*, 1934, p. 75). Both Solf and Schultz were Doctors of Philosophy. While in Africa, Margery took care to go back to and examine Dr Solf's speeches (MSS 81/22).

43 Although a lot of intimate information on the conduct of New Zealand's mandate of Samoa, which, as it turned out, formed the central part of Margery's research on this pre-African stage of her Rhodes Travelling Fellowship, emerges from the pages of her diary over the following six weeks, the scattered range of and frequent 'going back' to sources drawn on in New Zealand as well as in Samoa tend to make much of it diffuse and disconnected. A brief, consecutive note on Mau and its principal cast of Messrs Richardson and Nelson, on New Zealand's defence of her administration of Western Samoa before the Permanent Mandates Commission, and on the latter's turn-around from commendation to censure by the end of the first decade of the mandate is accordingly necessary to serve as background to the frequent addition of details of 'what I had come to discover' which provide the essence of the next hundred pages of her diary. New Zealand accepted the terms of a Class 'C' mandate (see part 1, note 56 above) for Western Samoa on December 17, 1920. In Wellington, Samoa was placed under the Ministry of External Affairs and not under the Ministry of Native Affairs and Cook Islands. Her administration was staffed by New Zealand bureaucrats seconded for up to

three years at a time from the home civil service. This was in sharp – and, as it turned out, sorry – contrast to Australia's comparable management of her mandated territory of New Guinea, where in as early as 1924 she had commissioned a special report from no less an authority than J. Ainsworth, CMG, formerly Chief Native Commissioner of Kenya, and went on to implement his proposals for establishing a system of Colonial Service-like career cadetships, with two years' probationary training in the field followed by a professional course in anthropology at the University of Sydney. The PMC, which, after the admission of Germany in 1926, consisted of ten members, met irregularly but generally twice a year (three times in 1926 and again in 1930) in Geneva. Sessions could extend to a whole month. New Zealand's first annual report on Western Samoa was submitted to the PMC's 2nd Session, held in August 1922. From then until the 16th Session (November 1929) – the climax of New Zealand's stewardship as far as this diary is concerned – Western Samoa regularly featured on the agenda. In passing, one may quote here a manuscript retrospective warning of Margery's, addressed to herself, on the mass of notes she had made from the PMC records for 1922–7 in Geneva, and later from the 16th Session (November 1929): 'Be careful not to quote what I could not have known!' (MSS 36/3, 50). At the 7th Session (October 1925) New Zealand succeeded in arousing the PMC's admiration for her 'broadminded' administration of Samoa, and was again commended at the 10th Session (November 1926). By the time the PMC assembled for its 19th Session (in November 1930, the year after Margery's Pacific journey), at which the unfavourable scrutiny of New Zealand's administration of her mandate for the period from 1926 to 1929 emerged as a major item on the agenda, the Commission was ready to take a very different view. Now they were of the opinion that, despite the 500-page report of the *ad hoc* 1927/8 New Zealand Royal Commission set up to inquire into the administration of Western Samoa following the Government's dissatisfaction with the record of General Richardson as Administrator (1923–8) and the outbreak of the Mau movement led by O.F. Nelson challenging his government of the island (reproduced in full, along with verbatim evidence, in the 1928 *Annual Report of the Government of the Dominion of New Zealand on the Administration of the Mandated Territory of Western Samoa*), the genesis of those troubles could not be said to have been fully identified; nor, clearly, had a solution been found. And once the Civil Service Commission Report of the New Zealand Government on 'The Finances and Staff of Western Samoa' (1929) had been communicated to the PMC in Geneva, the Commission lost no time in pointing to the hiatus 'in tone and tenor' (the phrase is Arnold J. Toynbee's) between the trenchant criticism in this report and the bland annual report on the territory's administration for the same period, written six months *after* the 'Finances and Staff' report. (There are lengthy summaries of these several reports, made by Margery on her visits to Geneva, in MSS 81/22.) The PMC at once publicly drew attention to these melancholy discrepancies (Minutes, 16th Session, pp. 207–8). While condemning 'the behaviour of the island's principal agitator, O.F. Nelson', it also expressed its belief that the administration had 'acted with great patience if not always with sufficient psychological insight'. The PMC implied that New Zealand had been at fault in imposing a system of administration 'without first carrying out a study of the traditions, customs and psychology of the native people'. One member went further, reproving the New Zealand accredited representatives, Sir Thomas Wilford and C. Berendsen, with the accusation that 'You are not governing the territory, you are sitting down and doing nothing'. It was these rebukes which caused Wilford subsequently to shrug off the charges as merely 'passing wrinkles on the brow of time'. Besides the extensive minutes of the Permanent Mandates Commission, there is a brief and useful account of New Zealand's appearance before the PMC sessions in J.V. Wilson's chapter in E.P. Walker's, *A History of the League of Nations* (1952) and again in T.C. Larkin (ed.), *New Zealand's External Relations* (1963). One final comment is of particular, and hitherto unsuspected, relevance to the present diary. To Professor Toynbee's long and detailed narrative of the PMC's examination of New Zealand's administration of Western Samoa for the crucial years 1926–9 (*Survey of Historical Affairs, 1929,* 1930, pp. 337–402) was added a two-page note headed 'Certain circumstances that might throw light on events in Western Samoa during the period under review'. It bears no authorship; it was 'communicated to the writer of the *Survey*'; and it was dated June 23, 1930. It is tempting, and far from implausible, to attribute this note to Margery. Such a dedication can be supported by the phrasing, thrust and content of a number of comments on the Samoan situation now made public for the first time in the present diary, e.g. the emphasis given to New Zealand's grave lack of any administrators trained along the lines of the British Colonial Service, the acknowledged sensitivities of the half-caste, and the insistence on the *radix malorum* being the strong personal antipathy existing between Richardson and Nelson.

44   The hotel was called the Casino. The German firm was the Hamburg Deutsche Handels-und-Plantagen Gesellschaft der Südsee-Inseln, founded in 1878 and generally known as DHPG. The territory's Administrator from 1928 to 1931 was Stephen S. Allen.

45   This is a remarkable, though none too rare, example of the exaggerated punctilio to which colonial society could lend itself. Superficially more reminiscent of the proverbial extremes of cantonment life under the Raj in India, in the event this was a New Zealand instance of gubernatorial formality. The wife of the British acting governor of Fiji was to behave little better.

46   The German gunboat SMS *Adler*, which had played a conspicuous role in the tridominium crisis of 1888 on Samoa, was one of the six ships reefed in the 'monumental' (Paul Kennedy) and 'stupendous' (Grattan) 100 m.p.h. hurricane of March 15, 1889, which blew for twenty-four hours across Apia Bay.

47   Throughout her life Margery was deeply affected by what today would be called the cause of 'animal rights'. She recorded her distress at a 'piscine tragedy' in the aquarium at Honolulu and again her concern on a sheep-shearing station in Australia. In later years she had phases of vegetarianism and wrote several letters to the press about – for example, the evil of battery hens (*The Guardian*, November 7, 1968).

48 Not surprisingly Margery, never one to spare herself, was beginning to feel the strain of her punishing itinerary, with its many moments of discomfort. When she at last reached Africa, she suffered severe bouts of illness. As she constantly revisited Africa throughout the 1930s, she just as regularly fell ill.

49 This outburst of *furor tropicalis* may perhaps have been as much attributable to her fraying nerves as to an upsurge of the 'colonial' racism she feared.

50 A memorable cameo of Margery stumbling on a secret meeting of the insurgent Mau in their 'no-go' forest headquarters and carrying it all off with a wave of the hand and a shouted hallo. This is in marked contrast to the threatening atmosphere she sensed at the Mau road-block later on. The 'official' Mau uniform (locally made by Nelson's import and export firm) was a violet *lava-lava* with white piping, worn with a white shirt.

51 This was Stephen Shepherd Allen (later knighted), appointed in the wake of the Richardson 'failure'. For the full gubernatorial succession, see the next note. The title, which Margery is technically incorrect to describe as governor, was changed from [resident] administrator to high commissioner in 1948. The appointment lay in the hands of the Governor-General of New Zealand.

52 General Sir George Stafford Richardson (1868–1938), whom Margery was to seek out and interview as soon as she arrived in New Zealand, was the country's third Resident Administrator of Western Samoa (1923–8). Richardson, who was born in Arundel, Sussex, had emigrated to New Zealand in 1891 as a gunnery instructor, after serving as a private in the British Army. By 1911 he had risen to the post of Director of Artillery, New Zealand, from where he gained admission to the Staff College, Camberley. He served with New Zealand troops in the First World War, earning no less than five military decorations. Unusually, he was one of the few resident administrators to learn Samoan – and within eighteen months, it was said! His diary is preserved in the national archives, Wellington (Dept of Island Territories, 1/33). A useful obituary appeared in the *New Zealand Herald* of June 13, 1938. Although Richardson's successor, Sir Stephen Allen (1925–31), was also a military man, the office was a civilian one from 1920, coming under the Ministry of External Affairs. Nevertheless, the New Zealand Government continued to appoint military men right up to 1935.

53 R.L. Stevenson bought the 300-acre property in January 1890 for £400, naming it Vailima after the three streams and two waterfalls that flowed through it from Mount Vaea. In some of his earliest descriptions of clearing the site, which lay along the clifftop 600 feet above Apia, he called it 'a home for angels'. Detailed descriptions of Vailima as it was in 1893 are to be found in the introduction by his stepson, Samuel Lloyd Osbourne (later US Vice-Consul in Samoa), to the Tusitala edition of Stevenson's works and in the memoir written with his sister, Isobel Strong, *Memoirs of Vailima* (1902). On Stevenson's death, Vailima was bought by the Vladivostock millionaire, Kunz. During the period of German overrule it became the official residence

of Governor Solf, at first rented but then bought by his successor Schultz-Ewerth for 150,000 marks. During the New Zealand occupation it housed Colonel Logan, the military administrator, and thereafter continued to serve as Government House.

54 Jim, whom I have not been able to identify, later wrote a letter to Margery, in which he said that, for all his knowledge of Samoa, he would never forget the twilight scene she and he had had the privilege to witness. In the original, but deleted from the revised version, Margery expressed how 'on the whole I was disappointed with the beauty of Samoa' (MSS 36/5, 1) – an impression that seems to have faded as time went by.

55 Small talk seldom stood out as one of Margery's social arts; she was in too much of a hurry to move on to 'facts and ideas'. Yet when she made up her mind to relax, she could do so as hard as she worked – and enjoy it just as much. Her diaries reveal her as always being ready for a game of tennis or bridge, and, less successfully, for golf or cricket.

56 A general conclusion in Geneva on the first decade of New Zealand's administration of Western Samoa was that it was well intentioned but totally lacking in any psychological insights, and had been handicapped by the poor quality of its personnel on the island.

57 In the original text Margery writes that the Samoans in Apia, unlike those of Pago Pago, were 'as near insolent as Samoans could be' (MSS 36/5, 58).

58 How right she was! Examples are too numerous to cite in full: occasions in Basutoland (*AA*, p. 98), South Africa (where she 'catechized Standard III', *AA*, p. 47), Kenya (*EAJ*, p. 75), and Tanganyika (where she 'made them all tell me how they would spend £100 if I gave it to them', *EAJ*, p. 69), and at Ibadan, Kano and Katsina in Nigeria (*WAP*, pp. 40, 64, 71 and 107), all within the next two years, must suffice as illustrations.

59 The London Missionary Society, which was founded in 1795, began its operations in the Pacific in 1797 when its ship *Duff* disembarked four clergymen in Matavai Bay. According to Alan Moorehead, the LMS was 'essentially a lower-middle-class organization made up of dissenting clergymen, of lay preachers and of respectable artisans and tradesmen who were Protestant to the core and who believed utterly in the Bible' (*The Fatal Impact*, p. 80). In C.H. Grattan's demonology, the LMS hated 'nudity, dancing, sex, drunkenness, anything savouring of *dolce far niente*, self-induced penury, war (except in God's name), heathenism and Roman Catholicism' (*The South West Pacific*, p. 197). Virtually all the Western Samoans, apart from a handful of Mormons and Catholics, were adherents of the Congregationalist LMS, known locally as the 'Church of Tahiti' because of its local historical roots. The first missionary, John Williams, landed on Savaii in 1830. He was later clubbed to death at Erromanga, New Guinea, and, *pace* the LMS history, was 'consumed by the natives' on November 20, 1839. Translation and publications in Samoan began in the same year, and a Missionary Institute was established at Malua in 1844.

60　Sixty years later the governments of the newly independent states were finding this incipient colonial dilemma of 'the diploma disease' just as intractable. Margery's interest in higher education overseas was to lead to her becoming a valued member of such bodies as the Colonial Office's Advisory Committee on Education in the Colonies, the Inter-University Council on Higher Education Overseas and the West Indies Higher Education Committee.

61　If the insensitivity of the Governor struck her at once, it was not long before she began to entertain doubts about the quality of the whole of the New Zealand staff posted to Samoa and their fitness to administer the mandate.

62　Yet this is where Margery, in collaboration with the Colonial Office Appointments Staff, essentially put her faith: cf. Sir Ralph Furse, *Aucuparius: Recollections of a Recruiting Officer* (1962), *passim*; the report of the Warren Fisher *Committee on the System of Appointments in the Colonial Service* (Cmd 3554, 1930); and her own confession of such faith in, for instance, her Introduction to Robert Heussler's *Yesterday's Rulers: The Making of the British Colonial Service* (1963).

63　Margery's condemnation reflects, perhaps not altogether by coincidence, the strictures of the 1927 New Zealand Royal Commission on the Samoan administration and the inferior quality of its staff.

64　Margery was probably not unaware of the fact that this was precisely what the Western Samoans had pleaded at a *faro* or council meeting to welcome the incoming Resident Administrator, Colonel R.W. Tate, in 1919: let us either be handed over to the American administration at Pago Pago or else be administered by the Colonial Office; but on no account by New Zealand. Six months later she was able to discuss with Sir Cecil Rodwell, who had been Governor of Fiji from 1918 to 1925, this idea of whether it might not have been better for the Western Samoans if the mandate had gone to Britain, with her trained and experienced Colonial Service, rather than to the New Zealanders, 'with no inkling of their own ignorance about native administration' (cf. Mary Boyd's assessment forty years later – 'Although the New Zealand public service lived in a biracial society, they had little experience of native administration' – in Ross, *New Zealand's Record*, p. 129). Rodwell told Margery that not only had he offered to help New Zealand during that initial period of the mandate but had 'actually found the right man for them, but they would accept neither help nor advice' (*AA*, p. 251). In Australia, things seemed to have been managed much better, for, following the recommendations of the Ainsworth report, the Department of Anthropology at the University of Sydney began to organize training courses for the cadet District Officers destined for New Guinea. The Department's respected journal, *Oceania*, served to support the now 'scientific' method of colonial administration based on anthropological appreciation – cf. William C. Groves, 'Anthropology and Native Administration in New Guinea', *Oceania* (September 1935), 94–104. Later, a School of Pacific Administration was established at the University of Sydney, whose aims were 'teaching, training and research in colonial affairs'. At the time, Margery was thinking of some kind of exchange system whereby British colonial administrators could be seconded for service in Western

Samoa while New Zealand officials were being trained in the United Kingdom.

65   Nevertheless, an outline is essential here. The armed Mau (Margery's own explanation of the word, in a manuscript note, is that it means 'testimony, in the sense of criticism'; C.H. Grattan has preferred 'opinion') rebellion dominated the years 1927-9, and was followed by a period of passive resistance to the Western Samoan Government. The *O Le Mau* or Samoan League was formed in 1927, its object being 'to endeavour to procure by lawful means the alteration of any matter affecting the laws, government or constitution of the territory which may be considered prejudicial to the welfare and best interests of the people'. Its leader was the wealthy, half-caste trader, O.F. Nelson. He was banished from Samoa by Richardson and Mau was declared an illegal organization. A copra boycott ensued, several hundred Mau police took over and patrolled the streets of Apia dressed in their own uniform, and on February 21, 1928 the Resident Administrator summoned two New Zealand cruisers with a complement of marines. Four hundred Mau members were arrested in Apia. The administration then found it did not have the gaol facilities to accommodate all those arrested. Later, a noisy mass demonstration was held to welcome home the Mau's spokesman from among the traditional authorities, Tupua Tamasese, who had also been banished to the mainland. However, by far the most serious riot occurred on December 28, 1929, 'Black Saturday', when the Mau turned out in force to welcome back A.S. Smythe, one of its European leaders and the third deportee. The police (the force consisted of only one European inspector, one European sergeant, two local Europeans and twenty-five Samoans) tried to arrest Mata'utia, the organization's secretary, but they had previously been reduced to a state of helplessness through the pressures of family ties and taboos. The police now opened fire on the Mau procession (with a Lewis gun in support sited at police headquarters, it was alleged). Eleven Samoans and one European constable were killed, among whom was Chief Tupua Tamasese. The administration now turned its full force on the Mau. The *Dunedin* was recalled to Apia and a landing party of 150 sailors was sent to round up the Mau ringleaders. Yet in late 1929, when Margery visited Samoa, the rule of law and order was still thinly spread, even in the capital, Apia. It was not until the Labour Government was returned to power in New Zealand in 1935 that the legislation declaring Mau a seditious organization was repealed. Nelson had twice postponed his return to Apia and did not come back until May 20, 1933. Following the recommendations of an official goodwill visit from Wellington in 1936, the Livingstone-O'Brien report brought about constitutional changes in Western Samoa which made room for Mau participation in the government of Samoa. From then on, the Mau, which had probably provided some sort of psychological outlet for the Samoans, began to evince a nascent sense of national consensus: while it did not yet positively co-operate with the New Zealand administration, it no longer actively hindered it. In admitting in her *Times* articles that the Samoans, 'with all their charm, are not easy to rule' (other writers have preferred to call it a self-assured combination of pride and perversity) Margery happily quoted the local proverbs about how God had

created the Samoans first, the Tongans next, and last of all the white men and pigs. The adage is to be found inscribed on the inside back cover of one of her field notebooks (MSS 81/22). In their authoritative *Oxford History of New Zealand* (1981) W.H. Oliver and B.R. Williams sum up the Mau revolt as 'the Samoan fiasco', a public 'humiliation' for New Zealand in the first ten years of her mandate (p. 320).

66   A bull's-eye was a kind of hurricane lamp or policeman's lantern, so-called because of its thick lens.

67   Olaf Frederick Nelson was born in 1883 of a Swedish father and a Samoan mother. He was one of the three European members, along with Messrs Williams and Westbrooke, elected to the Western Samoan legislative council in 1923. He founded the O.F. Nelson and Company Ltd, the heir to the pre-war German copra trading firm, DHPG. Nelson soon established himself as the leader of the Samoan protests against the New Zealand administration. He had, it seems, been something of a professional protester ever since 1910 when, along with S.H. Meredith, he had petitioned the Reichstag for some form of local council for Western Samoa (a good source for his anti-government activities before the Mau rebellion is the historical section of the *Report of the Royal Commission Concerning the Administration of Western Samoa, 1927*, Wellington, 1928). Five out of the six wealthy and influential European members of the citizens' protest group who went on to join forces with an equal number of high-ranking Samoan *matai* or traditional titled family heads to form the Mau leadership were married to Samoan women. Besides Nelson, the Europeans included A.G. Smythe, S.H. Meredith, E.W. Gurr, A. Williams and G.E.W. Westbrooke. The immediate good relations between Nelson and the new Resident Administrator soon began to deteriorate, and Nelson assembled a long list of grievances which he planned to present to the New Zealand Minister of External Affairs, W. Nosworthy, who was due to visit Samoa in 1926. When, on Richardson's advice, this visit was postponed till the following June, Nelson organized a Samoan delegation to travel to Wellington. However, Richardson refused to issue them with passports. A Royal Commission under New Zealand's Chief Justice, Sir C.P. Skerrett, was appointed to investigate Nelson's complaints against the administration. In its report submitted in November 1927 it exonerated Richardson. In the following month Richardson issued a five-year deportation order on Nelson and Gurr, with two years for Smythe. Across in New Zealand, Nelson, who was active as a pamphleteer, deliberately courted Samoan sympathizers in the opposition Labour Party and formed the idea of leading a delegation to present the Samoans' case to the League of Nations. After visiting Geneva, where he had a mixed reception from the PMC, he returned to Apia on May 20, 1933, but on the orders of General Hart, the new administrator, who had declared that he would discuss the Samoans' demands only if Nelson were out of the way, he was quickly rearrested. He was sentenced to one year's imprisonment concurrently with a banishment order for ten years. However, when the Labour Government under M.J. Savage came into office in New Zealand in 1935, Nelson found no difficulty in returning to Samoa. He landed at Apia in July 1936, this time in triumph – and at public expense. In 1934, one of his

daughters, Irene, married the brother of Tupua Tamasese, who had been killed in the Mau riot of December 28, 1928. Nelson died in 1944, and two years later his long-time promotion of the Samoans' cause culminated in a petition for self-government sent in November 1946 to the new United Nations and the consequent dispatch by the Trusteeship Council of a UN Visiting Mission to Samoa in 1947. Widespread local reforms in New Zealand's administration at once followed, and after the visit of the Second UNTC mission (T/792, dated August 15, 1950) and then more triennial visiting missions, Samoa became independent on January 1, 1962. For Margery's meeting with Nelson, see pp. 126 ff. One recalls that in his South Pacific short story *Rain* Somerset Maugham, *mutatis mutandis*, introduces the character of Fred Ohlson, 'a Danish trader who had been in the islands a good many years. He was a pretty rich man as traders go and he wasn't very pleased when we came. You see, he'd had things very much his own way. . . . He had a native wife. . . .'

68   As the *Oxford History of New Zealand* shows, New Zealand's fear of the 'Yellow Peril' was almost as unrelenting a racial dread as that reflected in her neighbour's 'White Australia' policy. Resident Administrator Logan is on record as having once advocated a policy of Samoan racial purity – but for Chinese, not Whites!

69   Although, as a 'C' mandate, the territory was not required to have an open-door policy for citizens of the former colonial power, they were not automatically kept out. In Tanganyika, with her enforced open-door policy as a 'B' mandate, the number of German settlers who returned after was understandably much higher than Samoa's handful. There by 1930 they had acquired as much as 20 per cent of the total agricultural land 'owned' by European settlers.

70   One cannot but be struck by the generous attitude shown by the several governors to a researcher who made no bones that she had come to inquire into the suspect quality of their administration – 'an inquisitive and critical young woman', as she described herself. Margery was sensitive enough to be worried by the thought of criticizing those who were not only her courteous and necessary hosts but on whose goodwill and co-operation she depended. One of her very few contretemps with service officials during the whole two years of her Rhodes Travelling Fellowship was with Major Eric A.T. Dutton, the well-known local mountaineer whose *Kenya Mountain* had just been published in 1929. Many years later she was to find among the Oldham papers a note from Dutton which prescribed *his* recipe: 'Margery Perham ought to be boiled in oil.'

71   Perhaps her understanding of German was at fault, and what she read as evidence of descent from the Plantagenets was a notice proclaiming that Nelson and Co. were the successors to the pre-1914 German copra-buying firm Deutsche Handels-und-Plantagen Gesellschaft.

72   Part of the blame for the influenza outbreak in Western Samoa in 1918 has been placed by historians on the reluctance of the respective medical

authorities to notify each other and so quarantine the ship *Talune* on her arrival in Apia from Auckland, in contrast to the strict health measures taken when she berthed at Pago Pago.

73 As will be seen, it is indeed the slightest and least informative section of this diary. Significantly, in the résumés of her Pacific travels which preface both her subsequent diaries (*AA*, p. 27 and *EAJ*, p. 12), Margery mentions Fiji as no more than a stopover in her itinerary. Exceptionally for her, Margery does not seem to have penetrated much beyond the colonial society, and, unlike in Samoa or New Zealand, for once we have no record of vehement policy discussions with top officials or vigorous talks with nationalist leaders. Indeed, there is not even a mention of the already prominent Fijian, Ratu Sir J. Lala V. Sukuna (1888–1956), who had graduated from Wadham College, Oxford, a few years after Margery had taken her BA, was by now a Member of the Legislative Council, and fifteen years later became Secretary of Fijian Affairs and ultimately Speaker of the Legislative Council in 1956 (for a biography, see Deryck Scarr, *Ratu Sukuna: Soldier, Statesman and Man of Two Worlds*, 1980). Margery's cool reception at Government House may have contributed to this 'failure'.

74 The original diary has 'utmost coldness' (36/6, 26).

75 This American criticism of British colonial officialdom, which clearly still rankled with her, is quoted on p. 73. Fiji had been a Crown Colony since 1874.

76 This was the interregnum between the governorships of Sir Eyre Hutson (1925–9) and Sir (A.G.) Murchison Fletcher (1929–36). Up to 1952 the Governor of Fiji was at the same time High Commissioner of the Western Pacific. Margery just missed Sir Cecil Rodwell in Government House, Suva (1918–25), but in the following February he invited her to dinner at Government House, Salisbury. 'I had heard strange things of this establishment,' she noted in her diary, 'and the stories were not exaggerated' (*AA*, p. 248).

77 The person she met was probably the Chief Clerk in the Colonial Secretary's Department, a Mr C.W.T. Johnson. The original reads slightly differently: 'The Governor was away, the Acting Governor on tour, and the Chief Secretary off for the day' (MSS 36/6, 3).

78 There is a copy of the standard Colonial Office letter of introduction in the Rhodes Trust files (2695). However, Margery had cause to complain to Lord Lothian in her first official report submitted to the Trustees that the copy the Colonial Office sent to her was not typed on headed paper, so that 'its appearance was very unconvincing'. She concluded succinctly: 'Fiji officials kindly took me on trust.'

79 In the original, we are told that Bishop (?) was one of these juniors, now 'a very small cub' in the Secretariat, and 'already seething with discontent' (MSS 36/6, 9). (See reference to G.W. Bishop in n. 3 above.)

80 Of these 'Big Four' commercial members on the Legislative Council, two

were knights and one a CBE. The most important were the representatives of the Colonial Sugar Refining Company, operating since the 1870s, and of Lever's Pacific Plantations Ltd. The former also operated on a big scale in Australia. Other leading names in the commercial sector were the Hennings brothers and Burns Philp and Lever, known locally as 'The Octopus'.

81   Unexpectedly, Margery does not mention that Government House had just been restored (in the very year of her visit) after the original building had been struck by lightning and burnt down some six years earlier. The Botanical Gardens adjoin Government House, and a street away lies Albert Park, a great recreation centre for cricket and football.

82   It seems that Petronius, though still very much a newcomer to the colony, had quickly succumbed to the colonial disease of gossip and backbiting. One admires Margery's social courage, without necessarily applauding her social grace, in refusing a 'command' invitation from Government House. The lady in question was possibly Mrs A.W. Seymour, wife of the Colonial Secretary, who would be acting pending the arrival of the new governor.

83   In origin, bach is especially a New Zealand term, used for a seaside cottage. The 'batch' here was obviously the Suva equivalent of the commonplace 'chummery' of Anglo-India and the Far East, where the newcomers (almost by definition bachelors) to government service as well as in the commercial firms would share a large house and pool resources in a common mess. There are interesting glimpses of the Suva 'Batch' in June Knox-Mawer (ed.), *Tales From Paradise* (1986), pp. 18–19.

84   Namely J.E. Caughley. This particular educationalist was, in Margery's book, clearly an improvement on his predecessor. New Zealand's considerable contribution to education in the Pacific is usefully described in C.W. Mann, *Education in Fiji* (1935), and in the chapter by F.R.J. Davies in Ross, *New Zealand's Record*, pp. 271–99.

85   In Fiji the CSR Company had nearly 150,000 acres under its control. In 1936 it initiated a schame at Drasa to train Fijian youths how to grow sugar.

86   At the time Gandhi was already well known to Indians for his launching of a cloth-spinning *khadi* campaign and his espousal of a non-co-operation movement (*satyagraha*) in 1920–2, which was followed by his release from prison in 1924. His famous salt march did not take place till the year following Margery's visit to Fiji.

87   The Wesleyan experiment was situated at Ravielan. Wesleyans had been in Fiji for nearly a hundred years, having first landed at Lakemba in 1835. The Methodists (Wesleyans), and to a lesser extent the Roman Catholics, dominated the education scene in Fiji. It was not until the implementation of the proposals put forward by the Education Commission of 1926 that the Government set up its own Department of Education and, two years later, appointed the first director.

88   Following the recommendations of the New Zealand trade commission to Samoa in 1920, the Government agreed to import up to 5,000 labourers from

China (the Germans had already established a precedent in the islands by Solf's importation of 2,000 Chinese indentured labourers at the turn of the century). The indenture system was strictly controlled and a Chinese commissioner was appointed. It came to an end in the mid-1930s under the Labour Government in Wellington.

89 Indentured Indian labour in Fiji grew from 600 in 1880 to 60,000 in 1917, when the system was terminated. By 1929, when Margery visited Fiji (and the year in which an Indian, Badri Mahraj, was for the first time elected to the Legislative Council), the Indian population had reached 70,000. Already by the time of Margery's visit, the Indian population was well on its way to equalling that of native-born Fijians, some 80,000 each. The Fijian population had declined severely in the decades following cession in 1874, registering 105,000 in 1892 and only 85,000 in 1911, but by the 1970s it was back to well over 200,000. As with the East African case, it was a matter of considerable local argument whether the Indian population was essentially made up of low-caste Hindu coolies or whether there was a goodish element of better class artisans.

90 Dr Ivor H. Beattie. He appears in June Knox-Mawer (ed.), *Tales From Paradise* (1986). I am grateful to P.A. Snow for this identification and for his help with the names of several Fijian characters of the time.

91 The Secretary for Indian Affairs was J.R. Pearson, CIE, who had retired from the Indian Civil Service in 1926.

92 The racial problem, which over the years generated the colloquial labelling of Fiji as 'The Little India of the Pacific' (the title was used by J.W. Coulter in his book published in 1942), had by no means disappeared as Fiji approached independence in the 1960s. In his study of Fiji (1963), Sir Alan Burns had identified the two main anxieties of the incipient new nation as a shortage of land and a surplus of Indian immigrants (p. 224). By the time of independence, in 1970, Indians totalled almost half the population of approximately 500,000. The new Fijian Government took a firm line and set about constitutionally excluding them from any proportionate rule in the administration, civil service and armed forces, with the result that a gradual emigration of the Indian population began to take place. In the first decade of Fiji's independence no less than 15,000 of the 250,000 Indians in the country (the total had grown from 60,000 in 1921 through 90,000 in 1938 and on to 135,000 by the end of the war) emigrated to Canada. The turbulent events of 1987 have brought ethnic rivalry to a head.

3 NEW ZEALAND

1 The *Tofua*.

2 This was Faumuina, one of the royal scions, who succeeded Tamasese as President of the Mau movement after the latter's death in the 1929 riot in Apia. In the shadow Cabinet of *Samoa mo Samoa* envisaged by Nelson, Faumuina

was to have been appointed Chief of Police. He is described in further detail shortly.

3   Probably Professor Siegerfors from Minnesota. In the original, Margery records that he ended up at the same hotel as she did in Auckland.

4   On the Southampton–New York voyage in June.

5   Another instance of Margery's characteristic dislike of anything that seemed to be beating about the bush, quite without regard as to how far such directness might possibly prejudice her chance of obtaining further information. As she notes later in her diary in regard to her 'direct approach' methods: 'I should never make a good journalist.'

6   Soon after Margery's visit, Faumuina returned to Upolu. He was seriously injured in the 'Black Saturday' riot of December 28, 1929. Margery believed this incident marked the point of no return in Samoan–New Zealand relations.

7   It seems that as Margery was writing up her diary on board the *Tofua* she looked out of her porthole and saw the RMS *Maunganui*, a much larger ship which operated on the Wellington–Sydney–San Francisco run, 'standing on her prow' in the storm.

8   Sir George Grey (1812–98) was only thirty-eight when he embarked on the first of his twenty years as Governor (1845–53 and 1861–7) and then Prime Minister (1877–9), thus going down as the outstanding figure in New Zealand's nineteenth-century history. In between times, he was Governor of South Australia (1841–5), Governor of Cape Colony (1853–61), and publisher of a collection of Maori legends. Interestingly, in view of her discussion (p. 128) on imperial policy and race relations with the Maoris, and of her subsequent commitment as a leading publicist of the theory of indirect rule, Margery does not mention Grey's own major contribution to this particular form of native administration. The allusion to Grey's 'reputedly disreputable home' is to the harem he was believed to have maintained on Kawai Island. She later refers to his reputation for 'moral delinquencies'. In Sir Keith Sinclair's assessment, Grey 'was such a strange mixture of man and superman that his career has had a never-failing fascination for posterity'.

9   Margery drew a little cartoon in her original diary (MSS 37/1).

10   This was during one of the League of Nations Mandates Commission sessions which Margery tells us (*EAJ*, p. 12) she had attended as an observer to help in the preparation of her course of lectures at Oxford. When the New Zealand Government realized that matters in Samoa were not going to improve as long as the deepening antagonism continued between Richardson and Nelson, they appointed a new Resident Administrator (Allen) in March 1928 and sent Richardson to Geneva as their delegate to the PMC. Ironically, Nelson, too, made his way to Geneva for the same session, to present the Samoan case for the transfer of the mandate from New Zealand to Great Britain. Although Nelson was able to meet and talk with some of the members unofficially, the PMC declined to let him appear before it on the grounds that he was not an accredited representative and that the PMC was not empowered

to receive oral petitions, only written representations. Nor would the Privy Council grant him an audience when he travelled on to London to plead the Samoan case before the King. On his return he published in 1928 two pamphlets, *Samoa at Geneva: Misleading the League of Nations* and *The Truth about Samoa*, including his letter of protest to the League over his exclusion, written in London on October 2, 1928, and a photograph of himself (O Tatsi).

11 Somewhat prematurely, in the light of the Mau outbreak, both the New Zealand Government and the Permanent Mandates Commission expressed themselves highly commendatory of Richardson's tenure of office in 1926. On the strength of this, his appointment was extended by two years. In the middle of it, Mau erupted.

12 In September 1927 the New Zealand Government set up a Royal Commission under the Chief Justice to inquire into the failure of the administration of Western Samoa as evidenced by the outbreak of the Mau resistance movement. To a considerable extent, the Commission vindicated the administration in its lengthy report. No sooner was this made public than Richardson deported the two European leaders of Mau, Nelson and A.G. Smythe.

13 Sadly, Nelson's prediction was only too accurate, for four months later the police opened fire in Apia and killed a number of Samoans.

14 The Permanent Mandates Commission had had its request for more powers rejected. Sir Austen Chamberlain (1863–1937) was British Foreign Secretary from 1924 to 1929, and was awarded the Nobel Peace Prize for his part in negotiating the 1925 Locarno Pact. Aristide Briand (1862–1932) was Prime Minister of France no less then eleven times between 1925 and 1932, and was also a Nobel Peace Prize winner, in 1926. His government fell on March 6, 1926, two days before the Special Assembly of the League of Nations opened in Geneva to consider the admission of Germany as its fifty-sixth member.

15 The Samoa Defence League had been set up in Auckland by A. Hall-Skelton, Nelson's legal adviser. It worked closely with the Mau office in Auckland, where Nelson settled following his banishment from Samoa in 1928, and together they organized a number of mass meetings calling for the release of Tamasese, the rescindment of all deportation orders, and a round-table conference in Wellington between the Government of New Zealand, Nelson and Tamasese. The SDL printed and circulated a large number of pamphlets and contributed a steady flow of articles, letters and general propaganda statements to the press. It also started to publish a powerful propaganda weekly, the *New Zealand Samoa Guardian*, successor to Nelson's own *Samoa Gazette* which he had established in 1927 as a counterweight to the pro-Government weekly *Samoa Times*. Nelson found much support among the Labour Party led by H.E. Holland, who himself supported the Mau cause in the press and on public platforms, including Parliament. It was from this triple alliance that, after that tragic 'Black Saturday' of December 28, 1929, the Permanent Mandates Commission began to be bombarded with requests for

the mandate to be transferred to Great Britain, or failing that, to the United States and so lead to independence for a reunited Samoa. In 1931 they even sent similar petitions to the three powers who had signed the Berlin Act of 1889 which had brought about the original partition of Samoa.

16   For a more sympathetic portrait of Nelson, but again ascribing the root of his personal problem to the burden of his half-caste status (Margery's own diagnosis, too), see Mary Boyd's description:

> As one of the wealthiest and most influential members of the Apia community, he was alienated by New Zealand's policy of racial discrimi-nation, which threatened his commercial interests, denied him the right to a voice in Samoan affairs, and deprived him of his whisky. His family home at Tuaefu, with its fine private library, lavish entertainments and open-hearted hospitality, rivalled Vailima as a social and cultural centre for all sections of the community. Yet the official stereotype of the 'half-caste' as 'the dregs of civilisation' made it impossible for him to achieve the social and political standing to which he aspired. (Angus Ross (ed.), *New Zealand's Record in the Pacific Islands in the 20th Century*, 1969, p. 147.)

When Sir Henry Luke visited Samoa in 1938 on his way to take up his appointment as Governor of Fiji and High Commissioner for the Western Pacific, he met not only Nelson, 'for many years past the stormy petrel of Samoan politics' but now a member of Legislative Council, but his two daughters, one married to a Samoan chief and the other practising as a barrister in New Zealand (*From a South Seas Diary*, 1945, ch. IV).

17   One hopes that among them was S.H. Meredith's popular tract, *Western Samoa (Formerly German Samoa): How New Zealand Administers the Mandate for the League of Nations* and Nelson's own 95-page *The Truth about Samoa* (1928), together with his shorter *Samoa at Geneva* (1929).

18   In a manuscript note, Margery, invoking Rewi Maniapoto's testament cited in G. Henderson's life of Sir George Grey (1907), admiringly asked 'Would any other fighting chief of a conquered native people ask that his bones be buried in the same grave as his conqueror?' The Maori authority Elsdon Best had a similar tale of Maori chivalry in war to tell her. She may also have been aware of Raymond's Firth's classic analysis of pre-European Maori culture, *Primitive Economies of the New Zealand Maori*, which was published in the year of Margery's visit.

19   The Arotia (properly Aotea, Aotearoa), taken from the Maori term 'The Long White Cloud' – which William Pember Reeves was to adopt for the title of his pioneering story of New Zealand, first published in 1898 – was one of the principal Maori ancestors, who reached New Zealand (Tiritiri o te Moana, 'The Ocean's Gift') in large ocean-going canoes a millennium or so ago. The Young Maori Party, which was to effect such a transformation in the welfare of the Maori people through self-help and adaptation, aiming at integration with the Pakehas or 'Whites' rather than pursuing a policy of separate autonomy, grew out of the efforts of a group of young professional men graduating from

the famous Te Aute College. This had been founded at Hawkes Bay in 1854 by Samuel Williams, who in 1891 went on to establish the Association for the Amelioration of the Maori Race. Six years later he created the Te Aute College Students' Association. Its organizing secretary was Apira Ngata, its medical officers Pomare and Buck (qq.v., p. 166), and its foundation members included a group of other prominent Maoris (listed at length in the *Oxford History of New Zealand*, p. 288). Buck was to examplify the ideology of Pomare's cultural slogan that 'There is no alternative but to become a Pakeha' (see Thomas K. Fitzgerald, *Education and Identity: A Study of the New Zealand Maori Graduates*, 1977). The YMP soon found itself yielding its popularity to a new Maori movement, the Ratana church. In 1931 a Ratana candidate, Eruera Tirikatene, won one of the Maori seats in Parliament, and within a few years Ratana adherents had secured all four Maori seats. It was not until 1947, under the Fraser government, that 'Maori' replaced 'native' in New Zealand's official usage.

20   The Treaty of Waitangi, 'The Waters of Lamentation', was signed on February 6, 1840; by it New Zealand became a British possession. Since 1960, Waitangi Day has been commemorated in New Zealand by a message to the nation from the Governor-General. The date of 1856–65 for the war that put a final *finis* to Maori resistance is more usually taken as the war of 1863–5 or 1860–1, though in his account of New Zealand's wars (1922) the prolific James Cowan does describe the whole period from 1845 to 1872 as that of the Maori Wars. See Keith Sinclair's classic study, *The Origin of the Maori Wars* (1957).

21   By the Ellis Islands Margery meant the Ellice portion of what had been known as the Gilbert and Ellice Islands since their annexation, as a protectorate in 1892 and then as a colony from 1915. They separated in 1975, and the Ellice Islands, renamed Tuvalu, became independent in 1978. The Gilbert Islands, now called Kiribati, followed suit a year later. The Cook Islands eventually became a British protectorate between 1898 and 1901 and were then annexed to New Zealand in 1901 and placed under a resident commissioner. They obtained internal self-government in 1965. The Tokelaus, a group of islands some 400 miles north of Samoa, became a British protectorate in 1877 and until 1899 were the responsibility of the Deputy Commissioner in Apia. During Samoa's German period, the Tokelaus were detached and in 1916 were annexed as the Union Islands and brought under the general authority of the British Governor of Fiji wearing his other hat as Commissioner of the Western Pacific. In 1925 the British Government asked New Zealand to assume responsibility for the administration of the islands, and the Resident Administrator of Samoa now oversaw the government of the Tokelau Islands. The name Tokelau officially dates only from 1946.

22   The figures quoted in the authoritative *Oxford History of New Zealand* give a Maori population of 42,113 in 1896 (its lowest ever), climbing to 56,987 in 1921 and, in 1951, reaching 115,000, the same total it had registered in the 1840s.

23   *Pa* is properly the Maori term for a stockade or fortified place.

24 Margery's papers and personalia provide substantial evidence of her passion for amateur photography. After her death in 1982, her nephew and niece came across literally a whole suitcase of snapshots taken by her on her travels. Unfortunately, there were far fewer of the Atlantic and Pacific sectors of her Rhodes Travelling Fellowship (and far fewer references in the text of 'snapping' people and places) than in the subsequent African passages.

25 *Whare*, house; *poi*, dance; *haka*, song.

26 The stringent labour law insisted that no servant should be expected to serve a meal after 7.30 p.m. (cf. Australia's labour unions' success of its Eight Hour Movement: eight for work, eight for recreation, eight for rest). Such a restriction was linked in the public mind with the legislation which, from 1914 to 1967, required all public bars to close at 6 p.m., thereby giving rise to the barbarous New Zealand custom of 'the six o'clock swill' (commonly known in Australia, where similar closing laws obtained, as 'the five o'clock swill'). Such legislation was needed, according to one line of entrepreneurial argument, to promote the stunted growth of licensed restaurants (outside those belonging to hotels) in New Zealand's cities. Hence the hoary Australian chestnut about the girl who, returning from a week spent travelling in North and South Islands, was asked what she thought of New Zealand. 'I don't know,' she replied. 'It was closed.'

27 This reference is one of the few dates immediately identifiable in this diary, i.e. September 6.

28 The *Encyclopaedia of New Zealand* coyly comments that the name Urewera 'commemorates a painful mishap' which befell the son of a sixteenth-century Maori chief. It means, literally, 'burnt penis'.

29 From time to time the New Zealand Government took measures to balance up either the occupational categories of immigrants (e.g. the ex-public schoolboy farmers mentioned shortly) or the sex ratios (e.g. the calculated increase of women in the 1920s). The non-Maori population grew from under 750,000 in 1890 to 1.5 million in 1940 and about 3 million in 1980. In general, New Zealand immigrants, though poor, have been said to represent the upper working or lower middle class (Edward Wakefield's 'anxious classes'), whose ambition was not so much to destroy any disliked social superiors but, in Sir Keith Sinclair's phrase, 'to equalize upwards'. The pioneers, he concludes, aimed at 'creating a society which was classless because everyone was middle class' (*A History of New Zealand*, p. 102).

30 *Tangi* is the Maori word for a funeral ceremony and all its integral social obligations.

31 Lasting intermittently for a decade, the Maori Wars included both the King movement (Kingitangi) of the mid-1850s and the Hau Hau uprising of the mid-1860s, so-called from the warriors' incantation when under fire as a protection against bullets – see W.P. Reeves's romantic chapter 'The Fire in the Fern' in his *The Long White Cloud* (1898). But it is the specific phase from 1862 to 1865 that usually describes the last Maori War. In this, which was centred

on the Urewera country, the protest was led by the prophet Te Ua Haumene, founder of the Pai Marire separatist movement, 'The Good and Peaceful Religion'.

32 In 1916.

33 Margery has illustrated the original with a neat pen and paint sketch of this unusual congregation (MSS 37/1, 51).

34 She was probably thinking of an apophthegm attributed to King James I of England and VI of Scotland by Archdeacon Plume: 'Dr Donne's verses are like the peace of God; they pass all understanding.'

35 This is unclear on two counts. First, there is no hint as to why Margery should have been 'turned out'; rather, it had been Margery's own idea to 'improve relations' and ride out after the pastor. A comparison with the original suggests that two lines have been inadvertently omitted. Second, only on this page come the first references to any companion or the morning ride or to the unexplained shift from 'I' at the start of the ride to 'we' and 'us' later in the day. It is possible that her companion was the teacher for Te Whaiti referred to earlier, though she is not mentioned in any detail until the next paragraph – and then not too kindly!

36 In fact, the Rewa sect at Maungapohatu had been at its most active a decade earlier when, in what has been called 'the last shooting of the Anglo-Maori wars', armed police entered the Urewera in 1916 and two of the sect's followers were killed. Rua (Rewa) Kenana was arrested. His prophecies included that of a visit from King Edward VII, who would bring with him enough money to enable the Maoris to buy back all their lost lands from the Pakehas. Nearer the time of Margery's visit another, and in the end more influential, breakaway Church was started by Tapupotiki Wiremu Ratana. He started preaching at his *pa* at Wanganu in 1918, and within a few years his separatist movement had become the second largest Maori independent Church. By the end of the decade, the Ratana, which now moved from religion into politics, was able to claim the adherence of every Maori MP. Ratana died in 1939.

37 Like the Polynesian *tapu* (taboo), the Maori word *mana*, indicating mysterious personal power and an aura of prestige, has become an accepted part of the standard English vocabulary.

38 Fortunately, the situation has much improved over the past fifty years. See, for instance, J.M. Henderson's *Ratana: The Man, the Church, the Political Movement* (1972). A good study of Hau Hau is Peter Clark's *The Pai Marire Search for Maori Identity* (1975).

39 This was probably Mrs Staples Brown, who had studied anthropology in London and had been entertained in College by the Principal, Miss Barbara Gwyer, and Margery in the Hilary term of 1929. On her return to New Zealand, as Margery goes on to describe, she became a leading interpreter of Maoridom.

40   As Margery expressed it in her original diary, 'She now bears the name but not, apparently, the man' (MSS 37/11, 65).

41   The original Ringatu religion had been founded in 1870 by Te Koati. Though his link with the Hau Hau movement was never proved, he was – like Kenyatta and the Mau Mau in Kenya some eighty years later – convicted of such an association. On his escape from imprisonment on the Chatham Islands, his adherents carried out a massacre of settlers round Poverty Bay. In the decade immediately preceding Margery's visit, another Ringatu-like movement had sprung up in the stormy district of Urewera, when the Ringatu answered the call of a messianic leader named Rua Kenana.

42   These made up the impressive Maori establishment of the period. Sir James Carroll (1857–1926), part-Maori and part-Irish, represented a European-designated seat in Parliament from 1893 to 1918. From 1900 to 1912 he was the first Maori to hold the office of Minister for Island Affairs, a post which was then to be held successively by Maoris throughout the next quarter of a century. Sir Maui Pomare (1876–1930) went on from Te Aute College to take a medical degree in the United States and then became the first Maori health officer. He was Minister for Island and Native Affairs from 1912 to 1928 in Coates's reform government and author of *The Maori Past and Present*. Sir Apiriana Ngata (1874–1950), who graduated in law from Canterbury University College and had been the first Organizing Secretary of the Maori Committee at the turn of the century and then an MP since 1905, had just taken over as Minister for the Cook Islands and Native Affairs at the time of Margery's visit. He had also recently published an article, 'Anthropology and the Government of Native Races in the Pacific', in *New Zealand Affairs*. A prolific scholar, one of his last publications was a commentary on the Treaty of Waitangi, *Te Tiriti O Waitangi*. The only name omitted from Margery's list of contemporary eminent Maoris, all graduates of Te Aute College, the Anglican School for Maoris at Hawkes Bay and, significantly, all knighted, is Sir Peter Buck (1875–1951), athlete, soldier, scholar and legislator.

43   The shadow of steely, sooty Sheffield, where Margery had taken up her first academic appointment in 1917 and where three years later she was to suffer a nervous breakdown, was obviously still haunting her. In a radio broadcast forty years later, she could still vividly recapture the oppressive atmosphere of 'winter slush and the clanging trams' (BBC Radio 4, January 11, 1970), and the cheap lodgings on the edge of the city, to which she unwillingly returned every evening after class, alighted at the nearest tram stop, 'walked half a mile, and sat down to the piece of steak and pudding, both of which I had cut into four portions to last for four days'. Her sole recreation was to 'walk out on to the rather grim moorland and sit down amongst the wiry, inhospitable heather which was grimed with soot, and contemplate, physically and mentally, the dark bare horizon'.

44   Like all the best College tutors, Margery took an almost possessive interest in the performance of her pupils in their final examinations – and a related pride in the reliability of one's own predictions! The first was probably that gained by E.M. Tostevin, one of the two women among the nineteen

firsts awarded in the Modern History Schools in 1929. Another of Margery's pupils recalls of her tutor that she was 'young, energetic and full of vitality for emergent Africa'. She was also 'reputed to have shot a lion and published a novel . . . none of which qualities impaired her scholarly integrity' – Renée Haynes, quoted in Penny Griffin (ed.), *St Hugh's: One Hundred Years of Women's Education in Oxford* (1986), p. 94.

45   Here there is a gap in the manuscript.

46   The principal figures in contemporary New Zealand politics frequently mentioned by Margery over the next thirty pages of her diary were as follows. William Ferguson Massey ('Farmer Bill', 1850–1925) was leader of the Reform Party and had been Prime Minister from 1912 to 1925. A slogan attributed to him is that New Zealand was the outlying farm of the Empire. Local tradition has it that when the telegram inviting this Auckland farmer arrived, it had to be handed up on a pitchfork to 'Farmer Bill' who was busy working on a haystack. Massey was succeeded in 1925 by Gordon Coates (1878–1943), also of the Reform Party. Winning on the slogan of 'Coats off for Coates', and later known as the 'Never Again PM', he was voted out of office the year before Margery reached New Zealand. Sir Joseph Ward (1856–1930) of the Liberal Party came to power in the general election of 1928, sixteen years after his previous spell as Prime Minister (1906–12). On his death in 1930, George William Forbes succeeded him as leader of the Liberals.

47   The story is that Ward, misreading his notes, promised the electorate he would be able to borrow £70 million from Great Britain immediately instead of the actual figure of £7 million p.a. over the next ten years. 'The error', Len Richardson comments succinctly in his chapter on 'Parties and Political Change' in the *Oxford History of New Zealand*, 'won the election' (p. 219).

48   C.A. (later Sir Carl) Berendsen (1890–1973) had just taken over as Secretary of External Affairs when the Mau disturbances erupted in Samoa in 1928. He had himself served there with the occupying New Zealand troops during the Great War. He had also been a member of the three-man commission of inquiry into the record of Samoa's administration under Richardson, which reported in 1929. In 1931 Berendsen was New Zealand's accredited representative to the Permanent Mandates Commission, and in 1932 became head of the Prime Minister's Department in Wellington, an office he held till 1943. Later he became Ambassador to the United States and New Zealand Representative at the United Nations, where it fell to him, on April 22, 1947, formally to invite the newly established Trusteeship Council to send a visiting mission to Western Samoa in accordance with his country's acceptance of the principle of international trusteeship.

49   Beachcombers, a common feature of the Pacific trade, were local resident Whites who acted as agents for visiting trading vessels. In the Colonial Office and Colonial Service circles in which Margery was soon to move so influentially, the term grew up to describe the officers who were from time to time seconded from the field (service) to Whitehall (office).

50   By signing the optional clause attached to the Protocol of Signature of the

Statute of the Permanent Court of International Justice, which came into being on December 16, 1920, a state declared its acceptance of the Court's jurisdiction in disputes of a certain defined character. However, flexibility lay in the 'all or any' listing of the four classes of dispute enumerated. In 1928 efforts were reopened to induce more states to accept the compulsory jurisdiction of the Court.

51   This was the occasion when, in February 1928, the Resident Commissioner, finding himself unable to maintain law and order in the face of the Mau boycott, requested armed assistance from the New Zealand Government. HMS *Dunedin* and *Diomede* were dispatched to Apia with a force of marines.

52   Philip Bouverie Bowyer Nichols (1894–1962) entered the British Diplomatic Service in 1920, having won the MC in the war. He was a year older than Margery, his birthday falling on the day after hers. In 1928 he was seconded to New Zealand for two years, the first of the new liaison officer posts created on the recommendation of the Imperial Relations Committee of the 1926 Imperial Conference. The consequent 'Balfour formula', confirmed in the 1931 Statute of Westminster, *inter alia* enabled the dominions, now *de facto* sovereign states, to post their own high commissioners to London and to each other's capitals. His role was less speculatorial than Margery supposed, being principally that of helping to iron out any wrinkles in the new procedures and protocol. The UK Foreign Office was to perform a similar tutorial job for the fledgling Ministry of External Affairs in a number of African states as they approached independence in the late 1950s and early 1960s. Nichols ended his career as British Ambassador to Czechoslovakia (1942) and then to the Netherlands (1948). He was knighted in 1946 and retired in 1951. He married Phyllis, elder daughter of the late Lt-Colonel the Right Hon. H.H. Spender Clay and his wife Pauline (née Astor) in 1932. He was not the elder brother of Beverley Nichols, as is suggested by Margery below, but the younger brother of R.M. Bowyer Nichols (1893–1944), poet, sometime playwright, and Professor of English Literature in the Imperial University of Tokyo.

53   The significance of the adjective 'pink' possibly refers to the fact that in Britain's African territories official telegrams were generally written out on pink forms.

54   Although no such scheme seems to have been formally implemented, nor did New Zealand ever agree to establish her own miniature Colonial Service, the Dominion Selection Scheme, extended in 1929 from Canada to the other dominions, proved hugely successful in the quality of men it recruited into the British Colonial Service from Australia and New Zealand.

55   Guy Hardy Scholefield (1877–1963) was the author of *The Pacific: Its Past and Future*. Published in 1920, it was likely to have been on Margery's list of prescribed reading for her Pacific tour. Parliamentary Librarian and Dominion Archivist, Scholefield was chosen to edit the pioneering volume *Dictionary of New Zealand Biography* (1940).

56   Richard John Seddon (1845–1906) succeeded John Balance as Liberal

Prime Minister of New Zealand during her would-be expansionist period of 1893–1906. In his introduction to *New Zealand's Record*, Angus Ross labels Seddon as 'the greatest imperialist of all the imperially-minded Prime Ministers of New Zealand' (p. 8).

57   One might justifiably conclude that he did (for his subsequent career, see note 52 above).

58   In the event, it was G.W. Forbes who inherited the Reform Party mantle in preference to T.M. Wilford, and he went on to be castigated as New Zealand's 'least impressive Prime Minister of the 20th century' (*Oxford History of New Zealand*, p. 220) and 'the most improbable' one (Sinclair, *History of New Zealand*, p. 255).

59   Margery's sorry impression of the New Zealand Parliament echoes that made sixty years earlier on Anthony Trollope when he attended a debate in Wellington. His conclusion was that New Zealand's parliamentary bores were the most boring in the world (*Australia and New Zealand*, 1873).

60   Gordon Coates, who had been unsuccessful in his bid to regain the premiership, spent the depression years as Minister for Unemployment Policy. His appointment to this unenviable portfolio may have reflected the slogan attached to his name in the 1925 general election, 'The Man Who Gets Things Done'.

61   William Downie Stewart was Finance Minister throughout the difficult recession years from 1929 to 1933.

62   He was suffering from tuberculosis, an affliction to which Polynesians were then tragically prone.

63   Colonel (later Sir) Stephen Allen succeeded General Richardson as Resident Administrator of Samoa in April 1928 and remained in the office until March 1931. A Cambridge graduate, lawyer and local mayor, educated and reserved, he was the antithesis of his ebullient, up-from-the-ranks predecessor, though both men were distinguished soldiers and totally innocent of the basic principles of native administration.

64   P. Verschaffelt (his name is confusingly and continuously misspelt by Margery in the original manuscript) was Public Service Commissioner. His two colleagues on the Samoan Administration Committee were A.D. Park, Secretary to the Treasurer, and C.A. Berendsen, Secretary of External Affairs – whence its common term of reference, the VPB report. The Commissioners had visited Samoa towards the end of 1928 at the request of the new Administrator, Colonel Allen, who realized that one of his priorities must be to raise the morale of his staff by improving the poor conditions of service. Its findings revealed a grave state of affairs in both the quality of recruitment and the level of remuneration, far below those obtaining in New Zealand. Among the proposals was one to revise the disposable revenue by abolishing a number of the services offered to the natives – hence Margery's condemnation of the report. The gloom of the VPB report contrasted so starkly with the optimism of the Royal Commission only one year earlier that the PMC in Geneva felt

itself obliged to query the apparently wide discrepancy and, in due course, to express its disappointment and disturbance at its findings (PMC Minutes, 16th Session, 1929). Margery's notes based on this report are extensive, covering some fifteen sheets (Perham MSS 81/22).

65 Colonel Sir James Allen (1855–1942) had been Minister of Defence in the Massey administration from 1912 to 1919 and then of External Affairs, 1919–20. As such, he was very much the right hand of the Prime Minister at the time of New Zealand's award of the Samoan mandate. From 1920 to 1926 he was High Commissioner in London.

66 Sir Francis H. Dillon Bell (1851–1936) had been Minister of External Affairs from 1923 to 1925 and then Prime Minister. He had been a staunch supporter of Richardson's administration. He was the New Zealand delegate to Geneva in 1922 and 1926. Responsibility for Samoa lay with this ministry until 1943, when it was switched to that of the Ministry of Island Territories until 1961, the eve of independence. Bell came from one of New Zealand's venerable oligarchic families, his father, Sir Francis Dillon Bell, being one of the gentlemen politicians whose civilized company was so enjoyed in the 1880s by Grey's successor as Governor, Colonel Sir Thomas Gore Brown.

67 The allusions here are to both the systematization of Lugard's indirect rule, by then in practice in much of colonial Africa and which had had its theoretical message spread through his *Dual Mandate*, first published in 1922 and now just reissued in a second edition (1929); and to the Malinowskian School of Anthropology as an important adjunct to scientific and humane colonial administration. Part of this thrust came from the International Institute of African Languages and Cultures (today simply the International African Institute), which was founded in 1926 and whose patron Lord Lugard was.

68 This was Colonel Hutchen.

69 The evening in question is described shortly when she recounts her meeting to W.D. Stewart. Margery's friendships with Westminster politicians, especially the successive Secretaries of State for the Colonies after 1935, were enviably non-partisan, encompassing as they did Malcolm MacDonald, Arthur Creech Jones and Alan Lennox-Boyd.

70 This is the Anglophile Wanganui Collegiate School at which HRH Prince Edward was to teach for a term.

71 For Lionel Curtis, see part 1, note 9. Eileen Power (1889–1940) had been a Fellow of Girton College, Cambridge, when Margery was an undergraduate at Oxford. After a year on an Albert Kahn Travelling Fellowship in 1920–1 she joined the staff of the London School of Economics, where she became Professor of Economic History in 1931. 'Young' MacDonald (1901–81) had, at this time and at his third attempt, just won his first seat as a Labour member for Bassetlaw, Nottinghamshire. In his subsequent career as Parliamentary Under-Secretary in the Dominions Office (1931–5) and then Secretary of State for Dominions Affairs (1935–9) and for the Colonies (1935 and

1938–40), and finally as Governor-General of Kenya (1963–4), Margery was to find her paths frequently crossing with his over the next thirty-five years. Lord Hailsham (1872–1950), son of Quintin Hogg, was Lord Chancellor in 1928–9 and Chairman of the British Delegation to the Kyoto Conference.

72   Colonel J.W. Hutchen was retired after his superior, General Richardson had left in 1928 as a result of the findings of the VPB report. He was then demoted by a posting to the War Graves Department.

73   Dr Ritchie's outstanding work for the improvement of the Samoans' health, especially in connection with the treatment of hookworm, had been warmly commended by both the PMC and by the Royal Commission of 1927. The latter endorsed the opinion expressed by Dr Buxton that the Samoan Health Department represented a service 'which might serve as a model to any small tropical country'. A few years later Dr Ritchie's work was again publicly applauded, this time by the Rockefeller Foundation.

74   Mrs Roberts, a qualified medical officer.

75   This was probably Dr Buxton's *Research on Melanesia and Polynesia* (1928).

76   William Morris (later Viscount Nuffield, 1877–1963), the industrialist and philanthropist, in 1912 produced at Cowley the first Morris Oxford motor car, on which his name and fortune were subsequently to be founded. For new insights into his role in founding Nuffield College (of which Margery was honoured by election in 1939 as the first Official Fellow), see chapter 6 of Sir Norman Chester's *Economics, Politics and Social Studies in Oxford, 1900–1985* (1986).

77   As Margery had already learned in Rotorua, where she had to go to bed supperless after a long and exhausting drive, New Zealand's primitive labour laws of the time made it illegal for domestic servants to be called upon to prepare a meal after 7.30 p.m. unless a separate night shift was involved.

78   Hence the term 'communalism' is today generally preferred so as to avoid such misunderstanding.

79   Informative comments on miscegenation are to be found in M.P.K. Sorrenson's chapter 'Maori and Pakeha' in the *Oxford History of New Zealand*. He draws attention to the fact that 'living as Maoris' and 'living as Europeans' were separate half-caste categories in New Zealand censuses at the turn of the century and 'an important reminder that racial interaction was a two-way process' (p. 192).

80   The Cook Islands had been annexed by New Zealand in 1901 during the expansionist Seddon administration. The first Resident Commissioner was Lt-Colonel W.E. Gudgeon. The islands became self-governing on August 8, 1965. A useful conspectus of their history as a New Zealand dependency is to be found in the two chapters by S.D. Wilson in Ross, *New Zealand's Record*, pp. 26–114.

81   The Imperial Conference of 1926 was dominated by General Hertzog and

Mackenzie King, with the latter's endorsement of a liberal measure of dominion independence being particularly strong following the furore of the Byng–King constitutional controversy (cf. Eugene A. Forsey, *The Royal Power of Dissolution of Parliament in the British Commonwealth*, 1943). The Canadian crisis was to have its memories vigorously revived in another dominion's constitutional confrontation between the Governor-General and the elected Prime Minister, namely Australia's Kerr–Whitlam controversy of 1975.

82   Ngata is quoted as once having observed of New Zealand's efforts, as the mandatory power for Samoa, to satisfy the League of Nations, 'Why do you not leave them alone and let them enjoy themselves in their own way [*fa'a Samoa*]? Is yours the only way in which a human being can enjoy himself?' – cited in Grattan, *The South West Pacific*, p. 455.

83   Although modern historians cast doubt on the 'fleet' theory of Maori settlement of Aotearoa ('the land of the long white cloud'), the Maori tradition of several canoes coming from Tahiti via the Cook Islands in the fourteenth century remains strong. The major Maori 'tribes' (*iwi*) trace their origin to the occupants of the original canoes – Ngapuhi, Waikato, Taranaki, Arawa, etc. (see the excellent map of tribal locations in the *Oxford History of New Zealand*, pp. 464–5).

84   Henry Edmund Holland (1868–1933) was Leader of the Labour Party and an outspoken critic of New Zealand's administration of her mandated territory. His publications on this issue included two short pamphlets of forthright denunciation, *Samoa: A Story That Teems with Tragedy* (1918) and *The Revolt of the Samoans* (1928).

85   The Beach: a reference to the waterfront community where Nelson also had an office.

86   Ngata's important 'Explanation' of the Treaty of Waitangi was translated by M.R. Jones in 1962. For a fascinating recent dissection of the 'meaning' of the Treaty of Waitangi, see Peter Cleave's article 'Language and Authority in the Ethnic Politics of New Zealand (Aotearoa): A Case Study of the Treaty of Waitangi', in Anthony Kirk-Greene and John Stone (eds), *Ethnicity, Empire and Race Relations: Essays in Honour of Kenneth Kirkwood*, special issue of *Ethnic and Racial Studies* (1986), 9, 3, 382–95. In the case against four persons for having insulted the Queen on her visit to New Zealand in March 1986 by baring their buttocks at Her Majesty, the defendants claimed that their action was a protest against the non-ratification of the Waitangi Treaty of 1840.

87   Elsdon Best (1856–1921) was ethnographer of the Dominion Museum, Wellington, from 1910 to 1931, having previously spent fifteen years in New Zealand's Native Affairs Department. Although Margery does not mention it here, in the original diary she had recorded that when Maggie Papakura, the Maori girl studying anthropology in London, had dined at St Hugh's College, Oxford, on January 31, 1929, she had named Best as one of the few anthropologists whom the Maori respected and trusted (MSS 80/21). Author of numerous works on the Maori and a long-time contributor to the *New*

Zealand Illustrated Magazine (est. 1899), a notable source and inspiration of the colony's intellectual life, his systematic and definitive survey of Maori culture, *The Maori*, appeared a few years before Margery's visit. She was conspicuously fortunate in her opportunities for consulting authoritative source material, for at the time of setting out on her Rhodes Travelling Fellowship two more indispensable and major studies were published: Felix M. Keesing's *The Changing Maori* (1928) and Raymond Firth's *Primitive Economies of the New Zealand Maori* (1929).

88 *Pakeha* is the Maori word used for 'foreigner', hence (pop.) 'white man'. In Samoa, they were known as *papalagi*. Pakeha Maori was a common colonial term for a European living with Maoris.

89 Johannes Carl Andersen (1873–1962) came to New Zealand from Denmark at the age of two. He was head of the Alexander Turnbull Library in Wellington from 1918 to 1937, and for many years edited the *Journal of the Polynesian Society*. Among his books were *Maori Life in Aotea* (1907) and *Maori Music* (1939). His *Myths and Legends of Polynesia* was published the year before Margery arrived.

90 Philip Snowden (1864–1937) was Chairman of the Independent Labour party from 1903 to 1906 and, once more, in 1917–20. He was Labour MP for Blackburn 1906–18 and Chancellor of the Exchequer in 1924, and then again from 1929 to 1931.

91 At least twice more on this Travelling Fellowship Margery was to encounter a case of mistaken identity. At a settlers' dinner which she seems to have gatecrashed in the New Stanley Hotel, Nairobi, on September 4, 1929, she was dramatically (if humorously) accosted by the settler leader, Lord Delamere, with the ringing challenge of 'Look! A spy!' (*EAJ*, p. 171). Again, on explaining her mission to the grim Moffat Thompson, Secretary for Native Affairs in Northern Rhodesia, with his 'bull-dog face . . . [who] barked out a series of questions about my business' (*AA*, p. 236), she found herself being taken as a Nosy Parker by the Aborigines Protection Society or a snooper by the ILO in Geneva. Most dangerous of all was the animosity of the white 'gauger' in charge of the dock labour in Durban, who suspected Margery was mixed up with the ICU trade union when she visited, alone, the mining compounds, her hand literally bloodstained (*AA*, pp. 32–3).

92 Probably Steven Ellis.

93 This was the VPB report.

94 In her Samoan diary there is no mention of her having met him there.

95 Massey had indeed fought for the award of the mandate to New Zealand at the Peace Conference. His historical reconstruction of the legitimacy of New Zealand's claim to Western Samoa, including the racial linking of Maori and Samoan, is quoted in full in Ross, *New Zealand's Record*, p. 9.

96 The composition of the League of Nations Permanent Mandates Commission, which rose to ten after the addition of a German member in

1926, enjoyed an unusual level of continuity. It had a single chairman for sixteen out of the eighteen years of its existence, Alberto Theodoli, Marchese di Sambuci (1873–1955), who served from 1920 to 1936 and had started life as a civil engineer. The Dutch member, Daniel F. Willem Van Rees (1863–1934), who had spent thirty years before the war in the Netherlands Colonial Service in the East Indies and became Secretary-General of the Dutch colonial Institute, sat on it from 1921 until his death, and Switzerland's Professor William Rappard (1883–1958), an economic historian who was Director of the Institute of International Studies in the University of Geneva, served from 1924 through to the final sessions in 1939. It was Scandinavia which sent the women members, the Norwegian Mlle Dannevig sitting for ten years. Portugal's second delegate enjoyed the same period. The mandatory powers were obliged to be in the minority. Belgium's Pierre Orts (1872–1958), formerly a diplomat, sat on the PMC throughout its whole existence and Lugard (UK) sat from 1923 to 1936. During the eighteen years, five French and three Japanese members were appointed.

97 On thinking back on her New Zealand days when she was in Africa, Margery recalled the astounding beauty of the air, 'so liquid-clear that every colour gets its utmost value as it never does in England' (*AA*, p. 40). It seems curious that nowhere in her New Zealand diary does she mention Henry Rayne, the husband of her adored sister, Ethel. As a boy he had run away from his home in New Zealand.

4 AUSTRALIA

1 RMS *Maunganui*.

2 Captain Richard Briscoe (1893–1957), Conservative MP for Cambridgeshire from 1923 to 1945, educated at Eton and Magdalen College, Oxford. He won the MC in the First World War and, despite his age, served with the Grenadier Guards in the Second World War.

3 In the event, she seems to have dropped even this minimal plan of acquainting herself with the exercise of the Papuan mandate and the principles of native administration in New Guinea. Instead, Margery concentrated what research time she had on aborigines and race relations in Australia herself.

4 Sir Dudley R.S. de Chair, whose official secretary was H.S.F. Campbell Budge.

5 John Laurence Baird, Lord Stonehaven (1874–1941), was Governor-General of Australia from 1925 to 1931, having enjoyed first a diplomatic and then a political career. From 1931 to 1936 he was Chairman of the British Conservative Party.

6 The Max Müllers were presumably of the family of Friedrich Max Müller (1823–1900), Taylorian Professor of Modern Languages and then of Comparative Philology at Oxford.

7 In strong contrast to her achievements in New Zealand, Margery's

government contacts in Australia seem to have been largely confined to the gubernatorial and bureaucratic rather than the elected level. With electoral uncertainty in the air, this was perhaps not the easiest time to interview the Australian political establishment. Indeed, 1929 was to find the country gripped by what has been called the greatest political debacle in her history (the judgement was made before the constitutional crisis of 1975), when the Bruce-Page Nationalist–Country coalition government was ignominiously swept from office and the Labour Party massively returned under J.J. Scullen. When Margery did try to ask political questions, all she got was abusive comment about the profound union intransigence and the 'Red' menace. With such a traumatic and topsy-turvy experience, and the storm-clouds unmistakably gathering down under, it is perhaps not surprising that Margery came away – and was aware of the potential bias – with such an unfavourable view of Australia.

8   Lachlan Macquarie (1761–1824) was appointed Governor of New South Wales in 1810 to put down the 'Rum Corps' rebellion, which had successfully toppled his predecessor Captain William Bligh (of *Bounty* fame) in 1808. He held office till 1821 and is credited with laying out inland Australia's oldest city, Bathurst, in 1815.

9   Alfred Reginald Radcliffe-Brown (1881–1955) was born and educated in Cambridge. After field-work in the Andaman Islands (1906–8) he became a Fellow of Trinity College (1908–14), during which time he made his first field trip to Australia (1910–12). After the war he became Director of Education in Tonga and then, in 1921, founding Professor of Anthropology in the University of Cape Town. In 1925 he moved to Sydney University as Professor of Anthropology, from where he went on to the University of Chicago in 1931, before being elected to the Chair of Social Anthropology at Oxford University in 1937. He retired in 1946. His work earned him recognition as the leading authority in the analysis of the social structures of 'primitive' societies, kinship and family organization.

10   Le Roy L.L.J. de Maistre (1894–1968) changed his name to Roy de (not Margery's le) Maistre when he left Australia permanently in 1930 and thereafter considered himself a British artist. He first exhibited in 1916. In Australia, his 'colour-music' style became part of Australia's art folklore as 'pictures you could whistle'. His memorialist in the *Australian Dictionary of National Biography* comments that 'from his family's position in society he helped to make modern art fashionable in Sydney, even in Government House circles, but his paintings became tame exercises in Fauvism and Post-Impressionism'.

11   In 1829 Captain Fremantle took formal possession of the territory round Albany on King George Sound, the first settlement of what was to become the start of Western Australia. The cities of Perth and Fremantle developed from the original Swan River Settlement date from the same year.

12   On only four occasions in 250 manuscript pages covering more than three months does Margery give such a date in this diary.

13 There was as yet no Chair of Anthropology at either Oxford or Cambridge. The leading name at Cambridge would have been A.C. Haddon, who was Reader in Ethnology, 1909–26. He was succeeded by T.C. Hodson, who became the first holder of the Chair of Social Anthropology in 1932. At Oxford, the Reader in Social Anthropology at the time was R.R. Marrett. A Chair was not established until 1936. I am grateful to Dr J.D. Pickles and Mr P.W. Moss of the Registries of Cambridge and Oxford Universities respectively for their help in tracing these appointments. Despite his idea of 'a joke', Radcliffe-Brown was elected as the first holder of the Oxford Chair.

14 The Laura Spelman Rockefeller Foundation, founded in 1913, had played a major part in rehabilitating the Samoa health programme after the serious setback caused by the Mau rebellion.

15 Margery did study under Malinowski at the LSE for a short time after her return to England, but seemingly with neither pleasure nor profit. 'There as the only student of history and colonial government, I had to endure being the butt of the master. . . . I was generally sinking out of my depth in the dark swamps of anthropology' – Presidential Address to the African Studies Association of the United Kingdom, September 1964.

16 Article 22 of the Covenant of the League of Nations stipulated, in memorably paternalistic phrases, that countries 'inhabited by peoples not yet able to stand by themselves under the strenuous conditions of the modern world' should be treated as 'a sacred trust of civilization'.

17 These would have included E.W.P. Chinnery in New Guinea and R.S. Rattray in the Gold Coast.

18 Anthropological surveys (over two hundred of them) became part of the fundamental planning for the reorganization of Native Authorities in Nigeria during the 1930s under Sir Donald Cameron's governorship. Unfortunately, the close linkage between anthropology and colonial administration, so attractive a partnership to thinking colonial officials between the wars, led to a reaction against anthropology by the new African governments of the 1960s, which stigmatized the science as being nothing more than the handmaiden of colonial administration. As a result, most of the new universities in Africa turned their faces against anthropology as a discipline (Khartoum was a notable exception) and opted instead for the more post-colonial science of sociology.

19 John Hubert Plunkett (later Sir Hubert) Murray (1861–1940) was Lieutenant-Governor of Papua (British New Guinea until 1906) for a remarkable span of more than thirty years, from 1908 to 1940. Educated at Sydney Grammar School, he went on to Oxford where he achieved a double First. After practising at the Bar and seeing service in the South African war, he was appointed in 1904 to British New Guinea as Chief Judicial Officer. Four years later he was promoted to Lieutenant-Governor. He pioneered the welfare administration of the territory at a time when Australia showed little if any consideration to the welfare of her own aborigines. He was a member of a three-man commission set up by the Australian Government to incorporate

the administration of the mandated (1920) territory of ex-German New Guinea with that of adjoining Papua. His recommendation in favour of amalgamation was the minority one.

20 George Gilbert Aimé Murray (1866–1957), younger brother of Hubert Murray, was Professor of Greek at Glasgow University from 1889 (appointed to the Chair at the remarkable age of twenty-three) to 1899, and then Regius Professor of Greek at Oxford from 1908 to 1936. Their father, Sir Terence Murray, had been President of the Legislative Council of New South Wales. Margery is perhaps more likely to have met Murray in his capacity as Chairman of the League of Nations Union, 1923–38, for whom she had done some lecturing in the 1920s, or possibly at Geneva, where Smuts from time to time included him in the South African delegation to the Mandates Commission, rather than in his Regius role at Oxford. Margery is incorrect in her use of a title; unlike his elder brother, he was not knighted.

21 Stanley Melbourne Bruce (1883–1967) led the National Party as Prime Minister of Australia from 1923 to 1929. He was educated at Cambridge, where he gained a rowing Blue and was well known on the towpath as 'Bruggins'. In 1928 he also took on the Ministry for Territories. He was High Commissioner to London from 1933 to 1945 and also represented the Commonwealth of Australia at the League of Nations, 1931–8. After the war he left Australia for good, feeling that there was 'no niche' for him back home. He accepted a peerage in 1947, like Casey on becoming Governor-General of Australia in 1965, and became the first Chancellor of the Australian National University, Canberra; it was not an office that demanded many return visits to an Australia with which he had become disenchanted. Like Menzies twenty years later, he was looked on as a 'King's man', content to follow Britain in foreign policy.

22 William (Billy) Morris Hughes (1864–1952) was the Labour Prime Minister of Australia from 1915 to 1923, when he was ousted by the new (1919) Country Party led by Dr (later Sir) Earle Page. In Australia's history his name is inseparable from the acerbic crisis over conscription for service overseas, culminating in the stormy national referendums of 1916 and 1917, and from his narrow-minded and ill-mannered behaviour at the Versailles Peace Treaty, where his truculence earned him Wilson's opprobrium of 'pestiferous varmint' and the London sneer of 'Little Digger'.

23 This was either Lieutenant D.W.D. Nicholl, or Captain Houston, ADC to the Governor-General, Lord Stonehaven.

24 Lady Stonehaven (m. 1905), daughter of the Earl of Kintore, had been Lady Ethel Keith-Falconer before her marriage.

25 The Australian Capital Territory (ACT) of Canberra had replaced Melbourne as the Federal Capital only the previous year (1927), when Parliament first met there. The site had been approved in principle in 1901, the year in which the Commonwealth of Australia had been inaugurated, and then definitely selected in 1908. This was followed by a designers' competition, which was won by the Chicago architect Walter Burley.

Preliminary work was started in 1912, but the advent of the war put a stop to any further progress. As we see from Margery's diary, even in 1929 much of the nascent capital was still in a very rudimentary stage.

26 There is no indication of his name in the original manuscript. The Director of External Affairs at the time was W. Henderson and the Secretary to the Prime Minister was J.G. McLaren.

27 This kind of remark is echoed by Margery when she reaches the mandated territories of Africa – e.g. in *WAP*, pp. 151 and 181.

28 Charles Edward Lane-Poole (1885–1970) was appointed Conservator of Forests for Western Australia in 1916, having spent the previous five years as Conservator in Sierra Leone. In 1922 he was invited to write a report on the forest resources of Papua and New Guinea. He was Principal of the Australian Forestry School in Canberra from 1927 to 1945 and became Inspector-General of Forestry in the same year. He was the son of Stanley Lane-Poole (1854–1931), Professor of Arabic at Trinity College, Dublin, from 1898 to 1904 and a prolific scholar, who had made a visit to Australia in 1890. Charles was a relative of the medieval historian Austin Lane-Poole (1889–1963), who capped his extended Fellowship at St John's College, Oxford (1913–47) by being elected as the College's President from 1947 to 1957. Another Lane-Poole (R.H.O.) was Captain in Command of the Royal Australian Naval College at Harvis Bay, NSW.

29 Probably Mr Osborne. Their house was called Lanyon.

30 Possibly J.W. Bleakley.

31 This is more likely to have been W.D. Walker's highly critical and unpublished 1928 report to the Minister for Home Territories on aboriginal conditions in the Northern Territory, or else Bleakley's own report of the same year, than the Wood report of 1927 or the unpublished Central Australian inquiry of 1928/9.

32 Norman Brookes (1877–1968) was a prodigious games player who made an international name for himself at lawn tennis. He first played at Wimbledon in 1905, and in 1907 won the singles, the doubles (with New Zealand's A. Wilding) and the mixed doubles championships, being the first overseas player – and the first left-handed player – to win the world title. In the same year Brookes and Wilding captured the Davis Cup from Britain, a trophy which Australia retained for the next five years. After the war, in which Wilding was killed on the Western Front in 1915, Brookes continued to represent Australia in the Davis Cup matches. He made his last appearance at Wimbledon in 1924. From 1926 to 1954 he was President of the Lawn Tennis Association of Australia. Known in tennis circles as 'The Wizard', he was knighted in 1939 in recognition of his long record of distinguished service to the game. Brookes's wife, whom he married in 1911, was Mabel Balcombe. For many year's 'Dame Mabel' was Melbourne's leading society hostess.

33 Margery's Sir William Macfarlane was properly Macpherson, in 1928–9 Premier (not Prime Minister) of Victoria. Perhaps, not surprisingly, in view of

the ineptitude revealed by his comment, this knight is not included in *Who Was Who*.

34   Wycombe Abbey is a leading girls' public school in Buckinghamshire, founded in 1896.

35   Lord (Alexander Gore Arkwright) Hore-Ruthven (1872–1955), later the 1st Earl of Gowrie (cr. 1945), who had won the VC in the Sudan in 1899, was appointed Governor of South Australia on his retirement from the British Army in 1928, the year of Margery's visit. Hardly had he taken up his next appointment, as Governor of New South Wales in 1935, than he was invited to be Governor-General of Australia (1936–44). Ironically, Lady Hore-Ruthven (1879–1965), *née* Zara Eileen Pollok of Co. Galway, married her husband in 1908 against the wishes of her family, who are said to have regarded him as 'the impecunious son of an impoverished family – and with indifferent prospects' (quoted in *Dictionary of Australian Biography*). The ADC was either Captain G.L. Verney or Captain the Hon. H. Grosvenor.

36   Two aboriginal 'horror stories' of the time, other than the Bleakley report, would have come to Margery's attention. The first concerned the murder of a man called Hay by aborigines at Nulla Nulla Station in the Wyndham neighbourhood and the subsequent 'disappearance' of some thirty 'abos' at the hands of a police posse. While 'protector' was a quite legal and honourable title in the Australian bureaucracy, here Margery's understandably disparaging reference must be to the *soi-disant* 'protective' responsibilities of the police to the aborigines. Some historians have argued that in Australia the police still bear the brand of 'the System', that is to say the Botany Bay Settlement of 1788 and all that went with it until the abandonment of transportation in New South Wales in 1840 and finally to Western Australia in 1878.

37   By the 1980s the aboriginal population did not amount to more than 200,000 out of a total Australian population of some 15 million, more than a quarter of whom lived in the two cities of Sydney and Melbourne, and 10 per cent of whom were non-British immigrants who had arrived in the 1945–63 boom.

38   'Fremantle' is clearly wrong, since it lies at least two full days' sailing beyond the Great Australian Bight. Margery means Port Adelaide.

39   Margery had left the SS *Demosthenes* at Sydney to travel to Western Australia overland, so the other passengers were already of several days' standing by the time she rejoined the ship.

40   Stephen Lackey Kessel (b. 1897) took a Diploma in Forestry at Oxford (there is no record of his ever having been a Rhodes Scholar) and later became Conservator of Forests, Western Australia. The Kessel family had a strong tradition of Government service in Western Australia, especially in the career of Alfred Colenso Kessel, who spent much of his life as secretary to the state's Premier. Surprisingly, perhaps, given the fact that New Zealand had produced thirty Rhodes Scholars between 1904 and 1928 (the number was raised from one a year to two after 1925) and Australia six a year from 1904

onwards, this is the first time Margery mentions them in her travels. Yet the Rhodes connection is a splendid visa for Oxonians, and, after all, Margery herself was travelling on a Rhodes Trust award, one element in which was to facilitate closer College contact between Rhodes Scholars and senior members with some knowledge of their home countries.

41 The Governor of Western Australia was Colonel Sir William R. Campion. Western Australia had been annexed in 1829, as New Holland.

42 In the event, Lord Stonehaven's successor in 1931 was not selected from this proconsular class but was Isaac Alfred Isaacs (1856–1948), the first Australian to be appointed the dominion's Governor-General (and then only after King George V had reluctantly agreed to Prime Minister Scullen's nomination). The aristocratic tradition was restored and advanced to the level of royalty in the appointment of the Duke of Kent in 1939 (though the outbreak of war prevented him from taking it up) and by that of the Duke of Gloucester in 1945. Not till 1965 did an unbroken line of Australian governors-general establish itself.

43 The senior official whom she met here was A.O. Neville. In South Australia, the office of Protector went back to the 1860s. At the time of Margery's visit, the Chief Protector was stationed at Darwin, Northern Territory. Margery's comment on the revealing undertones of the title of Protector probably echoed the growing opinion she had picked up in Australian circles concerned with the aborigines, namely that the office displayed what at the best (and almost by definition) could only be an unprogressive and negative attitude.

44 Probably the home of Stephen Kessel.

45 On the sea voyage from San Francisco to Pago Pago, Margery had recorded in her original diary, 'I almost dread Australia', with its news of continual strikes and its bleak reputation for what she neatly termed its motto of 'service with a shrug' (MSS 35/4). In sum, Margery just does not seem to have taken to Australia.

5 FACING AFRICA

1 The SS *Demosthenes* belonged to the White Star Line and was making the Australia–England voyage, heading now for Durban and then Cape Town. The voyage from Western Australia to South Africa took just under three weeks.

2 This was a Mr Abdy.

3 In view of the pithiness of some of her acute comments that follow in her diary, Margery was probably right to preserve the anonymity of most of her fellow passengers; but historians cannot ignore the challenge. The carnivore was one Orton, from Western Australia. The vegetarian from South Africa (the list of passengers at the same table is continued later) was called Quaife,

and the name of the Scottish veterinarian was Murray. Margery identifies 'enigmatic foreigner' herself.

4 Margery had been a strong games player when she was an undergraduate, representing her College at hockey and playing in tennis matches. St Hugh's College has several photographs in its archives of Margery in various teams.

5 His snapshot appears in the original diary (MSS 37/7, 9).

6 I have been unable to identify this party-piece. However, in her partly autobiographical novel, *Josie Vine* (1927), Margery describes the Laska recitation at some length (at pp. 53 ff.) as 'the story of Texas down by the Rio Grande, and the stampede of steers during which the heroine saved the hero by spreading her body above his'. The extra line is included there: 'We followed a grave. . . .'

7 The 'probably' was not to last too long, for Africa was indeed to become the focus of Margery's work and the location of her scholarly reputation over the next fifty years. This stemmed as much from an instinctive affinity with Africa as by the continent's beckoning of the intricacies of race relations and native administration. No sooner had she landed at Cape Town than she recorded in her diary the prophetic entry: 'For me it was the gateway to a continent.' Amerindians and aborigines, mandates and Maoris were now all put aside, despite years of study and research and a sizeable travel grant: she had fallen in love with Africa. Yet at the same time Margery, ever forthright, was to experience the curious sensation of a bitter-sweet, love-hate feeling towards Africa which, as she recounted in 1972, had remained as vivid, as inexplicable and as involuntary as it had been at the moment she stepped ashore at Berbera almost exactly fifty years earlier: 'I had an astonishing spasm of recoil, of something more than physical fear . . . a revulsion against the thought that I, so white, so vulnerable, so sensitive, so complex, was about to commit myself to that black continent across the water.' It was, this notable inquirer into race relations in action confessed, her one moment of racial fear. 'It passed, and I have never felt it again.' Instead, Africa was to become the place 'where I fulfilled so ecstatically my childhood's dream and found a guiding purpose for my life and work'.

Appendix

MARGERY PERHAM – A CALENDAR

(Compiled by A.H.M. Kirk-Greene with the assistance of Patricia Pugh)

1895   Born September 6 at Bury, Lancashire, youngest of eight children (only seven survived) and second daughter.

1908–13   Educated at St Stephen's College, Windsor, and St Anne's School, Abbots Bromley, Staffordshire, from where she won a scholarship to Oxford University but stayed on a year to be head of school.

1910   Her sister Ethel (b. 1887?) sailed to East Africa to do mission work and there married (1911) Major Henry Rayne, a New Zealand cotton-planter in Jubaland, East African Protectorate.

1914   Went up to St Hugh's College, Oxford.

1915   Death of Edgar (b. 1892), her youngest and favourite brother, at Delville Wood in France.

1917   Graduated from Oxford with First Class Honours in Modern History.

1917–19   Lectured to the army in northern France and on Salisbury Plain for War Office Educational Scheme.

1919   Appointed to a part-time Assistant Lecturership in History, Sheffield University.

1921   Wrote, produced and played the leading role in 'Aethelburga' (unpublished play).

1921–2   Granted a year's leave of absence following a breakdown in health. Spent a recuperative year in British Somaliland with her sister Ethel, whose husband was now a District Commissioner.

1922   Resumed teaching at Sheffield University.

1924   Appointed Fellow and Tutor in Modern History and Modern Greats, St Hugh's College, Oxford University.

1925   Published *Major Dane's Garden* (repr. 1970).

1927   First visit to Geneva to observe the League of Nations Permanent Mandates Commission in session. Published *Josie Vine*.

1929   Second visit to Geneva to attend League of Nations PMC. Began to establish close contact with Lord Lugard at

261

Abinger Hammer. Awarded a Rhodes Trust Travelling Fellowship for one year's research into 'the administration of coloured races' in North America, Polynesia, Australasia and Africa, travelling via USA (July), Samoa and Fiji (August), New Zealand (September), Australia (October) (for diary see *Pacific Prelude*, 1988) and Southern Africa (for diary, see *African Apprenticeship*, 1974).

1930   Travelling Fellowship extended for a second year, spent in Uganda, Kenya and Tanganyika (for diary, see *East African Journey*, 1976).
First articles in *The Times*, on Samoa (April).
Resigned her Tutorial Fellowship at St Hugh's College (May).
Moved to Ponds Farm, Shere, home of the Raynes.
First article in *The Times* on Africa (November).

1930–1   Covered Joint Select Committee for Closer Union sittings for *The Times*.

1931   Returned to St Hugh's College, Oxford, as Research Fellow.
Studied anthropology at the LSE under Professor Malinowski.
First major African lecture on Native Administration (International Institute of African Languages and Cultures, April).
First article on African administration (*Africa*, July).
First articles in *The Times* on race relations in Africa (August).
First visit to Nigeria and French Cameroons (November) (for diary, see *West African Passage*, 1983).

1932   Returned to Oxford from West Africa (April).
Awarded Rockefeller Travelling Fellowship by the International African Institute to visit the Sudan to study Native Administration but prevented from taking it up by ill-health.
First article in *The Times* on the Nigerian administration (December).

1933   First article in *The Times* on French colonial administration (May).

1934   First radio broadcast (BBC) on Africa (*The Listener*, February).
First article in *The Times* on the High Commission Territories problem (July).
First public lecture on indirect rule (Royal Society of Arts (March), for which she was awarded the Society's Silver Medal.

1935   Published *The Protectorates of South Africa* (with Lionel Curtis).
First letter to *The Times* on Ethiopia.
Appointed Research Lecturer in Colonial Administration, University of Oxford.

1936   Editor, *Ten Africans* (repr. 1963).
First visit to the Sudan.
Research Consultant to Lord Hailey for *An African Survey*, commissioned by the Royal Institute of International Affairs (pub. 1938), which she had helped Lord Lothian, Sir Reginald Coupland and in some measure Lord Lugard to plan.

1937   Visited Kenya, Tanganyika, Uganda and the Sudan (December–April 1938).
Observer of the De La Warr Commission at Makerere College.
Member, Colonial Office Social Studies Research Committee.
Member, Advisory Committee for Colonial Administration.

1938   Published *Native Administration in Nigeria* (repr. 1962).
Vice-Chairman, Oxford University Summer School of Colonial Administration (July).

1939   Vice-Chairman, Oxford University Summer School of Colonial Administration (June).
Elected first Faculty Fellow of Nuffield College, Oxford, and Official Fellow in Imperial Studies.
Appointed Reader in Colonial Administration, Oxford University.
Visited the Sudan and first article in *The Times* (June).
Member, Advisory Committee on Education in the Colonies.

1941   Published *Africans and British Rule* (repr. 1952).
Member of Oxford University's Social Reconstruction Survey Committee (Cole) and Director of the parallel Colonial Studies Committee in co-operation with the Colonial Office.

1942   Published *African Discovery* (with J. Simmons; repr. 1957 and 1963; Penguin abridgement, 1948) and *The Colonies* (reprinted from *The Times*).

1943   First radio broadcast (BBC) on the Colonial Service (*The Listener*, April).

1943–5   Worked closely with Sir Ralph Furse, Director of Recruitment at the Colonial Office, W.T.S. Stallybrass, Vice-Chancellor, and Sir Douglas Veale, Registrar of

Oxford University, on planning for post-war training for
the Colonial Service (Devonshire Courses).

1944   Published *Race and Politics in Kenya* (with Elspeth
Huxley; rev. ed. 1956).
First article in *Foreign Affairs* (April).
Member, Higher Education Commission and West Indies
Higher Education Committee.
Visited West Indies.
Lecture tour in USA on behalf of Central Office of
Information.

1945   Appointed first Director of the Institute of Colonial
Studies, University of Oxford (resigned 1948).
First article on Lord Lugard (*Africa*, July).

1946   *Colonial Administration* (Reading List).
Editor, *Colonial Economics* (P.A. Bower) (Select Reading
List).
Introduction, *The Economics of a Tropical Dependency*, I:
The Native Economies of Nigeria (D. Forde and R. Scott).
Preface, *Studies in Colonial Legislatures*, I, *The Development
of Legislative Councils, 1660–1945* (M. Wight).
Member, Executive Committee of Inter-University Coun-
cil on Higher Education Overseas (IUC).
Member of Council, Makerere College, Uganda.

1947   Editor, *Urban Conditions in Africa* (J. Comhaire) (Select
Reading List).
Preface, *Studies in Colonial Legislatures*, II: *The Gold Coast
Legislative Council* (M. Wight).
Editor, *Rural Conditions and Settlement in the British
Colonies* (P. Mayer) (Reading List).
Foreword, *Path to Nigerian Freedom* (O. Awolowo).
Member, Colonial Social Science Research Council.
First involvement with the Cambridge University Summer
Schools on Colonial Administration.

1948   Made a Companion of the British Empire (CBE).
Published *The Government of Ethiopia* (rev. ed. 1969).
Introduction, *The Economics of a Tropical Dependency: II,
Mining, Commerce and Finance in Nigeria* (P.A. Bower *et
al*).
Preface, *Studies in Colonial Legislatures*, III, *The Northern
Rhodesian Legislative Council* (J.W. Davidson).
Editor, *Colonial Law* (C.K. Meek) (Reading List).

1949   Visited Nigeria and the Sudan, where she advised on the
establishment of the School of Administration.
Member, Standing Committee of the Colonial Social
Science Research Council.
Member, Colonial Office Committee on Smaller Territories.

1950   Gave Lugard Memorial Lecture to Royal Empire Society/
        International African Institute.
        Colonial Government (Annotated Reading List).
        Preface, *Studies in Colonial Legislatures, IV: The Nigerian
        Legislative Council* (J. Wheare).
        Private and public involvement in the Seretse Khama
        affair. Visited West Indies on behalf of the IUC.

1951   Preface, *Studies in Colonial Legislatures, V: The Legislature
        of Ceylon* (S. Namasivayam).
        Preface, *Colonial and Comparative Studies, I: The Metro-
        politan Organisation of British Colonial Trade* (K. Stahl).

1952   Preface, *Colonial and Comparative Studies, II: The Sudan
        Question* (M. Abbas).
        Preface, *Studies in Colonial Legislatures, VI: The Legislative
        Council of Trinidad and Tobago* (H. Craig).
        Foreword, *East African Future* (Fabian Colonial Bureau).
        Hon. LLD, St Andrew's University.

1953   Foreword, *Colonial and Comparative Studies, III: The
        Making of the Modern Sudan* (K.D.D. Henderson).
        Public involvement in condemnation of the proposed
        Central African Federation.
        Visited Kenya and Uganda.
        Visited the Sudan.
        First article in *The Times* on the Mau Mau.

1954   Visited the Sudan.
        Foreword, *Colonial and Comparative Studies, IV: Britain
        and the United States in the Caribbean* (M. Proudfoot).
        Lectured at universities in Germany on behalf of the
        Foreign Office.

1955   First public lecture and broadcast on her work on the
        biography of Lord Lugard (*The Listener*, June).
        Visited Kenya, Uganda and Nigeria (sabbatical year,
        1955–6).

1956   Published *Lugard, I: The Years of Adventure, 1858–1898.*
        Foreword, *The Kenya Question: An African Answer* (T.
        Mboya).
        Visited Kenya.

1957   Visited East Africa.

1958   Visited Northern Nigeria.

1959   Editor, *The Diaries of Lord Lugard*, I–III (with M. Bull).
        Preface, *Colonial and Comparative Studies, V: Gezira* (A.
        Gaitskell).

1960   Published *Lugard, II: The Years of Authority, 1899–1945.*
        First article in *Optima* (March).
        Consultant, Oxford History of East Africa project.

Official guest at British Somaliland's independence celebrations.
Official guest at Nigeria's independence celebrations.
Visited Kenya.

1961 Convened foundation meeting of Oxford Colonial Records Project (OCRP) at Nuffield College.
Gave the BBC Reith Lectures, 'The End of Britain's African Empire'.
Elected Fellow of the British Academy (FBA).
The Colonial Reckoning (Reith Lectures).
Awarded Royal African Society's Gold Wellcome Medal.
Awarded Royal Scottish Geographical Society's Mungo Park Medal.

1962 Chapter in *Restless Nations: A Study of World Tensions and Development*.
Honorary Fellow, St Hugh's College.
Hon. D Litt, University of Southampton.

1963 D Litt, Oxford University.
Honorary Fellow, Makerere College, Uganda.
Visited Kenya, Uganda and Tanganyika.
Introduction, *Yesterday's Rulers* (R. Heussler).
Foreword, *Mau Mau Detainee* (J.M. Kariuki).
Official guest at Kenya's independence celebrations.
Retired from teaching at Oxford University.
Honorary Fellow of Nuffield College.
Chairman, Oxford University Colonial Records Project.
President, Universities Mission to Central Africa.
Presided over the amalgamation of the UMCA with the SPG.
Editor, *The Diaries of Lord Lugard*, IV (with M. Bull).
Elected founding President of the African Studies Association of the United Kingdom.

1964 Gave address at the memorial service of A. Creech Jones.
Hon. D Litt, University of London.
Honorary Fellow, School of Oriental and African Studies, University of London.

1965 Created Dame Commander of the Order of St Michael and St George (DCMG).
Introduction, repr. *The Dual Mandate in Tropical Africa* (Lord Lugard, 1922).
Introduction, *Principles of Native Administration in Nigeria* (A.H.M. Kirk-Greene).

1966 Published *African Outline* (expanded version of four talks given on BBC Radio 3, 1965).
First article in *International Affairs*.

Letter to *The Times* on the Oxford Colonial Records Project.
Hon. Litt D, University of Cambridge.
Broadcast on Nigerian crisis in BBC programme 'Personal View'.
Embraced the cause of animal welfare.

1967   Published *Colonial Sequence*, I: *1930–1949*.
Awarded Royal African Society's Wellcome Medal for distinguished service to Africa.

1968   Public involvement in the Nigerian civil war.
Visited Lagos and Biafran battlefront at the invitation of the Nigerian Federal Military Government.
Personal broadcast message to Colonel Ojukwu (September).
Retired from OXFAM's Africa Committee.
Elected Associate Member, Institute of Development Studies at University of Sussex.

1969   Open letter to General Gowon (January).
Visited Kenya.
Elected Member of the American Academy of Arts and Sciences.
Hon. D Litt, University of Birmingham.
Voted an honorary degree by Smith College, Massachusetts, but unable to attend the ceremony.

1970   Published *Colonial Sequence*, II, *1949–1969*.
BBC Radio 4 programme, 'The Time of My Life' (January).

1971   BBC Radio 4 programme, 'Travelling on Trust' (June).
Resigned from IUC.

1974   Published *African Apprenticeship* (Southern Africa diary, 1929–30).

1976   Published *East African Journey* (Kenya and Tanganyika diary, 1930–1). Elected a Daughter of Mark Twain.

1982   Died at Burcot, February 19.

[1983]   *West African Passage* (Nigeria and Cameroons diary, 1931–2).

[1988]   *Pacific Prelude* (USA, Samoa, Fiji and Australasia diary, 1929).

Principal Biographical Sources

Anon., obituary, *The Guardian*, February 22, 1982.

Kirk-Greene, Anthony, obituary notice, *African Research and Documentation*, 29, 1982, 1–3.

——, 'Margery Perham and Colonial Administration: A Direct Influence on Indirect Rule' in Frederick Madden and D.K. Fieldhouse, *Oxford and the Idea of Commonwealth: Essays Presented to Sir Edgar Williams*, 1982, pp. 122–43.

——, Introduction to *West African Passage*, 1983.

Oliver, Roland, in *African Affairs*, 81, 324, 1982, 409–12 (see Oliver in note *infra*).

Robinson, Kenneth, and Madden, Frederick (eds), Introduction to *Essays in Imperial Government Presented to Margery Perham*, 1963, pp. vi–viii.

H.M.S., 'Africanissima', *West Africa*, 1982, p. 933.

[Veale, D., and Madden, A.F.Mc.], obituary, *The Times*, February 22, 1982.

IN PREPARATION

Madden, A.F.Mc., contribution to *Dictionary of National Biography*, 1980–5.

Pugh, Patricia, Introduction to the handlist of Margery Perham's papers in Rhodes House Library.

Robinson, K.E., contribution to *British Academy Annals*.

Useful biographical information can also be found in the memorial addresses given by Professor Roland Oliver, Sir Norman Chester and Dr A.F.Mc. Madden; in Margery Perham's presidential address to the inaugural conference of the African Studies Association of the United Kingdom held at the University of Birmingham in September 1964; and in her talks given in the BBC Radio 4 series 'The Time of My Life' (1970) and 'Travelling on Trust' (1971). Surprisingly, there is no original material in the obituary notices contained in the *St Hugh's College Chronicle*, *1982–1983*, pp. 34 ff. The Nuffield College *Record* appears only quinquennially, the next issue not being due to appear before the present volume went to press. The papers of Margery Perham, bequeathed to the Bodleian (Rhodes House) Library at her death in 1982, are being catalogued by Patricia Pugh and should be open to inspection by researchers in 1988.

Index

Abdy, Mr (kangaroo trainer), 205
Aborigines, 12, 18, 22, 201
Aggrey, Dr, 49
Akeley, Carl E., 60
Albany, 37, 38–40
Alice, Princess, 28
Allen, Colonel Sir James, 159, 177, 178, 179
Allen, Robert, 159
Allen, Colonel (later Sir) Stephen Shepherd, 93–6, 97, 98, 99, 103, 108, 159
Amerindians, 12, 16, 18, 22, 37, 131, 172
Andersen, Johannes Carl, 174
Annie, Sister, 142, 143
Apia, 20, 27, 29, 90, 92, 93, 96, 101, 106–7, 109, 110, 171
Armstrong, General Samuel Chapman, 59
Arotia (Aotea, Aotearoa: Maori Association), 128, 129
Ashton, Hugh, 27
Ava (Samoan chief), 80. 83, 86, 110, 181, 182

Baldwin, Stanley, 168
Balfour, Arthur James, Lord, 168
Barrett, Mr, 25
Beattie, Dr Ivor H., 118
Bell, Alan S., 34
Bell, Sir Francis H. Dillon, 159, 177, 178–9
Bell, Sir Hesketh, 16
'Benedicta' (Aletta Lewis?), 80, 81, 89, 181, 183, 185, 186
Berendsen, C.A. (later Sir Carl), 150–4, 162, 177
Berkeley University, 64–5, 66
Best, Elsdon, 173–4
Bleakley, J.W., 196
Briand, Aristide, 127, 179
Briscoe, Captain Richard, 180–1, 187, 196
Brookes, Norman, 25, 197
Bruce, Stanley Melbourne, 190
Bull, Mary, 28
Butterick, Dr, 53

Cameron, Sir Donald, 16
Campbell, G., 62, 63
Campion, Colonel Sir William R., 200
Carroll, Sir James, 147
Caughley, J.E., 114–16
Cawley, Elwyn ('young English escort'), 62–3, 69
Centenary (aka Cente), 90, 93
Chair, Sir Dudley R.S. de, 184
Chamberlain, Sir Austen, 127, 179
Christchurch, New Zealand, 165
Clemence sisters, 138–40, 142
Coates, Gordon, 32, 132, 150, 151, 157–60, 163–4, 165, 166, 167–8, 169, 170, 171–2, 174–5, 176–7, 180
Coates, Mrs, 160, 163, 164, 168, 177
Cook Islands, 130, 166, 167
Coupland, R.T. (later Sir Reginald), 14, 16
Curtis, Lionel, 161

Davis, Jackson, 51–3, 55
Dawson, Geoffrey, 14, 15
Dorothy, Sister, 137, 145
DuBois, William Edward Burghardt, 48

Eden, Mount, 124
Ellis Islands, 130
Ellis, Steven, 175–6
Empson, Patience, 28

Faumuina, 120, 121–2, 124, 125
Field, Marshall, 60
Fishback, Miss, 44
Fisher, H.A.L., 14, 16, 23
Fletcher, Dr Robin, 34
Flexner, Dr Abraham, 37, 53
Forbes, G.W., 156
Forman, Laura ('graduate student'), 64–5

Gandhi, Mahatma, 115
Gauguin, Paul, 83
Gisborne, 142, 174
Godwin, Captain, 153
Goldman, Mr, 197–8
Graham, Mr (half-Maori), 128, 131

269